Leslie Stuart

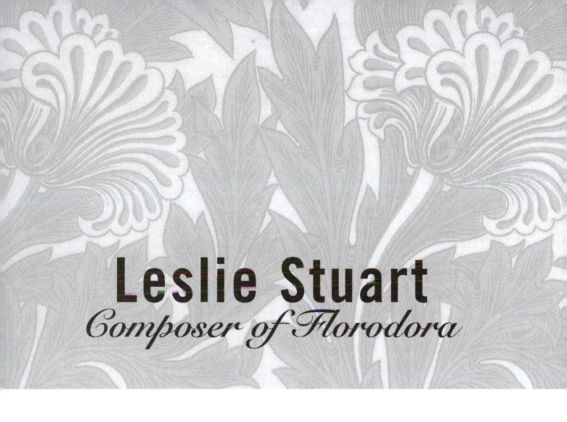

Leslie Stuart
Composer of Florodora

Andrew Lamb

FORGOTTEN STARS OF THE MUSICAL THEATRE

ROUTLEDGE
NEW YORK AND LONDON

Published in 2002 by
Routledge
29 West 35th Street
New York, NY 10001

Published in Great Britain by
Routledge
11 New Fetter Lane
London EC4P 4EE

Routledge is an imprint of the Taylor & Francis Group.

Printed on acid-free, 250-year-life paper
Manufactured in the United States of America
10 9 8 7 6 5 4 3 2 1

Cataloging-in-Publication Data is available from the Library of Congress.
ISBN 0-415-93747-7

To Helen, Susan, and Richard

Leslie Stuart (author's collection)

Contents

"Sic transit gloria spectaculi": Some Famous but Forgotten Figures of the Musical Theatre

Over the past few years, I have spent most of my time researching, writing, and otherwise putting together the vast quantity of text involved in the second edition of my now three-volumed *Encyclopedia of the Musical Theatre*. And, as the Lord Chancellor in *Iolanthe* exhaustedly sings, "thank goodness they're both of them over!" Part of this extremely extended extending exercise involved my compiling bibliographies of biographical works for the hundreds (or was it thousands?) of people whose careers in the musical theatre warranted an entry in the *Encyclopedia*. As I duly compiled, however, I became surprisedly aware of just how many outstanding figures of the historical stage have never, ever been made the subject of even a monograph-sized "life and works." Time and time again, I found that the articles that I have researched (from scratch, not only by choice but quite simply because no one has ever, it seems, done it before) and written for the *Encyclopedia* are the largest pieces of biographical copy up till now put together on this or that person or personality. And I do not mean nobodies: I mean some of the most important and most fascinating theatrical figures of the nineteenth- and early twentieth-century theatres.

This series of short biographies is intended to take the first small step toward rectifying that situation: to bring back to notice and, perhaps, even to their rightful place in the history of the international theatre, a few of the people whose names have—for all but the scholar and the specialist—drifted into the darkness of the past, leaving too little trace.

This is a very personal project and one very dear to my heart. And because it is so personal, even though the majority of the volumes in the series are written by my closest colleagues in the theatre-books world, rather than by myself, you will find that they do rather have me stamped on them in some ways. And I take full responsibility for that.

These books are not intended to be university theses. You will not find them dotted with a dozen footnotes per page and hung with vast appendices of sources. I am sure that that is a perfectly legitimate way of writing biography, but it's a way that has never appealed to me and, because I am being allowed to "do it my way" in this series, the paraphernalia of the thesis, of the learned pamphlet, has here been kept to a minimum. My care, in these biographies, is not to be "learned"; it is to tell the story of Lydia, or Willie or Alice, of Tom or Harry or of Dave, of her or his career in the theatre and (as much as is possible at a century's distance) on the other side of the footlights as well: to relate what they did and what they achieved, what they wrote or what they sang, where they went and with whom, what happened to them and what became of them. Because these people had fascinating lives—well, they fascinate me, and I hope they will fascinate you too—and just to tell their stories, free of any decoration, any theorizing, any generalities, any "significance" (oh! that word)—seems to me to be thoroughly justified.

The decoration, the theorizing, the generalities, and an exaggerated search for (shudder) significance will all be missing. Perhaps because I've spent so much of my life as a writer of reference works and encyclopedias, I am a thorough devotee of fact, and these books are intended to be made up wholly of fact. Not for me even the "educated guess." Not unless one admits it's just a guess, anyhow.

So, what you will get from us are quite a lot of dates and places, facts and figures, quite a lot of theatre bills reproduced word for word from the originals, quite a lot of songwords from the songwriters and singers, of text from the playwrights and actors, and, where we have been able to dig it up, as much autograph material from the hands of our subjects as is humanly possible.

What you won't get any more than can be helped is the "he must have felt that . . . " (must he, who says?), or the "perhaps she. . . . " There will be no invented conversations. No "Marie Antoinette turned to Toulouse-Lautrec and said 'you haven't telephoned Richard the Lionheart this week. . . . '" Direct speech in a biography of a prerecording-age subject seems to me to be an absolute denial of the first principle of biography: the writing down of the content and actions of someone's life. Indeed, there will be nothing invented at all. My theory of biography, as I say, is that it is facts. And if the facts of someone's life are not colorful and interesting enough in themselves to make up a worthwhile book, then—well, I've chosen the wrong people to biographize.

Choosing those people to whom these first six volumes would be devoted was actually not as difficult as I'd thought it might be. When Richard, my editor, asked me for a first list of "possibles" I wrote it down—a dozen names—in about five minutes. It started, of course, with all my own particular "pets": the special little group of a half-dozen old-time theatre folk who, through my twenty years and more working in this field, have particularly grabbed my interest and provoked me to want to learn more and more and indeed everything about them. The only trouble was—I was supposed to be editing this series, not writing the whole jolly thing. And there was no way that I was handing over any of my special pets to someone else—not even Andrew, Adrienne, or John—so I had to choose. Just two.

Lydia Thompson, to me, was the most obvious candidate of all. How on earth theatre literature has got to its present state without someone (even for all the wrong reasons) turning out a book on Lydia, when there are three or four books on Miss Blurbleurble and two or three on Miss Nyngnyng, I cannot imagine. Lydia chose herself.

Having picked myself this "plum," I then decided that I really ought to be a bit tougher on myself with my second pick. Certainly, I could take it easy and perhaps pot the incomplete but already over-one-million-word biography of the other great international star of Lydia's era, Emily Soldene, which is hidden bulgingly under my desk, into a convenient package. But then, why not have a crack at a really tough nut?

When I said I was going to "do" Willie Gill, almost everyone—even the most knowledgeable of my friends and colleagues—said "who?" Which seems to me to be a very good reason for putting down on paper the tale of the life and works of the man who wrote Broadway's biggest hit musical of his era. Tough it has been and tough it is, tracking him and his down, but what satisfaction to drag from the marshes of the past something that seemed so wholly forgotten. A full-scale biography of a man about whom *nothing* was known!

Having realized that these two choices were pinned to the fact that it was I who was going to be writing about them, I then also realized that I ought to be considering my other choices not from my own "pet" list, but to suit the other authors who were going to take part in the series. First catch your author.

Well, I caught three. The fourth, pretexting age, overuse, and retirement, got away. But I got the other three—my three (since the fourth is retired) favorite and most respected writer colleagues in the theatre-books business. Enter Andrew, Adrienne, and John: one from England, one from New Zealand, and one from the United States. A very judicious geographical spread. And the subjects for the four final volumes were, of course, chosen in function of what enthused them.

For Andrew, the choice was the not-so-very-forgotten English songwriter Leslie Stuart, whose *Florodora* songs stunned Broadway, and the rest of the world, in the earliest years of this century. For Adrienne, I went for the mysterious Alice May, whose career ranged from Australia and New Zealand to the West End and Broadway and who has gone down in history—when anyone reads that bit of history—as Gilbert and Sullivan's first (full-length) prima donna. For John, I earmarked two very different American writers: the musician Dave Braham, who, although his wordsmith Ned Harrigan has attracted repeated attention down through the years, has been himself left puzzlingly in the shade, and the prolific, ebullient Harry B. Smith, the writer who flooded Broadway with over two hundred musicals in an amazing and amazingly successful career.

I feel bad about the ones who have got left on the cutting-room floor—but, maybe later? If we all survive what I've discovered with some apprehension is the intensive work needed to extract from the past the life and works of someone long gone, and largely forgotten.

But it has been worth it. Worth all the work. I've enjoyed it enormously. I know my colleagues have enjoyed it, and are still enjoying it. And I hope those of you who read the stories of Lydia, Willie, and Alice, of Dave, Harry, and Tom, will enjoy them too. And I hope, too, that you will remember these people. Because I really do reckon that they deserve better than to be forgotten.

Kurt Gänzl

Acknowledgments

To write about Leslie Stuart has fulfilled a forty-year ambition. For all those years I have wanted to honor the Edwardian musical comedy whose melodies I have loved since childhood. That it is Leslie Stuart about whom I have written has also provided the satisfaction of revisiting Lancastrian haunts of my boyhood. For a dozen years I traveled most schooldays and workdays along roads that Leslie Stuart himself would have crossed daily during his boyhood.

To achieve such fulfilment I am indebted above all to my colleague Kurt Gänzl. Not only did he establish this series of studies and entrust me with contributing, but he tirelessly provided no end of information from his own encyclopedic knowledge and his searches through newspaper microfilm. The result would still have been sadly lacking a personal flavor had I not also had the kind and generous assistance of some of Leslie Stuart's descendants. Of these, I am indebted first to Ross de Havilland (son of the original "Little Dolly Daydream"), his wife Barbara and their son Piers. I have also been assisted no less generously by Alexandra Mayhew, granddaughter of "Sweetheart May."

Other fascinating first-hand material has come from the kind assistance of Maryann Chach of the Shubert Organization in New York. It was my very good friend Gerald Bordman who not only arranged contact with her, but (among other things) generously helped with photographic material and applied his vast erudition to an early draft of my typescript. David Taylor of the Central Libraries, Manchester, also provided more willing help than I could reasonably expect.

Others to whom I extend my warmest thanks for assistance of various kinds are Ellwood Anaheim; former President George H. W. Bush; Jerome D. Cohen; Lee Cox of the San Francisco Performing Arts Library and Museum; Andrew Farthing and Matthew Tinker of the Local History Unit, Southport Library; C. Harman of St. Anne's Library; Mitzi Kanbara of the San Francisco Public Library; Michael Kennedy; Father David Lannon; Peter Linnitt and Lucy McKenna of the BBC Music Library; my sister Catherine Mallon; Richard Mangan of the Mander and Mitchenson Theatre Collection; Rodney Milnes; Richard Norton; Eileen Organ and others at Liverpool Record Office; Mrs. P. M. Perrins of the Birkdale and Ainsdale Historical Research Society; Eric Sams; Father Chris Thomas; Mike Thompson; Malcolm Walker; and Meg Whittle, Liverpool Roman Catholic Diocesan Archivist. I am grateful also to staff of the British Library (St. Pancras) and the British Library Newspaper Library (Colindale), as well as creators of innumerable websites.

Not least I appreciate having found a helpful and understanding editor in Richard Carlin. To any others I have inadvertently overlooked I offer shamefaced apologies as well as redoubled thanks.

Andrew Lamb
Croydon, England

Chapter 1

Irish Ancestry, Lancashire Boyhood

For over 150 years, Ireland has been an exporter not only of Guinness and peat but also of people. In the early 1800s, over two-thirds of the Irish people were dependent on agriculture, and the potato was a major source of food and income. Alas, in September 1845 a fungus was found to be destroying the potato crop, having thrived in the warm, wet weather of the time. Years of famine followed. The less fortunate of the population died of starvation or diseases such as cholera or typhoid, while the more fortunate found a solution in emigration. Between 1800 and 1841, the Irish population had increased from around five to eight million; but an estimated one million people died during the famine, and some two million emigrated. By 1911 the Irish population had declined to less than four and a half million.

Many of the emigrants went to North America, creating the Irish populations that exist to the present day. Others made the shorter crossing to Liverpool, often moving on to find employment elsewhere in England. The opening of the Liverpool and Manchester Railway in 1830 made it an easy trip to Manchester, where the raw cotton that arrived from America by ship for transporting along the Bridgewater Canal was processed. The population of Manchester and adjoining Salford (towns separated only by the River Irwell) grew from about 95,000 in 1800 to over 455,000 by 1851. Irish-born immigrants formed a third of Manchester's population by 1867, when members of the Irish Republican Brotherhood (the Fenians), sworn to bring about Irish independence from England, stormed a Manchester police van and murdered a police sergeant in the course of releasing two Irish prisoners.

Among areas of Ireland most affected by the 1845–48 famine was County Mayo, in the west, where some 90 percent of the population were dependent on the potato. It was from Ballina in County Mayo that one Thomas Barrett immigrated to England. The name Barrett suppos-edly came from Spaniards who arrived on the west coast of Ireland a thousand years ago. Since the local people had no names for them, "the priest who offered up Mass in thanksgiving for their safe arrival chris-tened them Biretta, after the headgear which priests wear."[62]

Thomas Barrett was one of five brothers who emigrated to England, all apparently at one time becoming cabinetmakers in Liverpool.[62] In 1854, he was in Manchester, where on May 15 he married Mary Ann Burke at St. Mary's Church. On the marriage certificate, Thomas Barratt [*sic*] is described as a bachelor and a joiner by profession, the son of Henry Barratt, joiner, while his wife is described as daughter of Bernard Lester, also a joiner. She was from Athlone, in the center of Ireland. Though described as "spinster," she was actually a widow and was appar-ently always referred to by her second husband as The Widow.[65]

The marriage certificate records both parties as twenty-eight years old and living at 39 Dearden Street, Hulme. Hulme was then a separate township to the southeast, divided from Manchester by the River Medlock, and one of the working-class areas that fed the larger city. On June 11, 1855, Mary Ann gave birth to the couple's first child, a son named Stephen, and a second name, William, was added subsequently. On the birth certificate their name is spelled "Barrett," while Mary Ann is recorded as "late Burke, formerly Lister" [*sic*]. The birth took place at 3 Welcomb Street, a thoroughfare off River Street, Hulme, though Dearden Street continued to appear in the 1855 and 1856 Manchester street directories as the business address of Thomas Barrett, joiner.

Thomas's disappearance from subsequent Manchester street directo-ries brings a period of fourteen years when documentary evidence of the family's whereabouts is scarce. The gap is more regrettable because it covers the period when the couple's second son was born. Named Thomas Augustine Barrett, his first name came from his father, and his second from the saint who brought Christianity to Ireland. He was to become known to the world as Leslie Stuart, composer of *Florodora*.

We may assume that the family moved from Manchester to the Lancashire coast, because it was in the seaside resort of Southport, to the north of Liverpool, that Thomas Augustine Barrett was born. That much is consistently stated in his published biographical details, as is the date of March 15. Of the actual year there is no such consistency. In reference works, he gave his year of birth variously as 1864 or 1866, and the matter is further complicated by his 1928 death certificate, which gives his age as sixty-six, implying that he was born in 1862. His daughter, at whose home he died, admitted that she didn't know the true year, adding that "no-one seemed to care."[65]

Before state benefits, of course, people often had only a vague knowledge of their true ages. Members of the theatrical profession, especially, were inclined to knock a few years off. For Leslie Stuart, creating a mystery of his true age seemed to be an obsession. A magazine feature ended with the intriguing statement that "birthdays and similar anniversaries are never alluded to in his family."[77] On another occasion he stated, "There is no official record of my birth. . . . My parents being worthy Irish folk, they did not consider it any business of the registrar's when I was born or that I was born at all, and contented themselves with having me christened at the Roman Catholic Church and my birth recorded there. The church was eventually devastated by fire, and from that moment there was no longer a record of the day I commenced this mortal coil."[62]

It is true that there is no birth entry in the records of Britain's Registrar-General. Neither has any baptismal record come to light. Nor has the Roman Catholic church that was "devastated by fire" been identified. School records and 1871 census records have proved equally elusive. The most convincing evidence of Leslie Stuart's year of birth is provided by the April 1881 national census, where his brother is correctly shown as age twenty-five and he as eighteen, implying a year of birth of 1863. This is supported also by the age on his marriage certificate, and there is even confirmation of a kind in the 1891 census. Though he gave his age there as only twenty-six, he equally knocked two years off the ages of his wife and sister-in-law, whose true ages *can* be verified. Overall, the best estimate we can make is that he was born on March 15, 1863.

We can at least confirm the presence of the family in Southport around that time from the appearance of Thomas Barrett, joiner, in the Southport street guide of 1864–65. His address is given as Duke Street, in the center of the town. According to Leslie Stuart's own testimony, he was actually born in Birkdale,[56] which until incorporation into Southport in 1911 was a separate urban district. Situated a couple of miles to the south, Birkdale was heavily developed during the 1850s and 1860s, attracting wealthy businessmen from Manchester and elsewhere in Lancashire. Joiners from urban Lancashire would doubtless have been equally welcome for house building.

Thomas Augustine Barrett, alias Leslie Stuart, later commented on early signs of his musical talent: "Even during my first stay in Southport the nurse declared there were notes, especially an *ut de poitrine*, in my voice suggestive of Sims Reeves."[63] (An *ut de poitrine* is the high C of a tenor's chest voice, and Sims Reeves was the most celebrated English tenor of the second half of the nineteenth century.) However, he did not live in Southport long: "One month after my birth our family migrated to Liverpool, where my father entered the theatrical profession, he becoming the head stage-carpenter at the Amphitheatre. . . . "[62] Opened in 1826 in Great Charlotte Street, at its junction with Queen Square, the Royal Amphitheatre was a huge building, accommodating nearly 4,000 people. In its early days it was noted for equestrian performances and music festivals, but from the 1840s it housed a more conventional range of theatrical entertainment. Together with the Theatre Royal in Williamson Square, it was from 1843 under the management of William Robert Copeland and from 1868 that of his daughter, with Henry Leslie as director. Thereafter it encountered increasing competition from the newer Adelphi and Prince of Wales Theatres. In 1880 it was sold and rebuilt, reopening in 1881 as the Court Theatre.

It was at the Royal Amphitheatre that Leslie Stuart's memories of the theater began. His daughter May claimed that "at three years old he used to sit on an orange box in the flies and watch the greatest actors and actresses of the Victorian age."[66] Stuart himself recalled, "The house we lived in so commanded the stage door that we had full view of all that happened about it, and I have seen [Samuel] Phelps, [Tomasso] Salvini, Barry Sullivan, and their famous contemporaries pass under my gaze to play their parts. In fact I became a child super to some of them, so that my association with the stage began very early. These efforts ranged from 'Julius Caesar' to 'The Poor of London.' I was a child super remember,

Popular entertainment outside St. George's Hall, Lime Street, Liverpool
(The *Graphic*, May 5, 1877; author's collection)

not the lead."[62] There were other early memories linked to his father's theatrical activities. As he noted, "The first star trap through which demon-like individuals are usually shot on to the stage from below, was constructed by my father—at least in Liverpool. When the time for the big test had arrived, I was the person who was shot through it."[62]

The experience evidently gave Stuart a passion for all things theatrical. He recalled walking up and down the steps of St. George's Hall, "on his hands for pennies from his impromptu audience," an occupation that ceased only when "I happened to number my father in my audience."[62] Evidently it did not kill his initiative:

Being fired with dramatic ambition from the age of six or seven . . .
I found myself an infantile confederate with a hawker who used to
stand in the streets selling tiny champagne bottles that had the reputation of defying gravitation until he caused them to be submissive by
his agent. The cherubic or seraphic youngster—whichever it was I
most appeared with my flaxen hair and baby blue eyes—fortified with
a tiny piece of metal that I used to slip into the neck of the bottle,
was the agent of that deceiver of the British public. . . . This source of

revenue was also ungraciously destroyed for me just when I began to grasp the meaning of avarice. Gone were two perfectly good opportunities for making money through a father's untimely intervention while a worthy son was endeavouring to follow his bent.[62]

Alas, there is no obvious sign of Thomas Barrett senior in the credits for Royal Amphitheatre productions of the 1860s, even for the pantomimes that most obviously required elaborate properties. Nor is there any sign of him in Gore's Street Directory of Liverpool until 1870, when we find Thomas Barrett, cabinetmaker, at 13 Beau Street, Everton. The Barretts were no longer there in the April 1871 census, though, nor at 34 and 36 Wilde Street, the address given in the 1871 and 1872 street directories.

It may have been when the family lived in Wilde Street, which runs off London Road, that further signs of musical awareness in young Tom Barrett became apparent.

When I was a baby we lived in Liverpool within an easy distance of the headquarters of the Irish Brigade, who paraded every Saturday afternoon past the end of our street to a popular tune on the band. I am told that, after they passed, I used to imitate that band with marvellous accuracy, my people discerning four distinct instruments playing at the same time.... This was the first discovery by my parents of my great musical gifts....

It was not in the musical department of my profession, however, that my earliest achievements were accomplished. I had a great leaning towards the stage.... When I became old enough to read advanced literature I was permitted to study the touring managers' advertisements and the back page of the *Era*, and perceiving that I possessed all the requirements for success—inborn modesty and saintly humility—I became an author-actor-manager. I wrote my own version of *The Miller and his Men*, bought my own stage, scenery and characters, and two pennyworth of red fire for the explosion of the mill. My reason for stocking so much red fire was that I had recently been to a melodrama at the old Adelphi ... and I noticed particularly that when the play became dull and the comedian's scenes began to bore the audience they lit red fire and exploded something or other. This struck me as an excellent idea. They don't burn red fire for that purpose nowadays, they use composers instead. I had fitted up the proscenium in front of our wash boiler, so that I might sit in the copper and push on the cardboard characters on either side—a most uncomfortable position, yet commanding. I arranged a Saturday matinée as my first performance—eight boys in the neighbourhood having guaranteed me their halfpennies for admission. On the day of the show they presented a respectable queue outside our back door awaiting admittance to the Scullery Theatre.

It was rather unfortunate for me that my mother had delayed her shopping that afternoon—this was an unlicensed performance—as three of the boys—through waiting for the doors to open—fell to the allurements of the winkle man who was passing, and spent their admission money. I have noticed ever since then what a thin line divides first class drama from winkles. I opened the door when all was clear, admitting the three boys who had no money on their undertaking to applaud and encore at the smallest provocation. Knowing what an advantage it was for a manager to play all the characters, I spoke all the parts myself through the flies. The book soon palled on them, so I brought on the mill scene very early and burnt the red fire. The scene was encored, the deadhead *claque* in front overdoing it so much that my red fire was soon expended, and, having to fall back on my book to get me through, the audience very soon demanded another explosion. After addressing them over the top of the proscenium with that humility discernible in a manager only when addressing an audience, I appeased them by promising an extra special explosion if they would only stand my play to the bitter end, to which they agreed.

Having no red fire, I ignited two whole boxes of household matches, which subterfuge was at once detected, and a demand for the return of their money was unanimous, the most satirical and unfriendly criticism coming, of course, from the three deadheads. They threatened to acquaint my mother of the illegal performance in her absence, which weighed with me, so I disgorged. This was a waste of money on my part; the smell of lucifers and red powder was quite sufficient to betray to my mother that a bad play had taken place in her boiler, and after certain preliminaries she reduced the show to ruins, displaying unforgivable vandalism in burning the scrip [*sic*]—the first of many occasions when my compositions have been roasted. I have ofttimes observed, since then, that it is generally my friends who do the most roasting. A lot of my old-time companions must have become pressmen.[61]

Young Tom Barrett's schooling in Liverpool was at St. Francis Xavier's, a Jesuit Roman Catholic boys' school founded in 1842. There is no sign of his name in the incomplete surviving admission registers of the school, but he recalled that it was there that he "first conquered the alphabet."[62] Before he was in his teens, however, the family moved back to Manchester—this time not to Hulme, but to Ancoats, just northwest of the city center. Smoke-begrimed Ancoats was a working-class district with significant populations of both Irish and Italian immigrants. It was thus a strongly Roman Catholic area, and also a musical one. Many of the Italians who lived there were either ice cream makers or street musicians, making a living from their mechanical organs. From 1874 Tom Barrett senior appears in Manchester street guides as cabinetmaker at 7 Blossom Street, and later at number 88.

It was in Manchester that Tom Barrett junior's musical talents were really developed:

> I attended St Patrick's School in Livesey-street, a thoroughfare that connects Oldham-road with Rochdale-road, two of Manchester's greatest arteries connecting the city with the greater Cottonopolis. . . . The school was in charge of that inestimable body of men—all great scholars and the most capable of teachers—the Christian Brothers, with headquarters in Ireland. The weekly payment of sixpence entitled the student to a curriculum extending from the common subjects, to Euclid, algebra, and even music, the latter through the unselfish devotion to Catholic boys of Brother Lanagan.
>
> This delightful brother devoted himself in particular to developing any musical faculty he found a boy possessed. To this end he used to run a special hour when those boys with a musical bent met and rendered either vocal or instrumental efforts. At that time I had taken to the flute, but you have my word for it that no flautist on this earth ever had cause to regard me as a menace to his position.[62]

Fortunately his father's business had blossomed to the extent that it was necessary to make a display of keeping up with the neighbors by acquiring a major status symbol—a piano:

> Just to find occupation for the piano it was decided to send little me . . . to a music teacher, and after a short spell with one man I found myself being taught by Mr. Peter Conroy. I hope I shall be pardoned for this vanity, but Mr. Conroy was the first with joy to admit it, I very

soon competed with him to the amazement of everybody, and, most decidedly, myself. To be fair, I must frankly admit that this achievement was brought about by Brother Lanagan, who paid special attention to me as he saw me develop musically. . . . In order that I might concentrate on the study of music, the Christian Brothers, with their splendid psychological insight that enabled them to see that a boy was destined to follow the occupation he was naturally adapted to, relieved me from certain lessons on the schedule in which they knew I had little, if any, interest in order that I could profitably spend on music the time I would waste on algebra or political economy.[62]

For all their good intentions, of course, Brother Lanagan's methods were not best designed to produce a rounded person. "He never added up," declared Leslie Stuart's daughter May many years later. "Two and two made anything in the world but four."[65]

However, Tom's musical ability made him in demand in Ancoats:

Simultaneously with our piano a Glee Society was formed in connection with a church in our district; and, irrespective of my not being of their persuasion, be it said in justice, I was appointed as pianist by the conductor, who was also solo tenor and a debtor of my father's. My appointment will give an idea of the musical status of the society.

I soon learned why I was selected—a competent pianist would have been a great encumbrance. The conductor's sister-in-law was principal contralto, his sister's husband principal basso, and his father's aunt on the mother's side was solo soprano. The remainder of the society joined the board after allotment. A concert was duly organised for the alleged purpose of providing funds for the old poor of the parish, but, of course, primarily and solely to exploit the vocal efforts of the family quartet. When the bill of the concert was first issued I saw for the first time my name in print. I walked round and round the neighbourhood meeting those bills (I have found that a more difficult feat in later life), and, although my name was in the smallest type, even including the printer's, whose was as large as any on the bill, I considered that it struck the eye of every passer-by and that everyone read that name and no other.

A notice of the concert (written by the conductor) was promised in the *Parochial Monthly*—its next issue being, fortunately, three weeks hence, so that anyone present at the concert would not remember anything by which they would detect the glaring misstatements as to the abilities of the performers. On the morning when the notice was to appear I was out early to buy a copy of the *Parochial Monthly*, but could not discover a newsagent who had ever heard of it. I eventually went to the printer as the only one likely to possess a copy. I learned that it only had a circulation of three streets and that the ten pages of advertisements were gratuitously inserted to cover the lack of interest in the news matter. The notice was sandwiched in between a piece of poetry by the parson on "The Juice of the Apricot" and a "Further Appeal." I believed that at that moment the whole world was reading that notice of my wonderful performance, and, with ill-assumed nonchalance, I walked home to my people, who had been already vainly searching for the *Parochial Monthly*. I could meet no one who had read my notice, and had to resort to what I found out later to be quite the only process by which my friends were likely to see it. I had to read it to them myself.

I have always observed that your friends never do come across anything complimentary written about you in a newspaper; the day on which it appears is the only day on which they miss taking it. But let there appear anything to your disadvantage in the most insignificant paper in the remotest part of the world, and that becomes the most widely read amongst them.[61]

Soon young Tom's musical education spread out into Manchester's concert life:

It was my progress with my music studies that caused my mother to give me a shilling in order to attend my first Sir Charles Hallé concert. I was enchanted with his wonderful and elegant touch on the piano, and whatever I heard him play then, and at subsequent concerts, I managed to purchase by some means or other even though I was a long way behind the capacity necessary to play them or even read them.

Sir Charles Hallé so inspired me that I settled down to music fully determined to emulate him. Imagine what it meant when I eventually found that the man who played the piano as though he were some super-being, was to be my master. I do not remember experiencing any sensation of greater awe for mortal than when I went to him for the interview that was the prelude to my first lesson from him. Then came the day when he felt satisfied with his pupil to the degree of accepting that I had acquired the touch of the master himself.

And what age was I when I had thus been honoured by Sir Charles Hallé? I was but ten years old. At that age I had introduced musical classics into Blossom-street, Ancoats, and I had achieved a social distinction all my own.[62]

Tom's musical education was complemented by the books his father gave him to read. Tom Barrett senior was, his son recalled, "a man with romance playing a big part in his temperamental make-up. . . . He was the very double of Buffalo Bill, too, and because of his striking appearance, he was a very well-known figure in Manchester."[62] It was in 1868 that William Frederick Cody had gained fame as Buffalo Bill for his skill as a trapper and buffalo hunter in Kansas.

One of his father's gifts particularly encouraged young Tom's love of adventure. "It came," he once wrote, "while I was in bed with measles, or some other of the ills of childhood, shortly after we had settled down in Manchester. . . . As I lay tucked up in bed convalescing, my father entered the room one day and pitched on to my bed a bundle of travel books, entitled 'From Peru to San Francisco on Horseback.' . . . I devoured omnivorously, travelling every inch of the way on the very pummel itself of the daring rider. On we went through Mexico, Southern Colorado, Arizona, California, on to the north of the United States. I feel certain that this little act of my father caused more rapidly to develop any romantic characteristics which were my heritage, and which have manifested themselves in my compositions."[62]

Eventually the time came when Tom junior was forced to decide on a career. "When my father began to harass himself as to my capacity for future wage-earning, he, no doubt remembering my achievements in music and the drama, decided that he would make a cabinet-maker of me, and put me to find work amongst the men in his employ. But just as this (the finding of work) became, each day, more and more laborious, I displayed a corresponding tendency to learn the piano, the lesser evil, physically, of the two. . . . This brought me to the inevitable decision that a musical career was my bent."[61]

Help came from the Old Slip Inn, off Market Place, Manchester, a hostelry Tom Barrett senior used to frequent, where local singers aired their vocal talent, and where he one evening summoned his son:

There was at the Old Slip at the time I am referring to, a pianist of extraordinary merit. He was an old gentleman, and one night, as my father was seated in the "hotel," word came that the pianist had died suddenly and the evening's sing-song could not proceed. Just as I was being prepared for bed my father came rushing into our house with the sad intimation and ordering that I should go down with him and play. I protested and I had the support of my mother, but nevertheless I found myself conscripted into the service of the Old Slip. . . .

I have since tried in moments of reflection to understand how I got through that eventful evening playing songs for volunteer singers—songs of every kind and calling for various shades of accompaniment. I presume since I survived the ordeal that there must have been extreme toleration shown towards me. I took home with me that night all the music that was on the piano comprising standard songs varying from "Come Into the Garden, Maud," to "Tom Bowling" and "The Desert." Not being accustomed to accompanying singers, they were really songs beyond my capacity, or, rather, what had been till that evening expected of me.

My lines of study had been laid along a very different route. However, concentrating on these caused me to jump probably four years ahead of my time, but I never allowed myself to slide into a slipshod style, and I always determined to interpret accurately the various accompaniments, negotiating down to the slightest detail all their difficulties and characteristics. The result of it all was that I found myself engaged to remain regular pianist at the Old Slip. The wage, then unheard of for a boy of eleven years of age in that capacity, was two pounds and ten shillings per week![62]

Thus was his musical career launched.

Chapter 2

Early Career in Manchester

Tom Barrett's musical progress in Manchester was not achieved without hard work or the formation of strong musical prejudices:

Two of my young friends and musical contemporaries were fortunate in possessing well-to-do parents who expended many hundreds of pounds on their acquiring all the academical musical training that the best colleges and professors charged for. My limited resources caused me to become a musical heretic, and to be regarded as such by my two young friends. I practised my piano for as much as twelve hours a day, whilst they were cramming themselves with the golden rules of how symphonies were written. One was composing huge works for an orchestra demanding six oboes, eight bassoons, twelve horns, and three harps, with no earthly hope of ever hearing it performed. The other was discovering consecutive fifths in Mozart. They never went to the theatre—even grand opera was not high enough for their standard. I became more and more a diatonical mountebank.

I do not chronicle the following out of egotism, but simply to prove this. I became organist of a cathedral before I was fifteen years of age, and never had a lesson on the organ in my life. I played from memory almost every mass written by Mozart and Haydn and, on the piano, every one of Beethoven's sonatas, while they were drawing out diagrams of how they were written. They ceased to know me when I wrote a song that reached the barrel organs.[61]

Of his elevation to cathedral organist, he wrote more specifically, "I had been playing at the Slip Inn about three years when I became the youngest cathedral organist perhaps on record. I was only 14 years when I found myself immediately plunged into the midst of those works of indescribable grandeur of the greatest of composers, the masses of Haydn, Beethoven, Schubert, Mozart, and the others. It will be readily admitted the works of these composers were an extraordinary contrast to those with which I had familiarised myself at the Slip Inn."[62]

Tom had gained experience as organist at St. Patrick's Church in Livesey Street. Then, when the position at St. John's Cathedral, Salford, became vacant, he was appointed. This came after a "Father Raymond, himself a brilliant pianist, who had heard the boy play at a concert, recommended him for the post."[77] Although it is questionable whether this occurred, as he claimed, when he was just fourteen years old, he must have taken the post around 1880, when by anybody's reckoning he would have been no more than sixteen or seventeen. He applied himself to the position eagerly, proving adept in the training of the choir—especially the boys' voices, which became highly popular in the north of England. He claimed that "at one time the choir under my control had rehearsed and sung fifty-two different masses during the year. I conducted Sir Charles Hallé's orchestra at the age of fifteen at the Easter Sunday rendering in the Cathedral of Gounod's 'Messe Solonnelle' and Haydn's 'Imperial Mass.'"[62]

The Bishop of Salford from 1872 to 1892 was Herbert Vaughan, a powerful advocate of the right to denominational education, and a frequent speaker at public meetings on temperance, sanitation, and better housing for the poor. In 1892 he moved to London as Archbishop of Westminster, and he was named a cardinal in 1893. Tom remembered him with affection, not least for one particular occurrence:

His Lordship had positively no ear at all for music, and I frankly believe that when he noticed music at all was when it was not music—in other words, when some enthusiastic lady or gentleman in a country choir enthusiastically murdered one of the musical masters in endeavouring to interpret him. . . . The gratuitous slaying of Haydn and Mozart on one occasion was more than he could stand, and when he returned to the cathedral he sent for me and complained of the agony he had been compelled to suffer. He there and then instructed me . . . to set an example forthwith by indulging simpler music whereby the florid music that was so badly mutilated elsewhere might no longer assail his ears to the destruction of his nerves.

Now this was a real problem for me and most disheartening, seeing that I had devoted so much time to my choir that it could render at any time any form of church music in all its grandeur. However, . . . when the bishop . . . gave an order it was an order, so there was I left with the task of entirely reforming the music of the churches. . . . The injunction was equally disheartening to the then Rector Canon Beesley, and Monsignor Gadd, bishop's secretary, who were both very proud of their choir.

One day walking along Oxford-street I came across an old copy of a "Tantum Ergo" by Rossini. . . . [For] a shilling I purchased this thirty-odd pages of the most florid, extravagant, and theatrical compositions one could possibly conceive; certainly calculated to make one's hair stand on end if played in a church.

Nothing more opposed to the bishop's instructions than this could ever have happened, so that I rehearsed it merely experimentally with my choir, in his absence. . . . While rehearsing it one night, Canon Beesley and Monsignor Gadd, who had heard the choir from their rooms above, came and asked me what we had been rendering. So fascinated were they with the pyrotechnics of the composition they had me repeat it several times. Then Canon Beesley asked me to play it at Benediction the following Sunday, as his sister and brother would be present and he wanted to show off the choir. They assured me that the bishop would not be in Manchester that evening in time to come to the evening service, being engaged elsewhere. At their responsibility I put it on, and just as my choir were sending up the greatest musical skyrockets in the firework composition, my eye caught what I thought was an apparition by the cloister. . . . It was his lordship himself. How I continued I do not know, but I could not afford to break down in the service. I saw the bishop open his book, but, without reading it, close it again and listen. I imagined he was just endeavouring to gauge how far I would violate his instructions, and when the service was over I made for the front entrance of the cathedral instead of making my exit by the seminary, which was my custom.

Before I could make good my escape a boy came to me and told that his lordship wished to see me in his room. . . .

When I entered the room the bishop's first question was as to whose "Tantum Ergo" I had been playing. I stammered out some sort of an answer, and the sensation I was experiencing I thought had developed into madness when his lordship remarked: "That is the music I want in my churches. Anything more devotional and inspiring to prayer I have not heard for a long time. Procure more of that kind and let us devise some means of getting it to the choirs in my diocese so that they may adopt it."[62]

At the same time as he pursued his cathedral interests, Tom Barrett was continuing his secular activities. In doing so, he was to some extent following in his elder brother Steve's footsteps. Steve had taken his first steps on the amateur stage in Liverpool, and in Manchester he briefly joined the company of the Prince's Theatre, when it was still under the influence of the great Shakespearean actor Charles Calvert.[22] He had adopted the stage name of Lester Barrett, using the surname of his maternal grandparents. Between September and November 1877 he could be found at the Prince's Theatre, playing supporting roles to the likes of Adelaide Neilson and H. B. Conway, the Vokes family, Ellen Wallis and Edward Compton, and comedian J. L. Toole. Steve continued combining work in his father's cabinet-making business with establishing a performing career, not only in Manchester but in halls around Lancashire and Yorkshire in the winter, and in seaside resorts such as the Isle of Man and New Brighton during the summer. On October 10, 1881, the brothers began a whole week's entertainment at Manchester's Free-Trade Hall. It featured "Mr Lester Barrett, the Popular Comedian, Mimic, and Author, in his Novel, Amusing, and Refined Entertainment, entitled 'Homely Jokes for Homely Folks,'" with Mr. T. A. Barrett as accompanist.

Tom Barrett was evidently also composing songs from an early age. His friend Phil Herman, himself a variety theater performer, later reproduced the manuscript of what was supposedly the very first, "Rocking the Baby to Sleep," composed in 1876. Herman also provided the titles of other songs from those early days, including "John Malone," composed for the opening of Manchester Town Hall in 1877.[40] Tom set his sights high; and in music-hall song of the early-1880s they could be set no higher than George Leybourne. The creator of songs such as "Champagne Charlie" and "The Flying Trapeze," Leybourne was by common consent the greatest male music-hall entertainer of his day. Tom apparently approached him when he was playing in Manchester:

> [Tom] went to work with a will, producing a song that he felt sure would win the approval of "the master." In due course Leybourne granted an interview, and the composer spread himself over the piano and played for all he was worth. At the finish Leybourne said: "Thank you; that's admirable; really excellent—for oratorio or grand opera, but not a ha'porth of good for me or the public! Let me give you a tip, my boy. If you wish to compose melodies that the people are to sing, don't worry yourself about grand harmonies. Give them something pretty, something simple. Above all things, if you can manage it, start your air with a suggestion of a popular old melody. Then the public says: "That's very pretty; fancy I've heard something like it before, and then they go away humming it. That's the secret of all my successful songs!"[40]

Phil Herman also recalled Tom Barrett's appearances with Hamilton's Diorama.[40] Advertised as "Harry H. Hamilton's Panstereorama of Passing Events," this predecessor of the cinema consisted of painted scenes revolving on drums. It visited Manchester each summer during the early 1880s and attracted enthusiastic audiences. The two-hour show treated audiences to a guided tour of the world, the content frequently changing to embrace current events. On September 5, 1882, for instance, the *Manchester Guardian* reported that "a new feature was introduced last evening in the shape of a representation of the recent bombardment of the forts at Alexandria by the British fleet."

Musical interludes were an important part of the entertainment, and one of Tom Barrett's appearances was with his Cathedral Choir in September 1883, when he was seemingly still only twenty years old. It was of sufficient importance that he retained a framed silk program of the occasion for the rest of his life. It read,

LARGE
FREE-TRADE HALL

HARRY H.
HAMILTON'S
ORIGINAL EXCURSIONS AND GRAND

PANSTEREORAMA		120,000 MILES
OF		IN
PASSING EVENTS!		120 MINUTES

LAST

GREAT MUSICAL NIGHT

FRIDAY, SEP. 28, 1883

WHEN, BY KIND PERMISSION, THE

BOYS OF THE SALFORD CATHEDRAL CHOIR

Will again, by particular desire, appear under the Conductorship of

T. A. BARRETT, ESQ.

And render the following Choice Musical Items,

Assisted by Mr. JOHN CHILD, the Celebrated English Tenor.

MISERERE SCENE, "Trovatore"	VERDI.
"AVE VERUM"	GOUNOD.
SPANISH SERENADE	LACOME.
Grand Organ and Piano	Mr. T. A. Barrett

———————

The above RECHERCHE SELECTIONS will be given IN ADDITION to the

ENTIRE PROGRAMME of Hamilton's Extraordinary Confederation.

———————

Mr. BARRETT will play BACH'S GRAND POLONAISE IN E.
POSITIVELY THE LAST TWO PERFORMANCES,
MONDAY, OCT. 1ST, at 2-30 & 7-30.

EACH EVENING at 7-30. MID-DAY PERFORMANCES,
Monday, Wednesday, and Saturday at 2-30.

PRICES:—3s., 2s., 1s., and 6d.—PLAN AT THE HALL
AND AT FORSYTH'S.

When the diorama reappeared at the Great Free-Trade Hall the following year, Tom and his Cathedral Choir appeared again as a special attraction on Monday, September 15. This occasion, too, was remembered in a document handed down through successive generations of his family. This is a printed title page—alas, with no attached music—that incorporates a small, somewhat blurred, portrait of the composer, and reads: "Wake, Lady, Wake, serenade from T. A. Barrett to K. Fox, September 15, 1884."[67] This is the earliest souvenir we have of Tom's relationship with Kitty Fox, who some eighteen months later was to become his wife.

Before they married Tom continued to prove himself in the Manchester musical world. Resolutely billed as Mr. T. A. Barrett, and with a strong following inspired by his church activities and his sizable list of musical pupils, he took part in public concerts in Manchester. Enthused by the pianist Anton Rubinstein, who gave three concerts in the Free-Trade Hall in May 1881, Tom himself gave three piano recitals entirely from memory at Chorlton Town Hall during the 1880s. He quoted the program of the first as follows[21]:

Sonata op 3		Beethoven
Papillons		Schumann
Scherzo in B flat minor	|	
Ballade in A flat	|	
Valse in C sharp minor	|	Chopin
Nocturne in G	|	
Fantaisie Impromptu	|	
Polonaise in A flat	|	
Sonata "Moonlight"		Beethoven
Rondo Perpetual		Weber
Fantasia "Trovatore"		Schloesser
Rhapsodie No 12		Liszt

Tom was clearly no shrinking violet in making himself known to visiting musical celebrities. One was the bass Allan James Folley, known as Signor Foli, whom Tom met in 1885:

Signor Foli (Kurt Gänzl collection)

Nervously I approached him ... concerning a song I had written which I hoped would suit him, and asking him if he would honour me by permitting me to play it over to him.... To my surprise he said "Certainly, my boy." ... I played the song over, very nervously indeed, I know. He asked me to play it over again, and this firmed up my courage, and I brought the very best out of the song. Once or twice more, indeed, I played it, and then it was my intoxicating delight to hear the finest basso perhaps who ever lived sing a composition of mine.

He expressed himself as very pleased with the number, and invited me to follow him to London the next day. . . . Signor Foli then took me to J. B. Cramer's, then in Regent-street, so that he might sing the song over for them. This he did with all the melody and volume he was capable of infusing into my composition. In less than three days after this it was my intense pleasure to see displayed in the window of the establishment a bold announcement of the latest song to be sung by Signor Foli. That song was my song. Imagine the heights my hopes soared to when this great vocalist took my song to Covent Garden and gave it a classic rendering at the promenade concerts![62]

That was "Bounding o'er the Deep," the first nationally published song of T. A. Barrett.

Manchester was fortunate in having Sir Charles Hallé's concerts at the Free-Trade Hall to maintain a high standard of symphonic music making, but there was an enormous range of other concerts. While Hallé's took place on Thursday evenings throughout the winter season, on Saturdays there were Edward de Jong's popular concerts at the Free-Trade Hall, and those of J. A. Cross at the YMCA Hall. During the 1880s the city was looking to increased prosperity from the proposed construction of the Manchester Ship Canal, which would permit ships from America to bring cotton to Manchester directly. Based on these bright prospects, Tom Barrett—still no more than twenty-two years of age—announced a series of ten Monday evening popular concerts at the Free-Trade Hall:

MR. T. A. BARRETT'S

MONDAY CONCERTS

at the

FREE-TRADE HALL.

————

NOTICE.

The attention of the Public is solicited to the Novel Programmes which from time to time will be presented at these Concerts. They will include the favourite numbers from all the Popular Modern Operas; and although the very best Local Vocalists have been engaged to perform the Operatic Selections, the SERIES of TEN CONCERTS will be made unusually attractive by the appearance of TWO EMINENT VOCALISTS at each Concert.

Notwithstanding the great expense attending these Engagements, the

LOWEST POSSIBLE

PRICES OF ADMISSION

will be charged—viz.:

Reserved and Numbered Seats	3s.
Body of the Hall	2s.
The Entire Gallery	1s.
Area and Promenade	Sixpence.

Enabling all classes to hear the most Celebrated Vocalists of the Day, at prices never before instituted in Manchester, so that those who are debarred from hearing these artistes on other evenings can avail themselves of the opportunity provided in the

MONDAY CONCERTS.

The program for the first concert was typical of the series, with two eminent vocalists in Signor Foli and the soprano Clara Samuell. The items performed included excerpts from *The Mikado*, only eight months after its first performance.

FREE-TRADE HALL

MR. T. A. BARRETT'S

MONDAY CONCERTS

FIRST CONCERT, NOVEMBER 9TH (MONDAY NEXT)

PRINCIPAL VOCALISTS:

Miss CLARA SAMUELL,

Miss CONWAY, Miss HOWARD DUTTON,

Miss MAUDE YATES, Mr. SEYMOUR JACKSON,

MR. A. S. KINNELL, Mr. FRED GORDON

and

SIGNOR F O L I

PIANOFORTE—Mr. T. A. BARRETT.

CHOIR OF FORTY VOICES.

By permission of the Commanding Officers, THE BAND of the 4TH

DRAGOONS. CONDUCTOR—Mr. T. MARTIN.

PROGRAMME—PART I.

Overture	"Romantique"	Kéler Béla
The "Market" Chorus	"Masaniello"	
Song—Mr. Fred Gordon	"Time was when love and I were well acquainted"	"The Sorcerer"
Song (with chorus)— Miss Conway	"Poor wandering one"	"Pirates of Penzance"
Song—Mr. A. S. Kinnell	"Travellers all"	"The Siege of Rochelle"
Gavotte—Miss Maude Yates	"Mignon"	
Quintet—Miss Conway, Miss Dutton, Mr. Jackson, Mr. Kinnell, and Mr. Gordon	"She will tend him"	"The Sorcerer"
Song—Signor Foli	"Bedouin's Love Song"	Pinsuti
The Slave Chorus	"O, Caspian"	"The Sultan of Mocha"
Song—Mr. Seymour Jackson	"'Twas sad when I and Dolly parted"	"The Sultan of Mocha"
Duet—Miss Yates and Miss Dutton	"Sing hoity-toity"	"Princess Ida"
The Policeman's Chorus		"Pirates of Penzance"
"When the foeman bears his steel"		"Pirates of Penzance"

Solos by Miss Conway,
Miss Yates, and Mr. Gordon.

PART II.

Selection (Cornet Solo),	"Pré aux Clercs"	Band
The Election Chorus,	"Whatsoever may be won"	"Rip van Winkle"

Song—Mr. Fred Gordon	"The Castaway"	Barri
Duet—Miss Conway and Mr. Jackson	"Parigi o cara"	"La Traviata"
Song—Miss Dutton	"Alas, those chimes"	"Maritana"
Song—Miss Clara Samuell	"She wore a wreath of roses"	Knight
Song—Mr. Seymour Jackson	"My Queen"	Blumenthal
Song—Signor Foli	"The Diver"	Loder
Chorus,	"Behold the Lord High Executioner"	"The Mikado"
Trio—Miss Conway, Miss Dutton and Miss Yates,	"Three Merry Maids from School"	"The Mikado"
Song and Chorus—Mr. Jackson, Mr. Kinnell and Choir	"Perhaps if you Impress the Lady" "O, Dainty Triolet"	"Princess Ida"
March Cortège		"La Reine de Saba"

Admission 3s. (Reserved), 2s. (Body), 1s. (the entire Gallery);

and 6d (Promenade). Season tickets (transferable), admitting to

Ten Concerts, 21s (reserved), 15s., and 8s. (Gallery). Boxes, £1 5s. and £1 10s.
PLAN at HENRY ISON & CO's, DEANSGATE.

Doors open at 6 45   Concert at 7 30

The *Manchester Evening News* had misgivings about the prospects for the concerts. It wrote, "The *raison d'être* of the new undertaking is hardly clear, for the various entertainments which have come to be regarded as part of our musical curriculum appear to sufficiently cover the ground Mr. Barrett proposes to traverse. But this is mainly his concern, and if Manchester can be stirred deeply enough to be attracted by the singing of some first-rate—and all good—artists, so as to fill the Hall twice a month on Mondays, we cannot do otherwise than look on in appreciation and commend Mr. Barrett for his bold venture."

The *Manchester Guardian* was more welcoming. Mixing compliments with advice, it noted, "The accompaniments were played by Mr Barrett, and, considering that he is so young a man, he showed that beside good taste he possesses a considerable amount of experience. He will gain more as the season progresses. We may remark, for his information, that everywhere last evening there was a lack of sustained support in the accompaniments. Often the basses of the harmonies were scarcely audible, and everywhere we felt that there was indefiniteness in this respect which only needs to be pointed out to be remedied. In every other respect Mr Barrett showed himself to be an accompanist of judgment and discrimination."

The second concert, a fortnight later, offered the ballad composer Milton Wellings, accompanying a couple of his own songs. The third, on December 7, largely comprised the usual band items, together with operatic and comic-opera excerpts. At the fourth concert, on December 21, the chief attraction was the pianist Sidney Smith, while the fifth concert, on January 4, 1886, offered a "Grand New Year's Programme" that dispensed with the band and restricted itself to songs, choruses, and glees.

In his efforts to attract star names, Tom Barrett had even contacted veteran performer Henry Russell. Well into his seventies, Russell had achieved legendary status between the 1830s and 1850s with his tours of the United States and the United Kingdom, performing his own songs such as "Woodman, Spare that Tree," "A Life on the Ocean Wave," "The Old Arm Chair," and "Cheer, Boys, Cheer!" However, he had been retired for almost thirty years, and in a letter to Barrett dated December 1885, he replied, "I cannot again appear before the public. My nerves are gone."[36]

In the end it seems that Tom Barrett's hopes proved too high. On the Saturday before the scheduled sixth concert, on January 18, 1886, the *Manchester Guardian* published the following announcement from the booking agents:

MR. T. A. BARRETT'S

MONDAY CONCERTS

IMPORTANT NOTICE

Messrs. Henry Ison and Co. regret to have to announce that,

through indisposition, the result of the great exertions demanded by

these Concerts, Mr. Barrett is reluctantly compelled to POSTPONE

his SIXTH MONDAY CONCERT.

THE DATE OF RENEWAL WILL BE DULY ANNOUNCED.

It appears that the concert series never was resumed. It had been an astonishingly bold enterprise for one so young, but it seems that for once he stretched his youthful aspirations just a little too far. Almost certainly the termination of the series was due as much to financial as to health problems. However, those Monday evening Free-Trade Hall concerts were a declaration of intent for the future.

Chapter 3

Expanding Horizons

Tom Barrett's ambitions as concert impresario were temporarily set aside by his marriage on March 9, 1886 to Mary Catherine Fox, known as Kitty—the schoolteacher to whom he had dedicated a serenade some eighteen months earlier. The wedding was at St. Marie's Church, Failsworth, with Tom's brother Steve and Kitty's elder sister Constance as witnesses. Born in 1864, and thus seemingly a year younger than Tom, Kitty was the daughter of the late Michael Fox, a cashier. The Fox family, too, were of Irish Catholic origin, coming from Gort in County Galway, to the south of County Mayo.

The early months of his marriage found Tom immersed in Irish politics. For years he had been a supporter of Charles Stewart Parnell, whose Irish Nationalist Party had become a thorn in the flesh of the British government. Indeed Tom was sharing the platform with Parnell at a grand Irish rally in the Free Trade Hall in Manchester in May 1882 when news came of the murder of Lord Frederick Cavendish, the British chief secretary to Ireland, and his under-secretary, T. H. Burke, in Phoenix Park, Dublin.[62]

The British general election of November 1885 resulted in Parnell's party holding the balance of power, and when Liberal Party Prime Minister W. E. Gladstone's Irish Home Rule Bill was defeated in the summer of 1886 a further General Election was called, with implications for Tom's support for Parnell.

> He wanted to appoint me—and he then had the power to do so—member of Parliament for South Kilkenny. . . . I had to decline the honour because it was impossible for me, as there was no £400 a year thrown in with the job then, to accept the honour. Particularly forbidding was the financial side of the consequences of the acceptance since I had just married.
>
> With the spirit for politics that was very naturally bred in me, and the "wrongs against the distressful country" ever ringing in my ears, having youth and the fire of its enthusiasm, I launched out as an agent of Charles Stewart Parnell. . . . I must say that on the second election, when Parnell did not wish Gladstone to have too big a majority and he wished the voting to give him the balance on a division, I was given what certainly was the most difficult job of my life. I have composed tunes and written lyrics against time often enough, but they have been child's play compared with going out into an Irish community and asking them to vote Tory.[62]

Tom's marriage was far from the only major family event of the year 1886. It was the year in which his mother died, on October 15, of heart disease and dropsy. Her death certificate claimed she was fifty-four, but if this was so she would have aged only twenty-six years since her marriage thirty-one years earlier. Keeping track of birthdays was not a Barrett family strength! More happily, it was the year in which Tom's brother Steve also married. Though eight years the elder, Steve lagged behind Tom in marriage by a few months, marrying Henrietta Clara Burke in the summer of 1886. The surname she shared with Steve's and Tom's mother's first husband was, of course, a common enough Irish name. Following their marriage, widowed Tom senior moved in with Steve and Hetty.

Parenthood followed for both Steve and Tom before the year was out. Steve's and Hetty's first son, Harry Lester Barrett, was born within weeks of their marriage, but Tom and Kitty's first child was born a respectable nine months after their wedding, on December 4, 1886 at 116 Broad Street, Pendleton, a mile or so from Salford Cathedral. The

Church of the Holy Name, Manchester (The *Graphic*, October 14, 1876; author's collection)

child was a daughter, named Mary Catherine after her mother, and ever afterwards known as "May."

Tom, Kitty, and their infant daughter did not remain in Pendleton long. On November 12, 1887, a notice in the *Manchester Guardian* advised Mr. T. A. Barrett's current and prospective piano and singing pupils of his move to Lime Grove, Oxford Road. This new home was just around the corner from Owen's College, which later became Manchester University and whose campus now embraces Lime Grove.

Lime Grove was also just around the corner from the Church of the Holy Name, where Tom had now become organist and choirmaster. Though it may sound to be a step down from Cathedral organist, that was due to the historical accident that Salford was the head of the diocese, while Manchester was the faster-growing center. Following its opening in October 1871, the Church of the Holy Name had rapidly become Manchester's leading Roman Catholic church, and better financial terms helped induce Tom to make the move there, a move also facilitated by the fact that the priest at the Church of the Holy Name was Father Bernard Vaughan, brother of Bishop Herbert Vaughan, under whom Tom had served at Salford Cathedral.

From his new base Tom's varied activities continued unabated. In November 1888 came the announcement of his formation of a "Select Vocal Society" to practice "the best oratorios, masses, part songs, &c." Members democratically chose Wednesday for rehearsals, the first of which was scheduled for December 19, 1888. Of even greater significance than its announcement in the *Manchester Guardian* of December 15 was an adjoining announcement:

> MESSRS. J. B. CRAMER'S NEW SONG
> "CHERISHED VOWS," Music and Words by
> LESLIE STUART,
> Will be sung by BARTON McGUCKIN, SEYMOUR JACKSON,
> and all the London Tenors and Sopranos,
> In all keys.

Seemingly, this was the very first public appearance of the name Leslie Stuart, although its use was anticipated a few months earlier, when Tom Barrett christened his first son, born July 31, 1888, Thomas Leslie Barrett. He later described how the name of Leslie Stuart came about:

In those days people who attended music halls were not thought a great deal of socially because of the snobbery of the period and because, too, there was a lot of vulgarity in the numbers.

There then came to Manchester a comedian . . . of the name of T. W. Barrett. His great hit at that moment was a song entitled, "I am a Nobleman's Son." For his visit the city of Manchester was covered with posters showing a picture of Barrett that by some extraordinary coincidence of printing more closely represented me than it represented him.

This aroused the indignation of some of the superior members of the Catholic Church, who, believing I was the artist appearing at the music-hall, awaited on the bishop with a protest against any Catholic organist being retained while he played at a music hall. I was called on to the carpet, and the bishop enjoyed the joke.

My name, Thomas Augustine Barrett, it was felt by a music publisher, for whom I had just written a song, would have to be changed, and he asked me if I had considered an attractive name under which to publish my compositions. There was a copy of the *Era* lying on a table, and picking it up I turned to the back page.

There numerous cards of people on the stage were published, being alphabetically arranged.

In the middle of one column I saw the name "Fanny Leslie," and the name after that was "Cora Stuart." I saw the combination of the last names in each case. That is how Thomas Augustine Barrett became Leslie Stuart.[62]

It was some six or seven years more before Leslie Stuart fully ousted T. A. Barrett. In that period the pen name was used for no more than a handful of song compositions, and it was still T. A. Barrett whose musical activities proliferated. Most significant was another of Tom's solo piano recitals, given "entirely from memory" at Chorlton Town Hall on the evening of Tuesday, May 21, 1889. The program was similar to his first some years before. The critic of the *Manchester Guardian* confirmed "a numerous audience" and the fact that "Mr Barrett's efforts were warmly applauded." He added that, "Mr Barrett's reading has, however, a certain individuality about it—as, indeed, it should have—which will not probably in every case commend itself to his maturer judgement. The detached opening phrases of Chopin's B flat minor scherzo, for instance, need to be more firmly subordinated to the *tempo* if their full meaning is to be conveyed to the listener."

Tom's ambitions continued to expand. Press announcements on August 31, 1889 noted not only the resumption of his activities as music teacher and rehearsals for his vocal society but a series of Saturday evening concerts for the 1889–90 concert season. Evidently he had recovered from his unfortunate experience of four years earlier and was now ready to tackle something on an even larger scale, with no fewer than thirty weekly concerts at the St. James's Hall. Standing on Oxford Street, between Portland Street and Whitworth Street, the hall had opened in 1881 and was the largest of all of Manchester's concert venues.

The concerts were very much after the style of his earlier efforts: programs of unashamedly popular, short pieces featuring guest singers, choirs, and instrumentalists, with brass and military bands complementing his own piano accompaniments. The first concerts of the 1889–90 season had an especially homespun feel to them. There were contributions from Mr. T. A. Barrett's Opera Choir, and the concert promoter himself provided not only piano accompaniments for the vocalists but also occasional piano solos. Early concerts also included humorous numbers from his brother Lester Barrett. To retain his audiences,

St. James's Hall, Oxford Street, Manchester, c. 1890 (Manchester Central Library:
Manchester Archives and Local Studies)

however, he had to offer varied programs with bigger names. Besides a guest clarinettist, a local military band, and an orchestra of harpists, the concert of November 9, 1889 included the distinguished Irish operatic bass Charles Manners, who had created the role of Sergeant Willis in Gilbert and Sullivan's *Iolanthe*. The following week's "Grand Opera Concert" featured the French soprano Marie Roze. These monthly grand opera concerts were an especially successful feature of the season, the description "grand" perhaps applying to the concerts rather than the contents, which were primarily comic operas, with Gilbert and Sullivan prominent.

The ninth concert, on November 25, introduced the American *siffleuse* (whistler) Alice Shaw, whose contributions included the obbligato traditionally played by a flute in the mad Scene from Gaetano Donizetti's *Lucia di Lammermoor*. Shaw was to prove one of Tom Barrett's most loyal supporters. As he later wrote, "Apart from being a wonderfully clever woman, she possessed great beauty and the most attractive figure. . . . I have heard many whistling artists in my time, but I have never heard one who could approach Mrs. Alice Shaw. Her fee when playing for me was £25 per concert, and she was well worth the money because she was an immense favourite. So great a favourite was she in Manchester that if ever I had any misgivings over a programme ... , I used to send for Alice Shaw.... She never failed me, and always managed to bring home the bacon.[62]

The Saturday before Christmas 1889 brought another grand opera concert, featuring soprano Georgina Burns of the Carl Rosa Opera Company, with Gilbert and Sullivan items interspersed with numbers from two comic operas by Alfred Cellier. On Christmas Day itself there was an extra sacred concert, with Tom Barrett conducting soloists, orchestra, and chorus of 250 performers in pieces from George Frideric Handel's *Messiah*, Joseph Haydn's *Creation*, Gioacchino Rossini's *Stabat Mater* and similar works. New Year's Day 1890 brought a fun concert at which five local bands combined to produce a total of over two hundred performers playing Louis Jullien's *British Army Quadrilles*.

Increasingly Tom Barrett was able to attract performers of international renown. Marie Roze appeared at another grand opera night on January 4, 1890, and the celebrated American mezzo-soprano Zélie de Lussan was featured on January 25, February 22, and March 22. February 1, 1890, brought a "Grand Programme of Irish Music," followed by another, with Signor Foli, on March 15, 1890, to celebrate St. Patrick's Day. The program of February 22 included "We're Called Gondolieri" and the quintet "I Am a Courtier Grave and Serious" from the latest Gilbert and Sullivan comic opera *The Gondoliers*, which had premiered in London only ten weeks earlier.

The final scheduled concert of the season, on April 5, 1890, was another sacred concert, with a fifty-member orchestra. The first half was devoted to Rossini's *Stabat Mater*, the second to sacred selections by Rossini and Handel as well as by Haydn, Felix Mendelssohn, Jean-Baptiste Faure, and Ludwig van Beethoven. In the way of the times, this "final" concert was followed by the concert promoter's benefit concert the following week, featuring Marie Roze, Charles Manners, Alice Shaw, and many other star names from the series. Tom himself played Chopin's Valse in E-flat.

That first season of concerts at St. James's Hall was liberally covered in the press, both locally and in national musical journals. The quality of what was performed may have been variable; but there is no doubting the liveliness of its presentation or its popular success. Press reports refer time and again to the hall as "large" or "enormous" and the audience as "immense." Tom Barrett's claim in his publicity that over 200,000 people had attended the concerts was probably a slight exaggeration, because it represents the hall's full capacity of some 7,000 per concert; but it does give an idea of the huge audiences his concerts attracted.

Quite where he got the money for such a huge venture is unclear, but that first season was evidently sufficiently successful that he immediately announced a second season of thirty concerts for 1890–91, with even more ambitious plans. His soloists included not only old favorites but other outstanding singers of the time, such as the Canadian soprano Emma Albani and the American soprano Lillian Nordica. Another was contralto Antoinette Sterling, singing *The Lost Chord*, which Arthur Sullivan had composed expressly for her. However, the most significant newcomer of the 1890–91 season was a brilliant new thirty-year-old pianist, Ignacy Jan Paderewski. As the concert promoter noted,

> I had heard of the wonderful success he had achieved in Austria, but he had not then reached the stage when he could be regarded as an artist commanding high fees. I booked him for two engagements on two consecutive Saturdays at the fee of £30 per concert. I announced him as the greatest living pianist, well in advance. . . .
>
> As was somewhat naturally to be expected I was subjected to a good deal of criticism for giving this flourish of trumpets to Paderewski and particularly because I had, with others of that time, heralded various instrumentalists as being the greatest in the world.
>
> The consequences were that the advanced bookings at booking agents were dreadfully poor. I became very nervous indeed, as well might be expected, about my second Saturday's booking of the great pianist, and I immediately got into communication with the Liverpool Philharmonic Society and persuaded them to lease Paderewski from me. I was then happy to think I had thus cut my loss on my enterprise.
>
> As a preliminary canter, as it were, he gave a recital, arranged for after I had fixed my dates, on the Friday afternoon at St. James's Hall, London. . . . There he created a positive furore such as was never known for a performer on his first appearance in London. My concert was the next day, and the London correspondents of the Manchester newspapers gave him what for the period was an hysterical notice. . . . The effect of this sensation on my bookings was that from early in the morning special police had to be engaged to control the people outside Forsyth's and to queue them up in orderly fashion,

"easy execution"

Ignacy Jan Paderewski (*Vanity Fair* caricature by Spy; author's collection)

for when the premises opened hours after the first batch had assembled. I could have sold every seat in the house twice over.[62]

Tom seems to have been mistaken in his oft-expressed belief that he was the very first to engage Paderewski for England, apparently overlooking Paderewski's appearance in London in May 1890. However, he certainly did engage Paderewski before his reputation was established. The concert on November 15, 1890, at which Paderewski made his first Manchester appearance, also featured Durward Lely, creator of such roles as Earl Tolloller in *Iolanthe* and Nanki-Poo in *The Mikado*, and also Don José in the first English-language *Carmen*. The *Manchester Guardian* reported that "St James's Hall was crowded to the utmost extent on Saturday evening, and it was evident that M. Ignaz Paderewski—the latest sensational pianist of the day—was the chief attraction." However, his appearance was not without some anxious moments. As the *Guardian* noted, "When he should have appeared Mr Barrett had to announce that M. Paderewski had not yet arrived, and the public disappointment was most noticeable. However, after another item on the programme had been given the pianist duly put in an appearance. His first selection—Rubinstein's beautifully vocal 'Barcarolle'—seemed to fall rather flat on an audience who evidently had come to witness a display of technical fireworks. The 'Marche Hongroise' of Schubert and Liszt soon, however, supplied these, and the enthusiasm of the listeners was so thoroughly aroused that M. Paderewski was compelled to acknowledge the continued plaudits by returning to the piano and playing one of Brahms' 'Hungarian Dances.'"

During this second season, Tom Barrett provided a veritable feast of concerts over the Christmas and New Year period: a total of six between Saturday, December 20, 1890, and Saturday, January 3, 1891. He did not appear at all of them in person, but he gave himself the honor of conducting 250 performers from six local bands and a company of pipers in Jullien's *British Army Quadrilles* at the New Year's Day concert. Then, at consecutive concerts on January 24 and 31, 1891, he provided the special attractions of soprano Emma Albani and the Belgian violinist Eugène Ysaye, and a fortnight later the tenor Durward Lely and the great British baritone Charles Santley. The February 28 concert offered the novelty (to his own piano accompaniment) of the entire second act of *The Flying Dutchman*. Then, on March 7, "Mr Barrett's English Orchestra" (with, "by special permission, a good many members of Sir Charles Hallé's band") appeared, with Tom conducting the overtures to Carl Maria von Weber's *Oberon*, Richard Wagner's *Tannhäuser*, and Charles Gounod's *Mireille*, and waltzes by Johann Strauss and Joseph Gungl.

A third season followed in 1891–92, but this time with a break over Christmas and a total of just twenty-five concerts plus the inevitable final benefit concert. The grand opera night on October 17, 1891, featured two items from Sullivan's *Ivanhoe*, which had premiered in London less than nine months earlier. Paderewski made a return appearance on October 24, prior to sailing for America for his New York debut. He also gave a full-length recital under Tom's management on Wednesday, October 14, an indication of the gratitude he always showed towards the young man who had assisted his acceptance in Britain. Tom later wrote, that Paderewski "was a very grateful artist. Even when he could command the highest possible figure an artist was being paid, he contented himself to play for me at my concerts for a similar fee—£30—as he received on the first occasion."[62]

The continuing success of the Saturday concerts induced Manchester's weekly journal *Spy* to include a feature on Tom Barrett in its issue of November 21, 1891. This was based on a visit to the home in Lime Grove, where the Barrett family lived with three live-in servants—a cook, nurse, and domestic servant. His daughter May later recalled it as "a long, low, white house with a verandah nearly all round it, high railings, and a big iron gate ... and great bushes of rhododendrons." She also recalled how artists would call round to rehearse before their concerts.[66]

The *Spy* feature included a description of the reception room, "the artistically furnished *sanctum-sanctorum,* which is on the ground floor, and overlooks the pleasant grove off Oxford Road," noting, "A splendid pianoforte is in a corner, over which hangs a beautiful engraving representing the deathbed scene of Mozart's life. A bust of the famous composer of *Don Giovanni* and *Figaro* also stands near the window. ... A prettily got-up fireplace, and a gorgeously carved and gilt side console, which it is a pity one so seldom meets with in drawing-rooms nowadays, and plate glass to match, form the principal items of the tasteful furniture about. A special feature of the 'salon,' however, is a valuable collection of engravings and photographs, representing the living musical fame of Europe, from Patti, Sims Reeves, Paderewski, Mrs. Shaw, &c., downwards. Many of the photos are signed, and are from 'yours truly,' and go up even to 'yours affectionately.'"[58] *Spy* praised Tom's "genius—which does not only consist of a musical talent but also of a splendid business capacity." It referred to "his beautiful and popular ballad 'Hearts Ever True'" and to others, "some of which he writes under the *nom de plume* of 'Leslie Stuart.'" Among the "warm admirers" of his works is listed "the veteran song writer, Mr. Henry Russell, who justly predicts a great future for Mr. Barrett, and who is constantly in communication with Mr. Barrett on musical matters."[58]

Asked to what he attributed the success of his concerts, Tom referred to the great influx of people from the surrounding towns into Manchester on Saturday nights:

> "Well, of course, it is generally accepted that the prices of admission and the high-class programme are the causes of the success, although that in itself does not guarantee an audience such as assembles at St. James's Hall. When I commenced the scheme everyone said that at such prices of admission the better classes would not frequent the Hall. I may say that at first this was the case, but the persistency of my efforts has overcome this difficulty, and now the audience usually attending my concerts may be looked upon as truly representative.
>
> "Some state that my concerts have now assumed such a high-class pitch that the introduction of the 'whistling lady' or a humorous quartette is out of place on my programmes. But it is admitted that too much heavy and classical music during an evening's concert is a heavy mental strain, and unless there is a little brightness thrown in to relieve the mind, the concert becomes tedious to the average music lover. . . . Of course, I have myself had concerts exclusively classical, to preserve the high standard my programmes have attained. Such concerts are, however, never intended or expected by me to be financially successful. . . .
>
> "The day of successful orchestral concerts is a thing of the past. People now patronise individual sensations, such as a Paderewski or Nikita; there you may throw in the band for accompaniment purposes, &c., but to get up an orchestral concert pure and simple, means financial ruin. Were it not for the great personality that Sir Charles Hallé possesses, concerts such as his could hardly be carried on with any hope of *financial* success. Hallé's concerts, as they are now given, I believe will never survive when he retires—which we all hope will not be for many years to come."[58]

He also had comments on the recent opening of the Palace Theatre of Varieties, right next to the St. James's Hall. This was one of the chain of variety theaters that sprang up around the country during the 1890s to extend the music hall's appeal into family entertainment. He commented, "It is bound to injure theatres and concerts during the week, but will not harm the places of amusement so much on Saturdays . . . [when] . . . the great influx of people from the surrounding towns naturally crowds every place of entertainment. The question ... is ... what will become of the theatres and other places of amusement that have to depend upon the Manchester public to form good audiences on the other nights of the week. I think that in future the existing theatres will have to change their programmes twice a week regularly, viz., to engage two companies for the week, each company performing three successive nights only."[58] The answers show Tom Barrett's awareness of the need to respond to the rapid changes in entertainment against which he was promoting his enormously successful Saturday night concerts.

Chapter 4

Concert Promoter
and Song Composer

The November 1891 feature in Manchester's *Spy* referred to Tom Barrett as "the father of chubby youngsters." There were then three, with a fourth well on the way. May, almost five, and Leslie, aged three, had been joined on March 16, 1890, by Bernard Vaughan Barrett, named after the priest at the Church of the Holy Name. Known as Vaughan, he suffered an accident at birth, as a result of which he never spoke, could hardly walk, and failed to reach adulthood.[67] The fourth child, born on November 28, 1891, was named Marie Roze Barrett after the French soprano who had been so popular at the Saturday concerts, but was always known to the family as "Dolly."

That same month, Tom Barrett senior died at 8 Mytton Street. He had lived to enjoy his first grandchildren, teach them Irish songs, and instill in them pride in their Irish heritage. Always a convivial soul, he loved to drink; as his granddaughter May later testified, "No furtively slinking into places for a quick one. When Grandpa drank the town shook. He became gloriously, uproariously drunk. He fought all Ireland's battles over again. And Heaven help any Orangeman or Black Prod he came across! One summer, when we all went to the Isle of Man for our holiday, they left him in the care of the cook, Mary Kelly. She wrote Mother, 'You had better come home quickly. The old gentleman went out last night with his pants over one arm and a statue of St Joseph under the other, singing "God Save Ireland!" up and down Lime Grove. I sent for his Reverence the priest, and we made him sign the pledge, but, sure, we both knew he'd never keep it.'"[65]

Ultimately those convivial evenings proved too much for his system: his death on November 4, 1891, was certified as due to cirrhosis of the liver, haematemesis (vomiting of blood), and bronchitis. It seems to have been following Tom senior's death that "Lester" Barrett decided to give up the cabinetmaking business in favor of his performing career, refining his act into a full-evening's entertainment called "Hilarity," a "musical and mimical entertainment."

As for Tom Barrett junior's concerts, they continued with distinction during the 1891–92 season. The performance on November 28, 1891, the day of Dolly's birth, again featured "Mr. T. A. Barrett's Band of Fifty Performers," this time in a program that included Weber's *Euryanthe* overture and "Concertstück," as well as Wagner's *Tannhäuser* overture. The audience evidently braved inclement weather, for the concert announcement promised the heating apparatus in full operation, and curtains at the doors to prevent draughts.

On January 9, 1892, the leading British contralto Janet Patey appeared for the first time, singing "Che farò?" from Christoph Willibald Gluck's *Orfeo ed Euridice*. The eighteenth concert of the season, on January 23, 1892, featured the pianist Frederick Dawson and, once again, Charles Santley singing, among other things, the popular baritone solo "Ho, Jolly Jenkin" from Sullivan's *Ivanhoe*. Dawson returned on March 5, partnering Tom Barrett in Wolfgang Amadeus Mozart's Sonata for two pianos, and the promoter's benefit concert on March 19 included Marie Roze accompanied by Henry J. Wood performing one of the latter's own songs. The importance of Tom Barrett's concerts to Manchester's musical life was not in doubt.

Unfortunately, cancellations were a perpetual headache. The last-minute cancellation of "the world-renowned cantatrice Nikita" on February 27 caused special displeasure. The following week the promoter reproduced a doctor's certificate he had received, followed by the comment, "Mr. Barrett leaves the above to answer the numerous letters written by incredulous members of the audience. If the statement of the situation is not

Andrew Lamb

completely satisfactory, Mr. Barrett regrets to be unable to give further particulars, as he possesses none. The first intimation Mr. Barrett received of Nikita's illness was at 7.30 on Saturday evening." As the weekly journal *Spy* commented, "the public scarcely realise how arduous his duties must be."

All this, of course, was in addition to his duties as organist and choirmaster of Holy Name Church. In 1892, Robert Cocks published the first of a series of "Grand Motets and Benedictions" by T. A. Barrett under the collective title of "The Holy Name." Five of them appeared by 1894, with a further seven listed but seemingly never published. They were evidently only a small part of Tom Barrett's religious output, for in later years it was reported that "he wrote some hundreds of services, litanies, and anthems, many of which have been played and sung in Roman Catholic churches all over the world."[77] Phil Herman cited one hymn, *O Salutaris Hostia*, performed at the Holy Name Church, as having been transformed from something written originally as a regimental march song.[40]

Building upon the success of his first three concert seasons, Tom announced for the 1892–93 series what the *Musical Times* described as "an absolutely bewildering list of engagements, having apparently ransacked the whole musical world in search of novelty and talent." The first concert of the season, on September 24, 1892, was one of the popular "Grand Opera Programmes," featuring Fanny Moody and her husband Charles Manners alongside the usual complement of local singers. Heard in a comic duet from Sullivan's *The Sorcerer* and a solo from Jacques Offenbach's *Madame Favart* was an eighteen-year-old Manchester-born mezzo-soprano named Kirkby Lunn, who would become the foremost British mezzo-soprano of her time.

Items on the concert bill for September 24, 1892, demonstrate very well how operas and comic operas provided the popular hits of the day. In the comic-opera field, Walter Slaughter's *Marjorie*, Edward Solomon's *The Red Hussar,* and Reginald De Koven's *Robin Hood* (known in England as *Maid Marian*) had all been produced for the first time within the previous three years, as had the revised version of Solomon's *The Vicar of Bray*. In the operatic field, Pietro Mascagni's *Cavalleria Rusticana* had been produced in London for the first time less than twelve months earlier. Pyotr Ilyich Tchaikovsky's *Evgeny Onegin* was still awaiting its first British production, which it was to achieve the following month with Fanny Moody and Charles Manners in the cast.

The 1892–93 season was bedeviled by problems no less than usual. At least Paderewski's cancellation for the concert on October 8 had its compensations, because it permitted the first appearance in Manchester of Nellie Melba. Her program included "Il dolce suono" from *Lucia di Lammermoor*, with which she had made her mark at Covent Garden, as well as an aria from Herman Bemberg's opera *Elaine*, of which Melba had given the premiere at Covent Garden just three months earlier. Bemberg himself accompanied that number, and the star-studded program also included pianist Joseph Slivinski and Melba's regular accompanist G. H. Clutsam, future composer of the song "Ma Curly-Headed Babby."

The *Manchester Guardian* critic was full of admiration for Melba's "upper notes," which were "delightfully . . . pure and sweet," and for the "especially pleasing sustained . . . piano passages." He was less enamored of the concert running late, noting, "It is unfortunate that Mr Barrett does not adhere to his intention, printed at the head of every programme, of arranging the concert so as to terminate at ten o'clock. At that hour on Saturday there were still four items on the programme, exclusive of at least one certain encore."

The response was immediate. When Zélie de Lussan (singing the "Habanera" from *Carmen*) was engaged for a concert on October 14 along with the cellist David Popper, Tom Barrett—never one to mince words—concluded that day's announcement in the *Manchestet Guardian* with the following:

SPECIAL NOTICE

The above programme has been arranged to terminate shortly before
ten o'clock, allowing the opportunity to those of the audience who
have to leave by train of remaining for the end of the Concert. Mr.
Barrett hopes that this will also effectually deter that portion of the
audience who are in the habit of marring the entertainment of the
majority who remain to the finish of the programme, from leaving the
Hall during the singing of pieces.

On October 29, he announced further improvements to arrangements—namely, that the hall would be thoroughly heated for the remainder of the season, and new exits would be completed in a few days, while attention was directed to the prevention of drafts from the various entrances. When violinist Gabrielle Wietrowetz was announced to play the andante and finale from Mendelssohn's Violin Concerto on November 12, Barrett responded to claims that the sixpenny portion of the hall was being obliterated in favor of shilling-reserved seats. The *Manchester*

Guardian announcement included an assurance that unreserved accommodation for 3,000 people was provided on almost all occasions and went on to address accusations that the concerts were becoming too highbrow:

> To that portion of the public who so frequently indulge in the irritating practice of writing Mr. Barrett anonymous letters holding that the "popular" character of his programmes is "becoming extinct" Mr. Barrett will submit his programme for Saturday next. It should be noted that since the commencement of these concerts the patronage has increased by such enormous bounds as to allow of the engagement of every available eminent Vocalist and Instrumentalist, and the selections of these famous artistes are always those in which they have become famous elsewhere. If these selections should at times be regarded by lovers of "popular" programmes as "above their heads," the opportunity should be taken of hearing the grandest compositions of the great masters interpreted by the greatest performers. The selections of Fräulein Wietrowetz on Saturday next do not, for instance, include what is termed "popular" pieces, but they are those wherein the difficulties of the most difficult instrument are overcome by the artiste—an object-lesson to the student.

During all his years as a concert promoter, Tom Barrett only rarely used his concerts to promote his own compositions. It's unclear, even then, how aware Manchester audiences were that composer Leslie Stuart was the concert promoter himself. During his first season, the concert on November 30, 1889, featured a vocal trio, "Queen of the Night," sung by Clara Samuell, Louie Turner, and Fred Gordon, together with the song "Cherished Vows," for which the name Leslie Stuart was first used. Not until the concert on December 3, 1892, does the name seem to have reappeared, when Belle Cole introduced "The Vales of Arklow" and Charles Manners sang "Molly." Both songs had Irish content, the former celebrating the town of the same name in County Wicklow.

It seems these songs were inspired by a visit that Tom and his wife Kitty had just made to Ireland to trace their ancestors. After Kitty had gone to seek out relatives in Gort, County Galway, Tom went on to Ballina:

> When I arrived and made a friendly enquiry concerning my mission, I was immediately escorted by a thoughtful yokel to a shebeen. For those unaware of the meaning of shebeen, let me here make it clear that it is the name given to an institution where whisky is made and supplied without the excise officers being troubled about it.

The shebeen, I am happy to say, was run by a man whose name was Barrett, but he very clearly repudiated that his family had anything to do with me or my Barretts. However, bearing all the characteristics of a person bearing the name of Barrett, he was generous to the degree of sending out his darling daughter Maggie to round up the Barretts of Balina. Judging by the number that turned up at the rodeo of the Barretts, we must have represented the total population of Ballina with the exception of the railway employee who escorted me to the shebeen. However, after a lively consumption of the drink known as "two of malt," which, reduced to a common language, means a glass of whisky, I discovered that of all the Barretts, Ballina, the only one related to me was not in my party. However, hospitality was too good to have me left without a relative, so eventually a second cousin of mine was brought along. From him I learnt many things of the remarkable incidents in the life of my family in Ballina.[62]

According to Phil Herman, Tom hired a man, cart, and horse for that trip at a cost of 30 shillings per week (some £60 or £70 in year-2000 equivalents), exclusive of the cost of feeding the horse. Herman adds that the climax of the visit was an incident that Tom—referred to here as Leslie Stuart—always treasured. He notes, "He was introduced to the village organist—a man with the thick, long hair of the musical genius— an enthusiast to his finger-tips. He played some of his songs over to Stuart on the church organ, and then asked his guest to play something. Stuart sat down [at the piano] and played, with that caressing touch that thousands came to know, the overture to "Carmen." The next morning, when Stuart was about to leave, the organist came to him and said, 'I would like you to take my piano music—I'll never touch a piano again. I will keep to the organ.'"[40]

The 1892–93 concert season seems to have been one of particularly fierce competition, especially with the concerts of G. W. Lane at the Free-Trade Hall. At the end of the season the *Musical Times* commented of Lane's concerts that "the provision of vocalists has been so liberal that it is difficult to understand how even the crowded audiences could adequately repay the expenditure." Tom Barrett doubtless experienced much the same problem.

For the 1893–94 Saturday concert season, Lane scaled back his ambitions substantially, and so, to a lesser extent, did Tom, restricting himself to just twenty concerts plus the inevitable benefit concert. Paderewski reappeared on November 18. That day's *Manchester Guardian* also carried a tantalizing hint of Tom's other varied activities in the following announcement:

BARRETT v. LYTHAM PIER

AND PAVILION COMPANY, LIMITED.

Mr. T. A. BARRETT is pleased to announce,

with the Consent of

The Lytham Pier Company, that

HIS ACTION AGAINST THE PIER COMPANY

has been settled to his entire satisfaction.

It's unclear to what this related; but presumably it was some summer activity at the Lancashire seaside resort. It gives an indication of not only the range of Tom Barrett's activities but also the highly principled, sometimes litigious, stance he was wont to take.

On December 2, 1893, his concert series included a grand orchestral concert, at which he conducted a full orchestra of sixty performers in a program that again included the overture to *Tannhäuser*, plus a grand selection from Gilbert and Sullivan's *Patience* and Frederic Cowen's orchestral suite *The Language of Flowers*. He also conducted the full orchestra in Handel's *Messiah* on December 16, with a chorus of 350 and a distinguished team of soloists in soprano Clara Samuell, mezzo-soprano Belle Cole, tenor Ben Davies, and baritone Andrew Black.

The 1893–94 season was perhaps most notable, though, for the Sims Reeves affair. Reeves was regarded as the greatest British tenor of the age, and his name readily attracted the crowds. He was, though, seventy-five years old, and only poverty forced him to continue working. Suffering from numerous illnesses, he often failed to show up. Having announced him for the season's first concert on October 14, Tom was forced to announce on the day of the concert that "through an error on the part of his agent" Mr. Reeves had booked the wrong date. Fortunately he was able to reassure patrons that Reeves had "positively announced his intention to sing to-night fortnight, and the public may have reliance on this." Reeves duly appeared on October 28, singing Charles Dibdin's "Tom Bowling," Michael Balfe's "Come into the Garden, Maud," and Henry Bishop's "My Pretty Jane." The *Manchester Guardian* declared that "with what remains of his grand voice he produces effects unapproached by his younger rivals."

However, the *Guardian* also reported that Reeves had confided to a friend that he "has always found that the atmosphere of Manchester has a deleterious effect upon his very delicate throat." Tom was thus tempting fate when he invited Reeves back for another concert on January 6, 1894. Recognition of the risk he was taking is suggested by his announcement that "Mr Reeves has written an undertaking to be present on this night, so that no doubt need exist of the arrival of Mr Reeves." Alas, the great tenor failed to appear, and efforts to entice him to subsequent weeks' concerts were equally unsuccessful.

Not one to mince words then or at any other time, Tom Barrett took advertising space in the *Manchester Guardian* for a "no holds barred" explanation:

> MR. BARRETT regrets to have to announce, for the third (but certainly for the last) time this season, Mr. Reeves's non-appearance. When this engagement was made Mr. Reeves volunteered such an exceptional promise that whether in good or bad voice he would appear that Mr. Barrett had no doubt of its fulfilment. A letter (as published) was written to this effect. On Thursday afternoon Mr Reeves telegraphed, "Leaving by twelve train; meet me; rehearsal afterwards. REEVES." This morning another telegram: "Very sorry Sims Reeves seized yesterday with attack bronchitis. Cannot appear to-morrow evening. EMMA REEVES." This was too late to announce in evening papers. The patrons of these concerts may rest fully assured that Mr. Reeves will positively appear on the next occasion he is announced by Mr. Barrett.

Tom Barrett never announced Reeves again. Indeed there was very little at all to follow the 1893–94 season of concerts. Instead of a full season for 1894–95, he announced just six autumn concerts. They were, though, somewhat more adventurous than before, following a developing fashion for extended representations of popular operas, complete with costumes and scenery. Thus the first concert, on October 11, 1894, featured Zélie de Lussan and Barton McGuckin in act 2 of Ruggero Leoncavallo's *Pagliacci* and act 2 of Donizetti's *The Daughter of the Regiment*. The fifth of the six, on November 10, 1894, presented Fanny Moody and Charles Manners in a "grand production" of Gounod's *Philemon and Baucis*, which Sir Augustus Harris's Italian company had introduced to Manchester the previous year.

The last concert of the season was on November 17, 1894, when the *Manchester Guardian* reported that "the attendance was not quite so large as it had been at some of the earlier concerts." Evidently there were powerful counterattractions in the production of Gounod's *Faust* by Sir Augustus Harris's company at the Theatre Royal, and the appearance of Albert Chevalier, performing "My Old Dutch" and "Wot Cher" at the Free-Trade Hall. The *Manchester Guardian* also reported that Tom Barrett "had been unusually unfortunate in his arrangements" for the concert. Apparently he had hoped to feature the soprano Margaret Macintyre, the original Rebecca in Sullivan's *Ivanhoe*. When her return from South Africa was delayed, he announced the soprano Antoinette Trebelli, only for her to cancel due to indisposition on the day of the concert. Ultimately the one undoubted celebrity who did appear was the stalwart Signor Foli.

That concert, on November 17, 1894, was to prove the very last of Tom Barrett's concert promotions. Evidently the money had run out. "I . . . broke myself twice in bringing talent to the city of cotton," he lamented years later.[62] Yet that concert also pointed the way forward, in its inclusion of a new song he had written for Foli. He later described how grateful he remained to Foli for helping launch his career as a published composer with the modest success "Bounding o'er the Deep," and how he determined to write a song "that would be worthy of so great a singer and would contain an earnest of my gratitude for the interest he had taken in me."[62]

The inspiration for "The Bandolero" was the travel book series *A Ride on Horseback from Peru to California,* that Tom Barrett senior had given his son when he was ill with the measles. The composer was quick to stress that bandolero was not a word he had coined, but "a patois word among the Mexicans to describe the bandit type of Southern Mexico."[62] He was progressing pretty slowly with the composition in September 1894 when, late at night, he received a telegram from Doncaster. It was from his brother, who was currently performing in York, and who invited him to travel to Doncaster the following morning, assuring him that he would show him the winner of the St. Leger horse race. Tom sat up all night to complete the song in order to attend the race meeting. What's more, he and his brother backed the winner.[62] Newspaper commentators had to cast their minds back to St. Leger upsets in 1861 and 1882 to find comparisons with that of September 12, 1894.

The new Leslie Stuart ballad was published not by J. B. Cramer or Robert Cocks, but by Chappell, a leader in music for the theater as well as for the ballad concert. "The essence of bold bad banditry," as musicologist Eric Sams has colorfully described it, the song was to remain a favorite of baritones and basses for many years to come.

But this was not the only front on which things were looking up.

With his compositional activities as Leslie Stuart still scarcely started, Barrett had sought to add yet another string to his bow as composer of songs for the variety theater. This was doubtless encouraged by brother Steve's increasing success as north-country comedian Lester Barrett, not least in the summer seasons in Douglas, Isle of Man. From 1890, the music-hall song publisher Francis, Day and Hunter had published several songs and monologues "written, composed and performed by Lester Barrett," and now, it seems, his younger brother was seeking similar exposure in the variety theater.

He set out to do so in collaboration with Felix McGlennon, composer of the popular song "Comrades":

> Soon after my change of name from Tom Barrett to Leslie Stuart, I commenced seriously to write for the stage, or rather endeavoured with the aid of my old friend and collaborator, Felix McGlennon. . . .
>
> Every morning approaching the time the postman was due to arrive at my door my heart was suspended between Heaven and earth. If there were a thud as the more humble order of King's Messenger put his hand to the slit in the door, then my heart bumped to earth. If there were no noise at all, but a spooky suggestion that something light had tumbled to the mat below, my cardiac rating just soared among the angels. A letter at least might have contained an acceptance, and, at its best, a cheque. I have always believed in talking money. It is so convincing when it is backed up.
>
> Every morning after the postman had gone, my friend, McGlennon, would come along and ask: "Has there been any thud this morning, Tom?"[62]

For this further expansion of his activities, Tom Barrett chose to use yet another pseudonym. It seems he did so "under the spell of the prevailing spirit [that] to write good music for the music halls was absurd."[23] The name he adopted for the purpose was Lester Thomas, an obvious amalgam of his own first name and the surname of his maternal grandparents.

The partnership between composer Lester Thomas and lyricist Felix McGlennon produced the song "Katie, I Love You True," but does not seem to have lasted long. Soon Tom was composing to either his own words or those of his brother, and the *Manchester Guardian* of October 7, 1893, carried an indication that the brotherly collaboration was bearing fruit. Announcing forthcoming engagements of Mr. Lester Barrett, it proclaimed his song "By the Sad Sea Waves"—not to be confused with

Sheet music front of "By the Sad Sea Waves," attributed originally to Lester Thomas and later to Leslie Stuart, with portraits of Lester Barrett and Vesta Tilley (author's collection)

a similarly titled song by Julius Benedict—the sensation of the season and described the roars of laughter and thunderous applause with which it was being received.

What Tom Barrett really considered the turning point of his career was another Lester Thomas number composed in 1894. It had as its background his love of billiards and his friendship with another Lancastrian, John Roberts, an eight-time English billiards champion. After an evening session in Manchester, Roberts went to the Barrett home for supper. Afterward they had a game of billiards, during which Tom mentioned a popular song of the day, "Little Alabama Coon" by Hattie Starr:

Roberts said to me that that was the kind of songs I ought to write, adding there was plenty of money in that type of song writing. I replied that such songs were very easily written and did not appear to call for any serious physical effort. Then I made a bet with him that by the time we met the next night I would have written a song along similar lines, and that it would be published within a month.

I beat John Roberts at billiards, starting level. Fact. But it is perhaps only fair to mention that we played on a half-size table which I could use like a magician uses his box-table, and that the game was more cod than scientific. However, just to prove to Roberts that I meant what I had said and that my wager was not the outcome of pique or vanity, I sat up that night, and somewhere in the young hours of the morning "Louisiana Lou" was given birth to. When Roberts heard it, he did not wait till the end of the month. He said he believed I had written a certain winner and he paid over his bet. I think it was a cigar.[62]

"Louisiana Lou" was apparently first sung by an artist named Nellie Richards. However, Tom also took it to Ada Reeve, an up-and-coming twenty-year-old variety theater performer who in 1894 was engaged for the pantomime *Jack and Jill* at the Comedy Theatre in Manchester. She duly sang the song, thereby earning the composer's lasting gratitude.[49]

Encouraged by the reception of both "The Bandolero" and "Louisiana Lou," Tom Barrett determined to give up the organ loft as well as the responsibilities of concert promotion. On February 5, 1895, he made his customary appearance at the piano in Manchester's Free Trade Hall for an annual concert in aid of St. Bridget's Catholic Female Orphanage. Then, on May 18, 1895, the *Manchester Guardian* carried the announcement that "Mr. T. A. Barrett desires that all communications be in future forwarded to his London residence, 81 Albert Road, Battersea Park, S.W. or Gaiety Theatre."

He had received an offer of a songwriting contract from David Day of Francis, Day and Hunter, who were the leading publisher in the field of music-hall song, which was attracting new audiences with the opening of large variety theaters for family entertainment. The agreement included the provision that he should settle on what he described as "the more euphonious name of 'Leslie Stuart.'" In the words of a newspaper interview, "when he heard his songs whistled in the streets, he threw off his disguise, confounded the old fogies, and went back to the name he originally assumed."[25] Leslie Stuart was henceforth the name he used for all his musical activities.

Chapter 5

Leslie Stuart: Popular Songwriter

Leslie Stuart later gave the following reason for his decision to move from Manchester: "After a time the dull work of teaching palled on me. I had written one or two little things that people liked, and I was persuaded to give up my Manchester connection and go to London. I was to have gone to the metropolis, and to have written at my leisure, without any care for worldly matters, when, just as we had burned all our boats behind us, my best friend died. However, work conquers everything, and all came right in the end.[63]

The passage suggests that Stuart had found a backer to enable him to concentrate on composition in London. Who "my best friend" was is, however, unclear. Could it perhaps have been Sir Charles Hallé, who died suddenly on October 25, 1895? Certainly Hallé had encouraged Stuart and had apparently worshipped at the Holy Name Church where Stuart had been organist. At all events, if initially Stuart had to struggle hard in the capital, he had the determination, resources, and talent to succeed, and he was able to enjoy the new family home at 81 Albert Road, overlooking Battersea Park. The songwriter Harry Dacre, who wrote "Daisy Bell" ("A Bicycle Built for Two"), had found it for him, and he gave it the name Arklow, after the town in Wicklow, Ireland, that he had celebrated in one of his ballads.[65] His daughter May remembered,

> One afternoon … we trotted in a cab across Westminster Bridge: my mother and father and their five children. … With what excitement we children from Manchester leaned out of the windows to catch our first glimpse of the shipping on the River Thames! By another route went a procession of pantechnicons, drawn by heavy cart-horses, and laden with the family effects. They rumbled up the drive of a large house overlooking Battersea Park. My father superintended operations as the things were carried in. … Among the furniture they carried into the house on that day was—a harmonium. … The harmonium was a relic from his church organist days in Manchester. One of the surprising things about father was that some of his gayest tunes … were composed on that humble old harmonium.[66]

The family had reached five children with the birth of a son Stephen—always known as "Chap"—in 1894. It was completed in Battersea on December 2, 1896, with a third daughter, Constance Lola Stuart Barrett. Her first name honored her aunt, while her third name gave recognition to her father's new persona.

Fortunately for Stuart, it was a boom time for the popular musical theater. On the one hand, the glamorous musical comedies were replacing the diet of comic opera and burlesque that had been so popular during the 1870s and 1880s. On the other, the expanding chains of variety theaters allowed performers to reach family audiences, to tour not only Britain but also America and the British Empire, and from Christmas until March to appear in the much-prized annual pantomimes.

The most significant of Stuart's early successes as a specialist songwriter was with "Louisiana Lou." He recalled traveling from Manchester to London to take up an introduction to the London theater manager George Edwardes, who heard him play the song and agreed to include it in the Gaiety Theatre musical comedy *The Shop Girl*. This was the show with which the British musical comedy fashion really took off. The leading role was to have been created by Ellaline Terriss, playing opposite her husband Seymour Hicks (later Sir Seymour Hicks). However, Miss Terriss fell ill, and the show opened on November 24, 1894, with Ada Reeve in the title role. Ellaline Terriss finally introduced the song when she took over in April 1895. It was now republished, credited as written by "Leslie

Stuart," rather than "Lester Thomas," and the song's title also underwent a subtle change, becoming "Lousiana Lou"—without the first "i:"

> Lou, Lou, I lub you,
> I lub you, dat's true.
> Don't cry, don't sigh,
> You'll see me in de mornin';
> Dream, dream, dream ob me,
> And I'll dream ob you,
> My Lousiana, Lousiana Lou.

The song also became popular in America, where it was published by Francis, Day and Hunter's U.S. counterpart T. B. Harms. The composer's name was incorrectly shown as "Leslie Stewart," an error that was frequently to recur. In one interview among many, Stuart referred to the song's success in America during the 1890s, not least in relation to William McKinley, who was inaugurated as the twenty-fifth U.S. president in 1897 and reelected in 1901, noting, "In America, where they ought to know, it is regarded as the most characteristic coon song ever written. It aroused quite a controversy in New York as to whether a mere Britisher could have composed a song so thoroughly permeated with the spirit of Coon life. Only the other day a writer in a Philadelphian paper made the truly American discovery that Leslie Stuart is not a man at all, but the daughter of a well-known clergyman living in Philadelphia and a relation of President McKinley. This last part of the discovery is probably due to the fact that "Louisiana Lou" is the President's favourite song. He will go miles to hear it sung, and remarked lately that it ought to be America's National Anthem."[51]

However much truth there was in these claims, there is no doubt that the song was a noteworthy example of a British composer absorbing American styles. It was also a song that Leslie Stuart would use to demonstrate how he adapted the same musical ideas for sacred and secular. Sitting at the piano, he would play "Lou[i]siana Lou," and then, slurring the tune notes, repeat it in the form of a Gregorian chant.[16]

Ellaline Terriss's introduction of "Lousiana Lou" into *The Shop Girl* led to the insertion of another Stuart song in the same show. Seeking to rejuvenate his part, Seymour Hicks took on "The Little Mad'moiselle," another that had first appeared under the name Lester Thomas. It had been introduced originally in the variety theater by Vesta Tilley, who was to become one of the major performers of Stuart's songs. Daughter of a theatrical father, she had entered the theater as a child performer and became a major draw in variety theater during the 1890s with her male impersonations and "masher" songs. For many years she paid an annual summer visit to the Isle of Man, and it was probably there that she became friendly with Lester Barrett and his brother. W. R. Titterton eloquently described her appeal:

> There is the low buzz of a bell, and the conductor bends to his orchestra, the chorus starts again, and a dapper young man in an exquisite purple holiday costume strolls from the wings leaning on his bending cane. He comes to the centre of the footlights, and poses with crossed legs and staring monocle, the features deliciously quizzical and inane. It is a perfect picture—perfect in colour and composition, the quintessence of a seaside dandyism; but for a subtle hint of womanly waist and curving hips you might fancy it indeed a round-faced boy. . . .[72]

Other Vesta Tilley successes with Leslie Stuart songs were "By the Sad Sea Waves" and "Some Danced the Lancers," both attributed originally to Lester Thomas, and sung originally by Lester Barrett. During 1895, Tilley also successfully took up two more songs. The first was "The Limelighter's Lament," or "Oh, Venus, Let Me Call You Sal," the second "Sweetheart May," with its tender refrain:

> Sweetheart May, when you grow up some day,
> You may marry another and my love betray;
> But I'll wait for you and then we shall see
> What you will do when I ask you to marry me.

In the uncomplicated waltz refrain of "Sweetheart May," Stuart perhaps intentionally paid heed to George Leybourne's advice to start with a suggestion of a popular old melody. Certainly the first three notes of the refrain recall the grand waltz from Charles Lecocq's *La Fille de Madame Angot*, though in Vesta Tilley's interpretation the mood was very different. As W. H. Boardman indicated, "When she sang that rather inane piece of sentiment, 'Sweetheart May,' she actually had the audience on the verge of sloppy tears. . . . Vesta, without any pretensions to a great voice, could infuse into those lines a yearning that made every young man in the pit fumble for his sweetheart's hand and swear by the last instalment on his push-bike that he would gladly die for her."[6]

"Sweetheart May" was the first of two Leslie Stuart song successes inspired by his daughters. As a magazine feature later noted, "For many years the late Signor Foli, the great basso, had been a constant visitor at Mr Stuart's house. He was a great favourite with the two little girls, and on one occasion when he came to say good-bye to them, previous to going on tour in America, little May, who was then a small mite of four years old, said that she was his sweetheart and would marry him when he came back from America. There were circumstances in Mr Foli's home at the time which made the incident particularly pathetic and suggested to Mr Stuart the story which he subsequently worked up into the well-known song 'Sweetheart May.'"[51]

That neither "Sweetheart May" nor other Stuart songs remained as familiar as later Vesta Tilley songs is because they had passed from her repertory by the time commercial recordings arrived to preserve her interpretations. In her autobiography, however, Vesta Tilley—by then Lady de Frece—cites "By the Sad Sea Waves," "Some Danced the Lancers," and "Sweetheart May" as among her most successful songs.[71]

Vesta Tilley also tells a story that is informative about Leslie Stuart's readiness to help his friends:

One of my big hits, "Algy, the Piccadilly Johnny with the little glass eye," was written by a clever Manchester boy, Harry B. Norris, and the manner in which the song was brought to my notice is worth recording. Leslie Stuart and his brother Lester Barrett had written several very successful numbers for me, and Stuart was anxious that I should hear his latest effort. I was holidaying on the Thames at Bourne End at the time, and he wired me that he was coming over to play over the song "Sweetheart May."

I was delighted with the number and secured it at once. Then he told me of a bashful friend of his in Manchester, Norris, who had heard me sing at the Palace, Manchester, and was ambitious to write some verses for me; he had in fact sent on a sample to Stuart, asking him to be good enough to show it to me. He took the MS. from his pocket and, handing me the words, played the melody, remarking: "I don't think there is anything in it." I was struck with the lilt of the melody, although agreeing with Stuart that "masher" songs were rather overdone. However, I agreed to buy the sole rights for one guinea, and some weeks later tried it out at the Oxford. I dressed the part immaculately and made great play with the monocle, . . . with the result that I left the stage amid storms of applause, and Algy remained in my repertoire for many a year.[71]

Leslie Stuart's efforts to get his own songs performed were now bearing fruit on various fronts. On April 22, 1895, London's Trafalgar Theatre staged *Baron Golosh*, a two-act comic opera tried out the previous week at the New Theatre and Star Opera House, Swansea. An adaptation of *L'Oncle Célestin*, a comic opera by Edmond Audran, it had additional songs by Leslie Stuart interpolated into its score. Unfortunately, despite a strong cast, it achieved little and, because an English score was not published, it's unclear just what the Leslie Stuart additions may have been.

A more significant boost came at what was shortly to become the most fashionable theater in town. The George Edwardes musical play *An Artist's Model*, with a score by Sidney Jones, told of high jinks in the fleshpots of Paris, embroidered with the plight of a former artist's model who, when a rich widow, meets up with a former artist lover. It opened at Daly's on February 2, 1895; but a prebooking for another show forced its temporary transfer to the Lyric Theatre. It returned to Daly's on September 28 in a "second edition," refurbished with new songs. Among them was a waltz song by Leslie Stuart called "Trilby Will Be True," sung by Maurice Farkoa, a Turkish-born heartthrob of Anglo-French parentage. It was inspired by the huge success of George Du Maurier's novel *Trilby*, serialized in *Harper's Monthly* magazine in the first five months of 1894, and then adapted for the stage by Paul Potter. Potter's play toured America and enjoyed a season in Manchester before opening at the Haymarket Theatre on October 30, 1895. It was the wearing of a soft felt hat with a narrow brim and indented crown in the stage version of *Trilby* that popularized what we know today as a Trilby hat.

As was the norm with George Edwardes's musical comedies, the song content of *An Artist's Model* was extremely flexible, and along the way it also acquired two other Leslie Stuart songs. One was "The Military Model," which made no great impact despite a parallel life in the variety theater. The other was destined to become one of the greatest hits of British popular song. In his leading role of the Parisian artist, Hayden Coffin introduced a sarcastic ditty about "The Soldiers of the Queen" who loved to stop at home and let the others go out to fight.

The Daly's appearance was not the song's first incarnation. Though the precise details of its origins are a matter of debate, it was inspired by the Manchester Ship Canal, which opened to traffic on January 1, 1894, and was formally opened by Queen Victoria in a splendid ceremony on May 21, 1894. Theater musical director James M. Glover claimed that Stuart wrote the song in 1881 for an exhibition of the ship canal at

Blackpool.[30] However, it was not until 1882 that the idea of the canal was even seriously discussed. More convincing is a story claiming that Stuart was impressed by the ceremonial playing of the Marseillaise that greeted a visit to Manchester of Ferdinand de Lesseps, builder of the Suez and Panama Canals, and determined to write a song to rouse the English in similar fashion.[66] As a further variant, Phil Herman claimed that the song "originated in a curious ditty on the opening of the Manchester Ship Canal—sung by Stuart in private to a few of his friends. It started 'Going to the Ship Canal, and every man will bring a pal.'"[40]

As sung at Daly's Theatre in 1895, "The Soldiers of the Queen" still didn't catch on. Coffin returned the rights and, in Stuart's own words, it was "put on the shelf" yet again. Then, recognizing good material, he took it down and revised it further. Albert Christian relaunched it at the Oxford Music Hall in Oxford Street late in 1895, with stirring patriotic words that still impress today:

> Britons once did loyally declaim
> About the way we ruled the waves;
> Ev'ry Briton's song was just the same
> When singing of our soldier braves.
> All the world had heard it, wondered why we sang,
> And some have learned the reason why;
> But we're forgetting it, and we're letting it
> Fade away and gradually die.
> So when we say that England's master,
> Remember who has made her so.
>
> It's the soldiers of the Queen, my lads,
> Who've been, my lads, who've seen, my lads,
> In the fight for England's glory, lads,
> When we've had to show them what we mean.
> And when we say we've always won,
> And when they ask us how it's done,
> We'll proudly point to ev'ry one
> Of England's soldiers of the Queen.

Another significant breakthrough was with the variety artist Lottie Collins, destined to be forever associated with the song "Ta-ra-ra-boom-de-ay," a nonsensical song with a delirious dance routine that she would perform at four or five halls nightly. She also performed it in America during the intervals of comic opera performances, and it was after a long absence in America that she returned to London in July 1895 for a season at the Palace Theatre of Varieties. The theater was full to overflowing and gave an overwhelming welcome to her three songs, of which the third was Leslie Stuart's "I Went to Paris with Papa." The *Era*, in describing the occasion, wrote, "She bounds on to the stage dressed in a demure-looking frock to sing of the doings of a sly little puss whose knowledge of the world is much more comprehensive than she cares to confess. 'You've only got to see her when no one's in the way,' sums up the situation in a sentence. In the song we get just an echo of 'Ta-ra-ra.' The fair Lottie next impersonates a 'Little Widow' who has buried two partners, and is looking for a third to share her loneliness. In this selection the artiste exhibits an archness and piquancy that are irresistible; and in her last song, 'I went to Paris with Papa,' her unquenchable high spirits, her vivacity, and her chic style take the audience captive. The arts and graces of comedy are hers, and her dancing is delightful."

Another Stuart song for Lottie Collins that same year of 1895 was "The Gay Señora of Gay Seville." When she reappeared at the Palace Theatre of Varieties on September 7, 1896 the third of her three new songs was also his. It successfully recaptured the excitement of "Tar-ra-ra-boom-de-ay" while also adding something a little more sophisticated—to the extent that the *Era* considered the words worthy of quotation:

> The third song, written and composed by Leslie Stuart, was called "The Girl on the Ran-Dan-Dan." It has been pointed out as a grievance of the music hall bard that, for want of a book of the words in the hands of a critic, the poet's effusions are often superficially judged. We have much pleasure, therefore, in quoting the words of the last verse of the song, which may serve as a sample of its literary point and polish:
>
> > The dancing in Society
> > > Is rather free,
> > > But you'll agree
> > A lady—should dance like a lady.
> > The dreamy waltz goes rather flat
> > > With pas de quatre
> > > And such as that;
> > Though etiquette professes—as everybody knows,

Lottie Collins in "The Girl on the Ran-dan-dan" (author's collection)

To keep a proper level for your toes.
But up went mine at the ball the other night;
   Mamma was in a fright,
   Said "What an awful sight."

And oh! How she cried when I said "I'm not to blame,
Why the girl who sang 'Tarara' did the same"

The effect of these lines, delivered by Miss Collins with all the arch
"intention" which she knows how to put into her expression can easily
be imagined. Miss Collins's delicacy of handling, ladylike method,
and brisk activity in the dance were quite conspicuous.

The *Era* may have considered Lottie Collins's performance delicate
and ladylike, but a man named Edeveain presented a rather different perspective in the journal *Society* in December 1896. He accused Miss
Collins of vulgarity and gross bad taste. She sued for libel, and the case
was heard in the Queen's Bench Division on July 15, 1897, before Justice
Henry Hawkins. If the *Era* is to be believed, the judge was as ignorant
of popular events as is often the case with senior judges. It quoted his
interruption of counsel for Edeveain as follows:

"The two songs she sang at the Palace" —
"Where is the Palace?" asked Sir Henry Hawkins.
"Were 'The Little Widow' and 'The Girl on the Ran-dan-dan'" —
"How do you spell that?" asked the judge. . . .

Counsel for the defendant went on to quote the song's reference to "hon-
eymooney eye, and a spooney kind of face," and with considerable
expression read out another part of the song that ran, "A goody-goody
prude, who should never look at a man; / A slippety-winkety sort of a
girl on the ran-dan-dan." The jury returned a verdict for Miss Collins,
with damages of £25—equivalent to over £1000 in year 2000 terms.

Though Leslie Stuart was now settled in London, he continued to
produce material for Manchester, where Robert Courtneidge had taken
over management of the Prince's Theatre in 1895. Courtneidge recalled
how Stuart wrote numbers for several of his pantomime productions—
apparently without payment.[15] The program of *Babes in the Wood* in
December 1896 indeed contained the acknowledgement, "The Management desires to express its indebtedness to Mr Leslie Stuart for the
exclusive right of singing many of his most popular compositions. Mr
Stuart has also specially composed the Opening Chorus of Scene 7." He
contributed even more to *Puss in Boots* at the Prince's Theatre the following year. For all his increasing success, Leslie Stuart never forgot his
friends or his roots.

Among those friends, of course, was Signor Foli, for whom Stuart composed the last of his creations in 1896. He later recalled the number's origins, noting that Signor Foli "wintered as rarely as he could in England, and he went periodically to visit his sister in the Catskill mountains, near New York, the scene of Washington Irving's "Rip Van Winkle" legend. I told him during one of his visits there that I would write a song of the legend and have it ready on his return. He said it could not be done with any success in that time. It *was* done, and it occupies seventeen pages of music print. It is what is known as a scena. In my opinion, and in that of many others, it is the best number I have written."[62]

The year 1897 also saw Stuart's songs appearing in further stage shows. The debonair W. Louis Bradfield introduced "She May Not Be That Sort of Girl" into *The Circus Girl*, the successor to *The Shop Girl* at the Gaiety Theatre. There were also three songs in *The Ballet Girl*, a touring musical with music primarily by Carl Kiefert that was first performed at the Grand Theatre, Wolverhampton, on March 15, 1897. Just over two weeks later, on March 31, London's Shaftesbury Theatre staged *The Yashmak*, a show supposedly of Armenian origin whose London score was put together by Corfu-born musical director Napoleon Lambelet. The *Era* did not think much of the piece, stating that "one hour should be taken out of it without delay" and adding that "lengthy description of *The Yashmak* is precluded by the fact that there is very little to describe." In that context it was almost glowing praise for the paper to say that Mabel Love's singing of the Leslie Stuart ballad "The Silly Old Man in the Moon" was "deservedly applauded."

Within a month, the Duke of York's Theatre staged *Lost, Stolen or Strayed*, a British version of an American musical comedy that in turn derived from a French farce. Decima Moore, in the leading role, sang Stuart's "The Goblin and the Fay." Despite an attempt to popularize the show by renaming it *A Day in Paris*, it lasted little more than a couple of months.

In the variety theater, too, Albert Christian followed up "The Soldiers of the Queen" with a Stuart military piece in quickstep rhythm about "The Dandy Fifth." This was the U.S. Fifth Cavalry Regiment, which Buffalo Bill Cody had accompanied against the Indians at Warbonnet Creek in 1876 after George Armstrong Custer's defeat at Little Bighorn. Stuart's song tells of the regiment being mobilized in Philadelphia. Christian also introduced into the variety theater the song "An English Girl," previously heard in *The Ballet Girl*.

Vesta Tilley, too, included another new Leslie Stuart number, "Dear

Boy, Ta-Ta," in the pantomime *Robin Hood and the Babes in the Wood* at the Theatre Royal, Glasgow, at Christmas of 1896. In 1897 she shared with Lester Barrett a number entitled "In the Summer," and the following year she introduced "The Girl with the Roses Red," subtitled "A Story of Far Alsace." Stuart had another major success with a scena first performed by an American trio, the Sisters Hawthorne, at the Alhambra Theatre in 1896. This was "The Willow Pattern Plate," performed in Chinese costumes in front of a huge circular backdrop representing the plate.

Already by 1896 the magazine *Home Notes* was able to write, "Time was when music-hall songs were described as being vulgar, low, and commonplace. All this is now being considerably altered. Composers for the music-hall are beginning to write *genuine music*. Mr Leslie Stuart stands first in this movement."[66]

Already, moreover, those other songwriting successes were being outstripped by one other songwriting relationship. This was with Eugene Stratton, the blackface performer of "coon" songs, and it was destined to become the major creative relationship of Leslie Stuart's career.

Chapter 6

Eugene Stratton, and Musical Piracy

Eugene Stratton and Leslie Stuart were of similar age, but from very different backgrounds. Stratton was born Eugene Augustus Rühlmann, of Alsatian immigrant parents, in Buffalo, New York, on May 8, 1861. Small in stature, he gained varied experience as an entertainer in America before joining Haverley's Mastodon Minstrels in 1878, doing "Negro" sketches. At the end of the season he was invited to join the troupe, also acquiring the stage name by which he was thereafter known. In 1880 the troupe traveled to England, opening at Her Majesty's Theatre in the Haymarket on July 31, 1880, and appearing in London and the provinces with great success until the early summer of 1881.[4]

Instead of returning to America, Stratton then accepted an offer to join the Moore and Burgess Minstrels, run by George Washington ("Pony") Moore. Continuing a line of blackface minstrel troupes popular in London since the 1840s, they had been established at St. James's Hall in Piccadilly since 1871, and were still going strong over twenty years later when satirized by Gilbert and Sullivan in *Utopia Limited*. In late 1883, Stratton cemented his relationship with his employer by marrying

Moore's daughter Bella. While still with the troupe he made his name as a performer with his performance of the song "The Whistling Coon," distinguished by Stratton's electrifying ability to produce the shrillest whistle audiences had ever heard.[4]

Eventually, in 1892, Stratton decided to go solo. As a blackface performer he had great success that year with "I Lub a Lubbly Gal, I Do," written and composed by Brandon Thomas, who later the same year saw production of his play *Charley's Aunt*. In 1893, Stratton had further success with "The Dandy Coloured Coon," with words by Richard Morton and music by George Le Brunn, who then provided Stratton with "The Idler" in conjunction with John P. Harrington.

The first Leslie Stuart song that Stratton sang was "Is Yer Mammie Always with Ye?" which he introduced in the special Easter Monday program at London's Oxford Music Hall in April 1896. The report in the *Era* shows how well geared it was to showing off Stratton's strengths, not least his marvellously light-footed dancing. It noted, "Mr Eugene Stratton's newest item is entitled "Is your mammy always wid you?" a plantation song with a haunting chorus, which is chanted 'off' by a number of fresh young voices. 'Gene' introduces also a famous dance with a final back somersault—a feat that brings down the house." The song is a tender one, the very opposite of the raucous songs that epitomize the music hall, a point exemplified by music critic Neville Cardus. He quoted James Agate as having—by slowing down the rhythm and using German words "Bleibt die Mutter bei dir immer?"—deceived serious musicians into thinking it was a cradle song by Johannes Brahms discovered lining a drawer in his bedroom of the Tiergarten Hotel in Berlin.[13]

Stuart claimed that he never received any fee from Stratton for the songs he provided him, but "wrote them for the love of the thing."[62] He recalled with affection their close artistic relationship:

> There was an affinity between us that neither of us was able to explain the cause or the inspiration of, until one night—or late in the early hours of the morning—I asked him how he came to acquire his wonderful dancing ability. His dancing was, as I have always maintained, so magnificent as to rank him a male Pavlova. It mattered not how many numbers he danced to in the course of an evening, he never danced twice alike. He just danced as he felt like dancing. It is the fact that, wonderful though his dancing was there was no set arrangement about it, and, to use a stage slang term it was really

"gagging." Nevertheless, his dancing was grace itself, and his poetical gliding over the stage has never been surpassed for gracefulness, agility, and real tranquility of movement.

... [W]hen we discovered the cause of our affinity, the revelation was made in the most matter-of-fact manner. We found that the inoculation affecting us both came through admiration for a wonderful American actor named J. K. Emmet. Emmet was perhaps one of the most handsome men who ever trod a stage. He made periodical visits to England, and he appeared in a play called "Our Cousin Fritz." He sang, yodelled, danced, and played instruments, being perhaps the biggest attraction of his day throughout America and England.

When Stratton asked me where I obtained the style that I ultimately incorporated in the numbers I had written for him, I told him that I had been inspired in those irresponsible words and melodies by the never-to-be-forgotten impressions left by J. K. Emmet. Stratton immediately jumped to his feet and said: "Good Heavens, he has been my inspiration, too. I used to get a quarter ... to see Emmet when I was quite a youngster and he played in my home town Buffalo. My dancing is nothing more nor less than a replica of J. K. Emmet's performances.[62]

It was when Stratton had made his pantomime debut, singing "Is Yer Mammie Always with Ye?" in *Cinderella* at the Prince of Wales Theatre, Birmingham, at Christmas 1896, that Stuart wrote the first of his Stratton songs that remained widely popular. His account of how it came about tells the touching family story behind it:

I wrote a song called "De Baby am a-cryin'," which I played to Eugene Stratton. I shewed it to him and he liked it immensely, but I had no time to fix up definitely with him, as he was hurrying off to take a part in the pantomime at Birmingham. About six weeks afterwards I got a wire from him: "Come up to Birmingham tomorrow to rehearse song. Have been studying it." Now, this was distinctly awkward, for about a fortnight before I had disposed of the performing rights of "De Baby am a-cryin'" to someone else, while Eugene was evidently under the impression that I had promised the song to him. Something had to be done, and done quickly too, and I spent the next two hours casting about for a way out of the difficulty. After much botheration and brain-splitting this was finally discovered.

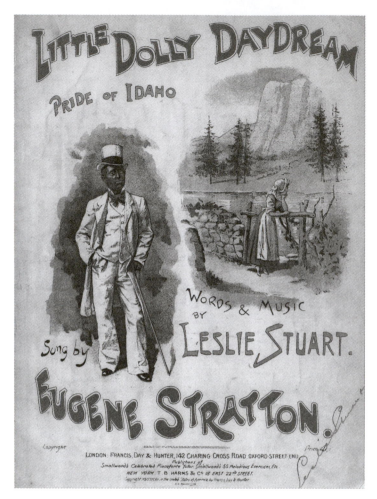

"Little Dolly Daydream" sheet music front, with portrait of Eugene Stratton
(author's collection)

My little daughter Dolly had only just begun to go to school, and,
like most children going to school for the first time, she seemed
greatly distressed at being parted from her mother for five or six
hours every day. On this particular evening she was more in the
clouds than ever, and didn't speak a word during dinner. At last my
wife said to her: "Come, little Dolly Daydream, you must find your
voice." That gave me the cue I wanted. Here I had, ready-made, a
taking title for a new coon-song, to take the place of "Baby am a-
cryin'." Before dinner was over I had the song mapped out in my
head, the words of it that is; the music was a different matter; but I

set to work about eight o'clock that evening, and by four o'clock next morning had finished the song, words, music, and dance.

Six hours afterwards I set off for Birmingham. Eugene met me at the station, full of the original song, but I told him I had something far better in my pocket. Luckily for me he was so taken with "Dolly Daydream," when I played it over for him, that he forgot all about "De Baby am a-cryin'." He had been singing "Dolly Daydream" for some months, before I told him the fate of the other song.[51]

"The other song," it might be added, had been sold for the musical play *The Ballet Girl*. As for "Dolly," it may be recalled that this was the name by which Marie Roze Barrett was known to her family. Stratton introduced the new song on his annual Easter appearance in London at the Oxford Music Hall in April 1897. It features a lovesick black man singing of his sweetheart in Idaho. When it later reached America, Stuart received letters from admirers, asking why it wasn't titled "Little Dolly Daydream, Pride of Manitoba" or "Little Dolly Daydream, Pride of Perkinsville." The answer was, of course, that "Idaho" suited the rhyme and meter better.[76]

There was better still to come. Even before it was publicly performed, their next song was clearly destined for popularity, as indicated by the *Entr'acte*, which wrote in its issue of July 23, 1898, "Mr Eugene Stratton's new song, 'The Lily of Laguna,' is sure to be a great success. It was produced at the Oxford on Monday evening, but those who had the opportunity of hearing the song at rehearsal could not resist the melody, and had it 'pat' before the song was publicly sung."

It was, indeed, the song of Leslie Stuart's that would charm Stratton's audiences the most, the story of the singer's love for his Lily, who "goes ev'ry sundown . . . callin' in de cattle up de mountain" and "plays her music to call de lone lambs dat roam above." "Laguna," the composer later wrote, "is a remote Indian village peopled only by cave dwellers, where the only language spoken is the native one. Lily, of the song, was a cave dweller in this spot about 100 miles off the main line *en route* for California proceeding from New Orleans."[62]

W. Macqueen-Pope later wrote affectionately of the impact the song created:

> Stratton did not so much sing the song, as caress it. Of all the myriads who have sung it since, nobody ever got near his perfect rendering. There he was, a coon carried away in an ecstasy of love,

discovered as the curtain rose, sitting on a gate, whistling away at a stick while the orchestra very softly played the introduction and then the verse.

But Stratton's thoughts seemed very far away from the music hall, they were with his Lily Girl. He whittled that stick by sheer force of habit, without knowing what he was doing, his mind fixed on his Lily and her sheep and cattle. And then, when the tension of watching that silent dreaming figure could hardly be borne, was at breaking point, he would begin very softly, to speak his thoughts, intertwined with Stuart's wonderful melody. Then came the lovely strains of "The Shepherdess Call," one of the best things Stuart ever wrote. . . . The words of the song . . . were just spoken thoughts and that is how Stratton sang it.

The song over, he would slide into his soft-shoe dance. . . . [It] was not so much dancing as movement expressing the words he had just sung. He made no sound, he moved like a spirit of the air, with perfect grace and rhythm. Yet he had no set routine, he danced as he felt, and at every performance he would improvise. One might see that dance a hundred times, and many did, and always it would be fresh and different.[38]

There was certainly no question now of simply following George Leybourne's advice to keep things simple. In "I Lub a Lubly Gal, I Do," Brandon Thomas had done just that, providing Stratton with a conventional old-fashioned number, with four bars of introduction followed by a sixteen-bar verse, eight-bar refrain, and four-bar postlude. In "Lily of Laguna," by contrast, a four-bar introduction prefaces a thirty-two-bar verse. Only after the sixteen-bar "Shepherdess's Call up the Mountain," with its oboe solo, do we have the twelve-bar refrain, after which we are led off again into a forty-four-bar dance and postlude. Where Brandon Thomas used a dotted rhythm that tended to reappear throughout, the verse section of "Lily of Laguna" introduces sharply contrasted rhythmic patterns. Crucial, too, are the strikingly inventive words. The lilting, effervescent tune leaves the listener feeling he has been taken on a thoroughly exhilarating mystery tour, with ever more intriguing twists and turns.

The fact that Stuart wrote both words and music was crucial to his songs' individuality. He later noted, "In my songs I wrote the words and music together to a large degree, and, consequently, I was able to get effects that the canons of the art lay down as being impossible. . . . There are only seven fundamental notes in music, and the sharps and flats are mere variations, but variations of the most desirable kind. . . . Now most authorities, forgetting the art of music, make it scientific, and declare that the set rules must be followed. Well, the set rules I set purposely on one side, and instead of ending where, say, the average poet would compel me by the metre of his verse, I, writing my own lyrics, add two bars more, and get an entirely new effect."[23]

Though the popularity of the songs for Eugene Stratton meant that sheet music sold in the thousands, their structural and rhythmic complexity meant that they were never the easiest of pieces for the amateur pianist. Grace notes and accidentals abound, and the basic key was rarely the simplest. When Francis, Day and Hunter published an album of nine of Leslie Stuart's most famous songs some years later, all but one ("Little Dolly Daydream") were notated in either three or four flats.

Similar characteristics were evident in Stratton's next Leslie Stuart song, which he introduced at the Oxford Music Hall on November 7, 1898. As the *Entr'acte* described it, "Mr Eugene Stratton's new song entitled 'The Cake Walk' is an unmistakable triumph and eminently special. Mr Stratton has a touch that is always recognisable, and it is his own. The music wedded to the "Cake Walk" is by Leslie Stuart, and is of a most uncommon and original order."

That evening's program was indeed a remarkable display of Stuart's talents. Also performing was Albert Christian, introducing Stuart's "The Little Anglo-Saxon Every Time," a number with choral accompaniment. Moreover, the *Entr'acte* describes a third Stuart contribution in the form of music for a dramatic sketch, "Drummer Dick." This was supposedly based on an incident in 1895, when a British expedition was despatched to quell a rebellion in Chitral in northern India (today's Pakistan). As the *Entr'acte* reported, "The boy hero, Dick, has misconducted himself, and the captain of his regiment threatens to take his drum from him, a punishment that presses very cruelly on the boy. But Captain Holt's sweetheart, Aileen Fitzgerald, intercedes for the young offender, and this turns out to be good diplomacy, for in the throes of a subsequent mutiny, and when Alice is borne away by revolting Indians, Dick snatches the drum and gives the alarm, which attracts the British forces to the spot, where they bring the disloyal Indians to their senses. Unfortunately, Dick's presence of mind causes the death of the brave drummer boy, who expires, surrounded by the friends who appreciate the value of his services."

Beatrix M. De Burgh wrote the sketch and played the part of Aileen Fitzgerald, with Evelyn Hughes as Dick, Albert Marsh as Captain Holt, and Wyndham Guise as Sergeant O'Neill.

Stuart's relationship with Stratton had meanwhile become as close a personal as an artistic one, as he later recalled, "Every morning when we were in London he either called for me in a hansom cab or I called for him, and we used to go to the Vaudeville Club, and while I endeavoured to emulate John Roberts on the billiard table, Eugene Stratton would entertain himself while waiting the result later in the day of one race or another on which the plunge had been made."[62] Stuart's daughter May elaborated, "They were just like schoolboys—mad parties at home when all the servants were sent to bed or out, and we children and Mother locked away in the nursery wing. Waiters from the Vaudeville Club, all the great men of the music halls behaving like crazy kids. Guns used to be fired, Father and Gene thinking up fantastic new games."[65]

The gatherings at Leslie Stuart's Battersea home evidently became something of an institution; as May recalled, "All sorts of stage folk and musical celebrities became our friends; they crowded into our Battersea home morning, noon and night—into that spacious Victorian house with its lace curtains, its aspidistras, its harmonium and grand piano, . . . and its boisterous father, and its pretty charming mother." She added that "Mother was always utterly unimpressed by my father's musical triumphs. But she was the most perfect hostess: the ideal housewife to remain at home, and look after the comfort of a genius. . . . "[66]

One major variety theater star who attended some of those gatherings, but for whom Leslie Stuart never wrote, was Marie Lloyd. He remembered meeting her in early 1898, when she was about to appear in her only musical comedy, *The ABC*:

> One night at the Tivoli (London), she was seated with my old friends Stratton, Little Tich, Harry Tate, and others in the little alcove where they were having the usual bottle. My wife and I had been in a box during the performance, and as we were leaving I saw this crowd of stars sitting in the alcove. Had I been alone there is not the slightest doubt about it, I would have been in the party. . . . I was endeavouring to clear off home with my wife, knowing how long the night would run if I then joined the party, and she was tired. . . . Marie came after us and insisted on us returning to the alcove. . . . We returned and I never remember a more amusing and entertaining three hours in my

life than those we spent with Marie Lloyd on that occasion. . . . Her wit and bubbling comments were a perfect joy. I frequently invited Marie to my Sunday evening dinners at my home afterwards. . . .[62]

There was, though, one major irritant in Leslie Stuart's increasingly successful and affluent life in London. His rise to fame in the 1890s had come on the back of an enormous increase in popularity of the variety theater and its songs as family entertainment. However, that same popularity gave opportunities to the unscrupulous to exploit it illegally. Copyright existed in respect of both performance and publication, but the practical operation of the copyright law was a problem. Composers could sell their creations to specific performers and publishers, and it was relatively easy to extract a performing fee from reputable concert societies or theaters, and a royalty on copies sold. However, it was an administrative nightmare to collect a performing fee from anyone who chose to perform a popular composition in some out-of-the way hall.

For the latter purpose the French had set up the Société des Auteurs, Compositeurs et Éditeurs de Musique (SACEM) in 1851, with appropriate administrative and legal support. Other European countries followed; but Britain and America chose not to. The result was that, following Britain's accession in 1886 to the Berne Convention for the Protection of Literary and Artistic Works, SACEM could employ agents in Britain to collect performing rights on French compositions, even though there were none on British works. As a concert promoter, Leslie Stuart had experience of this. In September 1890, his fellow Manchester concert promoter, J. A. Cross, had stood firm against a demand from SACEM for payment for performance of a French march.[14] Hence the assurance that, as Mr. T. A. Barrett, he had given ahead of his 1890–91 concert series that he had "made special arrangements . . . with the Society [*sic*] des Auteurs for the free use of all the French Operas and Songs in their repertoire."

As far as printed editions were concerned, publishers were prepared to turn a blind eye to the unauthorized copying of lyrics. However, the rising demand for printed editions of popular songs during the 1890s encouraged certain individuals to start issuing pirated editions of words and music that vastly undercut the legitimate article. Printed music was covered by the same copyright law as books; but, whereas the process of setting up in type, printing, and binding books was an expensive one, popular music of two or three pages could readily be photographed or lithographed in any old shed or barn.

What really got the pirates going was the huge popularity of "The Soldiers of the Queen" generated by Queen Victoria's Diamond Jubilee celebrations in June 1897. The authorities had sought to match the golden jubilee celebrations of a decade before, with a huge procession across London, featuring regiments and bands from all over the Empire. Leslie Stuart recalled, "When the second Jubilee was being arranged, . . . composers were . . . invited to send in suitable quicksteps. I scored 'The Soldiers of the Queen,' and by good luck it was accepted by every bandmaster whose band took part in the procession.[57]

According to Phil Herman, its selection was less by good luck than good management. He noted, "Stuart set about boosting it with remarkable energy. He approached all the regimental bandmasters, and the result was that on the occasion of the Jubilee, regiment after regiment came swinging along to the tune of 'Soldiers of the Queen.'"[40]

Stuart was left with the most popular—and potentially the most profitable—song in Britain; but he soon saw the rewards being creamed off as pirated copies flooded the streets. The whole music piracy issue was aired with the Music Publishers' Association and the Music Trade Section of the London Chamber of Commerce, but it was left to individual owners of copyrights to find their own remedy. Thus Francis, Day and Hunter took out a civil action in conjunction with the firm of Charles Sheard and Company, on which the *Era* reported, on September 4, 1897, "Mr David Day, of Messrs Francis, Day, and Hunter, has for some time been utterly unable to discover the source from which the penny copies of the firm's 2s. songs were flooding the kingdom. That experienced investigator, Inspector Littlechild, has at length solved the mystery. Step by step, by inquiries extending over nearly a couple of months, the inspector unearthed the printing establishment supplying the depôt from which the street vendors obtained their copies, and secured the necessary evidence. The legal proceedings that were instituted were not seriously resisted, and injunctions were granted in respect of 'Soldiers of the Queen,' 'Sweetheart May,' 'Let us be sweethearts again,' and 'The Song of the Thrush.'"

That it was "The Soldiers of the Queen" that was the real focus of the pirates' activities is confirmed by the following week's report in the *Era*, which noted, "Messrs Francis and Day have now obtained a perpetual injunction against one of the printers of pirated versions of their popular songs. The injunction orders the delivering up of all copies of the illicit edition, and the payment of costs by the defendant, the plaintiff firm continuing to waive damages. The printer declares he is now going

"Soldiers of the Queen" autograph voice and piano score (author's collection)

to leave the pirate line, and become an honest merchantman. A holocaust of copies of 'The Soldiers of the Queen' took place in North London on Wednesday morning. The plates from which they were printed were also hammered to pieces."

This was, however, little more than the beginning of the story. The potential profits from piracy far outstripped the impact of the penalties, and the demand for cheap editions of popular numbers could only increase. As Leslie Stuart recalled, the response of himself and David Day on one occasion led them into a spot of trouble:

The business went so far and was so disastrous to me that one day when out for a walk with Mr. David Day, the bare-faced nature of it so affected us that we got hold of some of the hawkers and tried to pound a sense of honesty and fair play into them. Some took the hammering well, no doubt believing that the game they had been profiting by really deserved it. One however, positively numb to all sense of decency, took out a summons against us, and this culminated in my friend and myself figuring on that stage of so many human dramas—the floor of Marlborough Street Police Court....

We listened to the sensational evidence against us, the court appeared grave, and the beak, toying ominously with his snow white handkerchief instead of with the black cap, we saw ourselves knocked down like a doubtful bargain lot for forty shillings and costs.[62]

Happily, most of Leslie Stuart's efforts to accelerate revisions to copyright were within the law. When on March 21, 1898, the attorney general asked in the House of Commons for the true facts on the issue, Stuart responded at once. His letter to the attorney general was published in the *London and Provincial Music Trades Review*'s issue of April 15, 1898. It is reproduced in part here, and it should be noted that there were 240 pence (*d.*) or twenty shillings (*s.*) to the pound (*l.*), and that monetary amounts need to be multiplied by over forty times to arrive at year 2000 equivalents:

Emboldened by the futility of the publishers' actions, an alarming development was made in April last ... in issuing not only the words but also the exact reproduction of the music of the most popular songs of the day (still without printer's name and address). A song of my composition (words and music) entitled "The Soldiers of the Queen," which was then in great demand by the public, was the first to be attacked. Hawkers were obtaining from 2*d.* to 6*d.* per copy—the streets of London and all the principal towns in the kingdom being literally swarmed by the men disposing of this song.

The legitimate musicsellers pay from 10*d.* to 1*s.* 4*d.* per copy to the publisher of my songs—I receiving a royalty of 2½ *d.* per copy.

I estimate my loss on this one song as already 250*l.*; and that of the publisher still more.

My publisher and myself, after much trouble and expense in the employing of detectives (four months in the process), discovered the printer. He had, we estimate, already disposed of 100,000 copies to hawkers. We found only about 800 copies in his possession, confiscated them, destroyed his plates, and injuncted him.

He printed in a small house (tenanted by his wife), his effects were not worth 5s., and no damages were obtainable from him, although over 100*l.* was spent in his detection. We could not confiscate the copies in the hands of the hawkers, although they continued to sell them long after the injunction on the printer. We have since discovered stereotyped copies on the street, which leads us to assume that they are still being printed elsewhere. . . .

Since last June all the most popular songs of the day have thus been pirated, many prominent publishers and composers being the victims of the process. I am the principal loser amongst composers, as three of my principal songs have been pirated simultaneously. I am compelled to withhold the issue of new songs, knowing this outrage will be committed should my new compositions obtain popularity.

The publishers whose songs are being pirated are receiving daily complaints from the musicsellers with whom they trade that they cannot dispose of the songs they have in stock while they are being sold at their door for twopence. They refuse to purchase these songs from the publishers in any quantity, as they find the demand decreasing enormously. New songs are not being purchased by the traders in any quantity, as they expect they will receive the attention, in due course, of the pirate. The loss to publishers and composers during eleven months past is estimated at many thousands of pounds—my individual loss I estimate at 5*l.* per day. . . .

Nothing short of criminal penalties will deter these men, as, being of no substance, injunctions prove no terrors for them. . . .[45]

He subsequently had several meetings with the attorney general, Sir Robert Finlay, and later recalled, "I tried to get him to give his fiat in magisterial proceedings which might then in the early stages of piracy have resulted in summary convictions. . . . I was instructed that my action was not necessary, and that Parliament would readily see that such an iniquitous state of things would meet with immediate legislation."[24] During July 1898 a select committee of the House of Lords heard representations from publishers in connection with an amendment to copyright legislation proposed by Lord Herschell. However, matters were to drag on for years.

While the publishing debate continued, moreover, there appeared a manifestation of Stuart's concern to protect his output on the performing side. It took the form of an advert published in the *Era* on December 3, 1898, and subsequently in the *Entr'acte*. Though it mentions Francis, Day and Hunter as publisher, the notice is in the name of Leslie Stuart, of 81 Albert Road, Battersea Park, and gives his home telephone number:

NOTICE

Managers are hereby acquainted that Proceedings will be Taken on the unauthorised use of the under-mentioned Songs, Written and Composed by me, and that the including of any portion of them in concerted numbers is in Strict Violation of the Conditions upon which Permission is Given for their Performance. It will be further regarded as Actionable if the Titles, Words, or Music are Altered to Suit a particular "situation" or character in Pantomime. On no account is Permission Granted unless the Entire Song (or no Less than Two Verses) is to be Sung.

LESLIE STUART

There follows, with artists' names in brackets afterwards, a list of his principal songs. Francis, Day and Hunter had seemingly already published these songs, with just two exceptions. The first was the song "The Down on the Butterfly's Wing," sung by Elaine Ravensberg, the second, "I Must Love Someone; It Might As Well Be You," supposedly sung by Vesta Tilley. It is far from clear whether Vesta Tilley actually did sing the latter song; but it seems to be the first mention of a number that was soon to create a sensation as the major hit of the musical play toward which Leslie Stuart was currently building.

Chapter 7

Florodora

Such was Leslie Stuart's status by the end of the 1890s that he earned the distinction of being one of the earliest artists to perform for the newly invented gramophone record. It was only in 1897 that the Gramophone Company set up in London to exploit Emil Berliner's European gramophone patents. On May 16, 1898, basement premises were taken at 31 Maiden Lane, behind the Strand, and on August 2, 1898, Berliner's young recording engineer and talent scout Fred Gaisberg made his first recordings. Just over five months later, on January 10, 1899, Leslie Stuart entered the Maiden Lane studio and recorded a piano solo version of "Little Dolly Daydream."[53]

Evidently the experiment was deemed a success, because some three months later—on April 7, 1899—he returned to cut a further, more significant, set of recordings. This time he had with him two of his most important interpreters. With Stuart at the piano, Eugene Stratton first sang "Little Dolly Daydream," followed by "Is Yer Mammie Always with Ye?" Then Albert Christian set down "The Soldiers of the Queen," after which Stratton returned to sing "The Cake Walk," and finally added his individual style of whistling to Albert Christian's recording of "The Dandy Fifth." Three weeks later the composer was back for a further four sides comprising piano versions of "The Cake Walk," "The Coon Drum Major," "Lousiana Lou," and "Is Yer Mammie Always with Ye?"[53]

Of these final four numbers, "The Coon Drum-Major" had been heard for the first time that very same month, when Eugene Stratton introduced it at the Oxford Music Hall on Easter Monday, April 3, 1899. It was another marvelous example of Stuart's invention, being a vigorous march number in which Stratton led a squad of black-face military men:

> I'm Drum-Major of de Band,
> Drum Major of de Band,
> The leader of de coon brigade;
> I'm Drum Major of de Band,
> And don't we make a loud zing boom
> Along de esplanade!

Stuart recalled the circumstances of the song's introduction as follows:

When I wrote . . . "The Coon Drum Major" Stratton was out of London; he was in pantomime in the Provinces where he commanded a huge salary. . . . I had rehearsed "The Coon Drum-Major" and had the scenery painted, leaving Stratton only to learn the song. Everything was prepared for his performance; twenty-four men were engaged as supernumeraries, and when he saw them go through their evolutions for the first time he was dumbfounded at the precision of their drill. The curtain went up on his new number, leaving the audience in a similar state of wonderment as to how it had been possible to obtain such remarkable military unison and deportment from the material among the "super" type usually at the disposal of "producers." The smartness of the men in their American military uniforms and blackened faces won the approval of critics and audience alike.

Little did they know of the secret of that success until some time later. Every man in the military party was a British Guardsman, and they performed their evolutions under the command of one of their own non-commissioned officers. Through the kindness of the officer at Knightsbridge I was permitted to employ, each evening, the number of men I have mentioned, and their honorarium was half-a-crown a man per night. To the boys this represented good spending money and there was competition for the reliefs.[62]

Later in April 1899, at the London Pavilion, came "My Little Octoroon," of which Stuart was especially fond:

> I must say that, to my mind, it is the best song in the series I wrote for Eugene Stratton, as it is based on a pathetic and true-to-life fact among negroes. As is generally known, an octoroon is an eighth degree remove from the real negro, and some very handsome women can be numbered amongst these octoroons. It is taboo in the Southern States for any white woman to marry an octoroon because of the consequent social complications that would follow. It is a strange freak of nature that the first issue of a marriage—despite the fact of the white colour of either of the parties whether man or woman—if one is an octoroon, enters the world as black as ebony. . . .
>
> In the States I have particularly referred to the man or woman as ostracised who marries out of his or her colour, but north of the Ohio river this is condoned and accepted. However, the story of my song is based on this physiological concession.[62]

The object of the protagonist's affection is an "octoroon" with whom he has been brought up. She decides to cross the Ohio River to where she is regarded merely as a "dark brunette" but where he may never venture. A tender outpouring after the manner of "Lily of Laguna," the song provided a sharp contrast to "The Coon Drum-Major":

> She ain't as black as she ought to be,
> Dey made her white, so's you could see
> Dat she could smile like you and blush as soon,
> But she's as much a nigger as a coal-black coon.

That Stuart's output during the first half of 1899 was otherwise negligible may have been, at least in part, a reaction to the pirating of published editions of his songs. The projected reform of copyright legislation had made little progress, and it received a particular blow when Lord Herschell died suddenly in the United States on March 1, 1899. Lord Monkswell took up the issue, and a committee of the House of Lords began a further enquiry. On May 15, 1899, David Day gave evidence to a select committee, proposing legal power to search for and seize unlawful copies. He produced pirated copies of several popular songs, among them "The Soldiers of the Queen" and "Little Dolly Daydream." He also produced innumerable letters of complaint addressed to Francis, Day and Hunter from music dealers from all parts of the kingdom and particulars of injunctions obtained at great expense in the High Court. It was to little avail.

That Leslie Stuart should now seek success as a composer of scores for the musical theater may have been in part a reaction to the piracy he was suffering, because royalties for theater performances were so much easier to collect and protect. It was anyway a natural extension of the dramatic scenas he had successfully composed for Stratton and others. It was two theatrical entrepreneurs, named Ben Nathan and Walter Weil, who formed a company for the purpose. Nathan, himself a variety performer, had known Stuart for many years, having sung Lester Barrett's song "Ada's Serenade" on the variety stage a decade before. Nathan and Weil linked up with Tom B. Davis, who had taken over the licence of London's Lyric Theatre in 1898. On June 29, 1899, a production company named Pheenia Limited was incorporated with Davis as a director.[54]

The first announcement that Stuart was to compose a musical play came at the end of May 1899 and brought a biographical profile in the *Era* issue of June 3, 1899, with the announcement that the work was to be produced in the West End in September. Two weeks later came the information that it would be produced at the Lyric Theatre, and that the book author would be Owen Hall, the pen name of James Davis that humorously acknowledged his perpetual shortage of money. Hall had written several of the most successful British musical comedy books of the 1890s, including that of Sidney Jones's *The Geisha*. The lyricist was announced as Adrian Ross, and the setting as India, but neither of these was actually to materialize. On August 26 the *Era* named the new work as *Florodora*, and on September 9, it noted that, notwithstanding the success of De Wolf Hopper's imported production of John Philip Sousa's *El Capitan* at the Lyric, the new production could not be delayed beyond the middle of November. The score, moreover, was "nearly finished."

Stuart did take time off from its composition to attend the first day of the race meeting at Goodwood in Sussex on July 25, when the main race, the Stewards' Cup, was won by a twenty-to-one outsider. It happened to be owned by a financial backer of *Florodora*, the journalist and entrepreneur Horatio Bottomley, who was eventually imprisoned for fraud. Stuart described his day out:

My conductor [Carl Kiefert], a German, was a great analyst of racing form up to the Goodwood meeting every year. . . . One day he told me that I ought to back Horatio Bottomley's horse Northern Farmer as it was certain to win the Stewards' Cup despite all other tips and the wagering in the favour of others.

My brother Lester was then playing a season at Douglas, Isle of Man. We had formed a party—my wife, a friend and his wife—to drive to Goodwood, and before we left London in the morning in the coach, having no account with a bookmaker, and knowing that we would be in the carriage enclosure far from the madding crowd that gambled, I telegraphed to Lester asking him to place two pounds each way for my friend and myself on Northern Farmer.

Just before the big race my friend and I left the ladies on the brake strolling over to the ring to see the boys. There we found Eugene Stratton. . . . I don't know why Stratton asked what I thought would win the Stewards' Cup; he had never had any reason to accuse me of being a highly successful backer of horses. But I affected the manner born of the man in the know; pulling my mouth one side and speaking through my teeth from behind my hand I said "Northern Farmer."

I thought Stratton, who was then a great gambler moving in a circle of jockeys and trainers who made history on the British turf, some of the undesirable kind that ended in their being warned off, was going to savage me for my apparent stupidity. He pulled me at one side, said the favourite was a certainty, hauled me over to a bookmaker and told him that I was on the favourite to a fiver each way, the account to go down with his. So here I was with a fiver each way with a horse I never intended backing with a prospect of owing a tenner in the next few minutes. . . .

As the horses passed it appeared fifty to one on the favourite. Stratton looked at me as much as to ask me what I thought of myself and my information when up in the frame went the number of "Northern Farmer." I became one of the most unpopular fellows among the stage folk at Goodwood, as they all believed through Horatio Bottomley being a patron of "Florodora," I must have had a good tip about the winner. They would not believe me when I told them that the information had no greater inspiration for its source than the man I have mentioned. . . . I was very pleased to find when I got back to London that Lester had received my wire, and more, had carried out the commission.... It took a bottle of wine or two to wash out my alleged shortcomings among the stage boys.[62]

As was frequently the case, the evolution of the book of *Florodora* was determined less by any high artistic muse than by the performers who were available. Ada Reeve in particular was added to the cast at the last moment after falling out with the management at Daly's Theatre during rehearsals for Sidney Jones's musical play *San Toy* and taking an engagement at the Palace Theatre. When Owen Hall chanced to meet her, he offered to bring Tom B. Davis to her dressing room to discuss a part in *Florodora*. As she later recalled, "When they arrived at my dressing-room at the Palace that evening, my first question naturally was: 'What is the part?' 'Well, what sort of a part would you like?' said Owen Hall cheerfully, 'it isn't written yet.' So the curious situation arose that Lady Holyrood, who eventually became the outstanding feminine character in *Florodora*, was not an intrinsic part of the plot at all!"[49]

The bulk of the lyrics of *Florodora* were written by a young actor and author named Ernest Boyd-Jones. However, Stuart himself wrote those for the more elaborate production numbers, while the lyrics for Ada Reeve's songs were written by Paul A. Rubens, who also composed the music for one of them. Like Stuart, Rubens had contributed a song to *The Shop Girl* at the Gaiety, and, though still in his early twenties and thus a dozen years or so younger, he was already making his name as a musical comedy composer.

Production of what Owen Hall described as a "society piece" was finally fixed for November 11, 1899. The *Era* claimed that the show had "not only a primary plot but a secondary one also; and Mr Hall considers himself to be in the position of a sportsman who, if he misses with one barrel, can bring down his bird with the other." A scent of the plot was provided in the announcement that when the show opened "a new perfume, bearing the same title, will be introduced to the public, and a small sample will be presented to everyone in the audience on the opening night." Throughout the show's run the perfume continued to be available from attendants in the theatre at 2 shillings, 6 pence per bottle.

Produced by Tom B. Davis at the Lyric Theatre, London,
on 11 November 1899

FLORODORA.

A New Musical Comedy. Written by Owen Hall.

Lyrics by Ernest Boyd-Jones and Paul Rubens.

Music by Leslie Stuart.

Cyrus W. Gilfain	(Proprietor of the Perfume and of the Island of Florodora)		
			Mr Charles E. Stevens
Frank Abercoed	(Manager for Cyrus Gilfain of the Island of Florodora)		
			Mr Melville Stewart
Leandro	(Overseer of Farms)		Mr Frank Holt
Captain Arthur Donegal (4th Royal Life Guards—Lady Holyrood's Brother)			
			Mr Edgar Stevens
Tennyson Sims			Mr Roy Horniman
Ernest Pym			Mr Ernest Lambart
Max Aepfelbaum	(Gilfain's Clerks)		Mr Alfred Barron
Reginald Langdale			Mr Frank Haskoll
Paul Crogan			Mr Sydney Mannering
John Scott			Mr Frank Walsh

AND

Anthony Tweedlepunch (A Showman, Phrenologist, Hypnotist, and Palmist)

Mr Willie Edouin

———

Dolores			Miss Evie Greene
Valleda			Miss Nancy Girling
Inez			Miss Lydia West
Jose	(Florodorean Girls, heads of the various Farms)		Miss Lily McIntyre
Juanita			Miss Fanny Dango
Violante			Miss Blanche Carlow
Calista			Miss Beatrice Grenville

AND

Angela Gilfain			Miss Kate Cutler
Daisy Chain			Miss Edith Housley
Mamie Rowe			Miss Jane May
Lucy Ling	(Friends of Angela Gilfain)		Miss Nora Moore
Cynthia Belmont			Miss Beryl Somerset

| Lottie Chalmers | | | Miss Nellie Harcourt |
| Claire Fitzclarence | | | Miss Nina Sevening |

AND

Lady Holyrood   Miss Ada Reeve

Florodorean Farmers, Labourers, Flower Girls, Welsh Peasants, etc.

Pas Seul in Act II by Miss LILY MCINTYRE

ACT I.   FLORODORA, A SMALL ISLAND IN THE PHILIPPINES

ACT II   ABERCOED CASTLE, WALES

Full Orchestra under the Direction of the Composer.

Production by SYDNEY ELLISON.

In Act 1, on Florodora, a group of flower pickers are praising the island's floral beauties ("Flowers A-blooming so Gay"). The "Florodora" perfume is made from these flowers in a factory belonging to the island's American owner, Cyrus W. Gilfain. His return from England is eagerly awaited, because he alone knows the perfume's secret formula.

While they wait, a group of clerks come from the counting house, claiming it is their bookkeeping that is keeping the operation afloat ("The Credit's Due to Me"). The farmworkers, though, have unkind words about one of their number, Dolores, who neglects her work but gets her wages doubled. Abercoed, Gilfain's manager, sends for Dolores and she enters, dreaming of love ("The Silver Star of Love"). It is soon evident that the two are deeply attracted to each other. However, Abercoed reveals that he left England to escape a fiancée he didn't love. Being engaged already, he can only express in vague terms who he's now in love with ("Somebody").

The ship from England brings various visitors, including Gilfain, who receives the welcome his status demands ("Huzzah! The Master Comes!"). He declares that he enjoyed England so much that he bought a castle and estate there from an impoverished aristocratic family. Also from the boat is a group of English girls who are friends of Gilfain's daughter Angela. Gilfain's clerks agree to show them the island ("Come and See Our Island").

Another visitor is the widowed society lady Lady Holyrood. She knows Abercoed and breaks the news to him that his fiancée has now married someone else; she also reports that his uncle has died and he is now Lord Abercoed. She explains that she has come to find a wife for her brother, Captain Arthur Donegal of the Fourth Royal Life Guards, but it is clear that Gilfain's wealth was a factor in persuading her to accompany him from England. When she realizes it is Dolores with whom Abercoed is in love, she ponders how to introduce her to London Society ("When I Leave Town"). Dolores, though, becomes jealous at seeing Abercoed chatting to Lady Holyrood.

Angela Gilfain meanwhile has wanted to marry Arthur Donegal, but her father has declared that she should instead marry his manager, Abercoed. When Angela learns the latter is now Lord Abercoed, she reveals that Abercoed Castle is the place her father has bought as European headquarters for selling the Florodora perfume. Abercoed makes it clear that he has no interest in marrying Angela, whereas Donegal stresses he is in a hurry to do so ("Galloping").

The final arrival from the boat is Anthony Tweedlepunch, showman, hypnotist, palmist, and phrenologist. He tells Gilfain that by phrenological examination he can discover nature's affinities and thereby pair people off. This is just what Gilfain wants, and they come to a financial arrangement that Tweedlepunch's "science" will arrange for Angela to be paired with Abercoed. When Lady Holyrood chances upon their conversation, she adds her own wish to remarry ("I Want to Marry a Man, I Do"). Gilfain's clerks then arrive, paired off with the English girls, and enquiring who Angela feels romantic about. She gives an enigmatic reply ("The Fellow Who Might").

It becomes clear that Tweedlepunch knows that Gilfain has stolen the secret of the "Florodora" perfume. Tweedlepunch realizes that Gilfain's plan to marry himself to Dolores, and Angela to Abercoed, is part of a grand scheme to regularize matters. For the present, Tweedlepunch goes along with Gilfain's scheme and uses his science to advise that Gilfain should pair off with Dolores, and Angela with Abercoed ("Phrenology").

Lady Holyrood, Donegal, and Angela are not impressed ("When an Interfering Person"). As for Abercoed, he has packed his bags, promising Dolores that he will return and that meanwhile she will always be in his thoughts ("The Shade of the Palm"). When Dolores vents her anger on Tweedlepunch, he realizes she is the young lady he has come to the island to find and why Gilfain is keen to marry her. While Gilfain claims Dolores as his own, everyone else tries to persuade Abercoed to stay ("Hey! Hey! A-lack a-day!").

In Act 2, at Abercoed Castle in Wales, the folk are indulging in a country frolic ("Come Lads and Lasses, Trip Your Light Airy"). All the major characters are there, with Lady Holyood expounding what is more important than money to survive in Society ("Tact"). Gilfain, of course, has no such money problems ("The Millionaire"). His clerks have followed the English girls back home, and the two groups pay each other polite compliments ("Are There Any More at Home Like You?"). As for Angela, she assures Donegal that he is the only man for her and that she'll whistle when she wants him ("Whistling" [words and music Paul Rubens]).

Then Dolores and Tweedlepunch arrive in disguise and convince Gilfain they are wandering entertainers ("Mysterious Musicians"). As for Lady Holyrood, she is increasingly confident that she will land Gilfain and his wealth for herself ("I've an Inkling" [words and music Paul Rubens]). Abercoed, meanwhile, has gained admission disguised as an old harpist, and he declares his intention to return to Florodora for Dolores ("Land of My Home"). However, Lady Holyrood mischievously tells him to hang around.

Tweedlepunch and Dolores reappear, now dressed as Parisian minstrels. Having ascertained from Tweedlepunch the truth about Gilfain's theft of the "Florodora" recipe, Lady Holyrood agrees to hire him to help punish Gilfain. At dinner Tweedlepunch appears as the ghostly Bard of Abercoed Castle and pronounces the ancient curse of Ethelwynda that hangs over anyone in the castle accused of crime and treachery. Terrified, Gilfain confesses to stealing Florodora and its perfume from Tweedlepunch's old friend Guisara, Dolores's father, and agrees to hand them back. Now the young people are all free to marry their true loves ("And the Nation Will Declare").

Three cheers from the gallery greeted Leslie Stuart as he made his way to the conductor's rostrum on the opening night. That he conducted was significant in itself, because the new generation of musical theater composers were divided between those who were musical directors—Ivan Caryll, Sidney Jones, and Howard Talbot—and those who specialized in songs with a popular touch—the likes of Lionel Monckton and Paul Rubens. Leslie Stuart was the exception: as popular a songwriter as any, and yet able to take charge of musicians in the orchestra pit. After the first night, of course, that role went to Carl Kiefert, who as a specialist theater orchestrator presumably also did the show's orchestrations.

The press reaction was uniformly enthusiastic, and from the first night the success was scarcely in doubt. The *Stage* reported that "tempestuous laughter [greeted] nearly every sally and topical allusion in Owen Hall's book, full of that writer's mordant humour and insolently audacious cynicism." The *Era* described the piece as "a refined variety show, set in a light frame of plot" and went on to say, "*Florodora* is certainly the brightest, liveliest, and most amusing entertainment of its kind which is at present being offered to the London public. The book is cleverly contrived and ingeniously invented; the lyrics are gaily, neatly, and crisply written; the music is full of dash and brilliancy; the stage pictures are extremely pretty; and each of the principals has plenty of opportunities."

The report described the dresses as "very handsome," the stage picture as "admirable," and expressed a widely held view that, as Tweedlepunch, veteran comic Willie Edouin was the mainstay of the evening: "The part is admirably planned to allow of that liberal expansion which Mr Edouin likes to give to the characters entrusted to him; and he is irresistibly droll in it. It is impossible not to laugh—and laugh most heartily—at the strong pseudo-scientific style of Tweedlepunch in the first act, and at the business which Mr Edouin introduces in connection with the phrenological examinations. But it is in the second act that he really lets himself go.' To see him, in a wonderfully current replication of the violinist of the Parisian Minstrel Troupe, dancing in the most grotesque fashion, and playing so frantically that his instrument goes to pieces; to witness his denunciation of Gilfain, accompanied by savage twangings on the harp, is to be convulsed." As for the score, the *Era* described it as "exhilarating in its buoyant gaiety."

The music's quality is indeed evident from the opening number. In two parts, it begins with airy chords accompanying the islanders' languorous tribute to the floral aromas and pretty maidens that bedeck the island. Underneath those chords is a melodic theme that, complete with castanet accompaniment, is taken up in lustier bolero tempo in a second section in which a group of Spanish farmworkers make their entrance and sing of the scented delights of "Flora! Florodora!" It is, in effect, the score's leitmotif.

In Dolores's entrance song, "The Silver Star of Love," the audience welcomed glamorous twenty-one-year-old Portsmouth girl Evie Greene. In waltz tempo and with an introductory section sung offstage, it is one of the numbers for which Stuart provided his own lyric, and it was all the more successful for that. Praised no less warmly was the flowing romantic baritone solo "In the Shade of the Palm," with its big waltz refrain, "Oh, My Dolores!" The *Graphic* also commented that the audience was particularly pleased with Rubens's "capital whistling song" for

Ada Reeve as Lady Holyrood in *Florodora*, London (author's collection)

popular light soprano Kate Cutler, as well as the first of Ada Reeve's lightly pointed, scarcely sung numbers, "Tact."

For all its trademark dotted figure in the accompaniment, "Tact" lacks Leslie Stuart's usual free-flowing style and, in truth, sounds more like a Paul Rubens composition. Presumably its fourth verse, with its references to Goodwood and roulette, was designed to reflect the composer's predilection for gambling and the race course.

The song was to serve Ada Reeve well, to the extent that she used it for the title of her autobiography, *Take It for a Fact*. The *Graphic* understandably felt it a song more appropriate for the variety halls, but that paper's similar categorization of "The Fellow Who Might" is more surprising. Sung by Kate Cutler as Angela in act 1, it is in the line of theater songs about tentative wooing that runs from "I Know a Youth" in Gilbert and Sullivan's *Ruddigore* to "Bill" in Jerome Kern's *Show Boat*. Its lyric (by J. Hickory Wood) is uninspired, but its musical setting is captivating, with an elegantly floated melody and delicate key shifts. Theatrical precedents are apparent, too, in the longest number in act 2, the duet "Mysterious Musicians" for Dolores and Tweedlepunch. With the performers showing off their talents in various song styles, it is a comic counterpart of Nanki-Poo's "Wandering Minstrel" in Gilbert and Sullivan's *The Mikado*, even down to containing a nautical section.

Not all reporters were as astute as the one from the *Times*, who noted the other substantial act 2 number, writing, "Perhaps the most ingenious number is a so-called concerted piece in which a little scene of courtship is gone through by six couples at once; strange to say, this number 'Are There Any More At Home Like You?' made a great hit...." In the rhythmic mould of "Lily of Laguna" but more upbeat and carefree, it has those same dotted rhythms and that same sense of meandering aimlessly on, oblivious to the conventional structures of popular song. It would soon become a theatrical sensation, better known under its opening line, "Tell Me, Pretty Maiden," or simply as the "*Florodora* sextet."

Neville Cardus once more came up with lofty musical comparisons for the number. "No popular music has equalled the beautiful and unexpected phrasing and transitions of this part-song in *Florodora*," he declared.[13] He recalled how "it begins with a long phrase, rather like the opening bars of a Brahms symphony. It is extraordinary to find music such as this in a musical comedy ... the men with their morning-coats and walking-sticks, the women with their big hats and long dresses (not an inch of leg showing)." He suggested the piece was "just as perfect a composition, on the plane of musical comedy, as is the quintet in *Meistersinger*...."[18]

Stuart himself gave a recipe for the number that at once recognized his own church music background and the piece's similarity to Eugene Stratton's minstrel songs, explaining, "For the business, take one memory of Christy Minstrels, let it simmer in the brain for twenty years. Add slowly, for the music, an organist's practice in arranging Gregorian chants for a Roman Catholic church. Mix well and serve with half-a-dozen pretty girls and an equal number of well-dressed men...."[27] His background was equally apparent in the staging, with chorus ladies and gentlemen, dressed as for racing at Ascot, meeting and crossing in the manner of acolytes moving across the altar at High Mass in a Roman Catholic Cathedral.[66]

Seemingly this double sextet was the number "I Must Love Someone; It Might as Well Be You" that Stuart had advertised almost a year previously as sung by Vesta Tilley. If so, and he held it back for *Florodora*, it casts doubt on his accounts of the number's origins, which suggest he composed it shortly before the show opened. Asked how he came to write it, he replied, "It came to me suddenly, I suppose. I had a great desire to write a concerted number for six men and six girls." Asked, "And why six?" he replied, "Because they would just comfortably reach across the stage."[76] Later in life he gave this more detailed account:

> About this time a niece of my wife, a Miss Agnew, was on holiday in England from Brisbane in Australia, her father being the mayor of that city. . . . The pretty Australian girl eventually decided to look up her aunt in London. . . . She had not very long installed herself in my house than I found her conducting a mild telephonic flirtation with one of the officers of the ship on which she had made the journey from Australia. Assuming all the dignity I could in manner and tone, I addressed the pretty and dashing colonial miss in terms that made it perfectly clear as I thought, that since she was under the chaperonage of her aunt and in my temporary guardianship, we would be remiss in our duty if we did not insist on abrogating the rights of her parents over their charming daughter and show our disapproval of the sweet little affair.
>
> However clear I thought I had made myself, you may accept it from me that I was completely fogbound compared with the clearness of the young lady in what she did say to me. Rage was pacific slumber by comparison with the display of the sweet little thing, and, when I managed to recover from the effect of the tirade sufficient to be able to frame words, I blurted, "Are there any more at home like you?"
>
> Like a flash it then came to my mind—there is the title you have been looking for. I went up to my study and wrote the song in about three hours. Its title was "Tell Me, Pretty Maiden."
>
> I brought this number down to the Lyric Theatre, and I told all those concerned with the production that I felt sure I had now the remedy for the hiatus in the second act. It was unanimously condemned on what I regarded as being the quaintest grounds for

turning down any enterprise connected with the theatre—that it was a departure from those things that were done on the stage. In other words, its great and only fault was its originality! Who cares to say he can beat that?

It was suggested by my collaborator, . . . Owen Hall, that instead of twelve people, six ladies and six gentlemen, singing the number, it should become a duet for a lady and a gentleman who were principals. The measure of my annoyance may best be gauged by my subsequent act. I simply put the manuscript under my arm and walked out of the theatre telling them they might make use of the music I had already written, rounding off with the prophecy that it would yet make history in the form of theatrical or musical comedy.[62]

His daughter May, who was twelve at the time, later recalled,

He came home to mother, said, "Kit, there's going to be no *Florodora*. Pack the children's things. We are all going to the seaside." Mother was rather pleased. She wasn't too enthusiastic about his music anyway. Why wasn't he something nice like a doctor, a lawyer, or a bank manager? She thought *Florodora* crazy anyway—"such a name, like a children's game."

We went next day to Bognor. Letters simply poured in—some pleading, threatening, lawyers' letters. Emissaries were sent down to beg Father not to be silly . . . a thing he never was. At last a telegram—one day a telegram from the author, Owen Hall, of whom he was very fond. It read: "Do you know what you're doing, Leslie?" He wired back: "Yes. Have just made a 100 break at billiards." That was the end! In force they came down. He could have the sextette, anything—only for pity's sake come back and let them get on with the rehearsals.[65]

Great as was the acclaim for Leslie Stuart as composer of "Tell Me, Pretty Maiden," the number also made a name for its choreographer, Sydney Ellison. London born and thirty-two years old, he had appeared at Daly's Theatre in Sidney Jones's *An Artist's Model* and *The Geisha*, but found his true vocation when asked to restage the former for New York. He went on to mount *Cupid and the Princess* for Tom B. Davis, leading to his engagement as director and choreographer for *Florodora*. The success of the double sextet saw Ellison praised for revolutionizing musical comedy chorus work "by putting action and special rhythm into it." He was thereafter much in demand for similar work on both sides of the Atlantic.[28]

By a curious chance, *Florodora* was first produced in London in the same month as Arthur Sullivan's last completed comic opera, *The Rose of Persia*, thereby permitting an assessment of stylistic similarities and differences. For all that Stuart was thoroughly familiar with Sullivan's work, the differences were surely greater than the similarities. Sullivan would never have contemplated a number so dependent on staging as "Tell Me, Pretty Maiden," or so strongly dependent on rhythmic allure rather than the words of his librettist. However, we are so conditioned to having musical theater works measured against the standard of Gilbert and Sullivan that it is interesting to read a comparison from the opposite perspective. Tom B. Davis had a vested interest as the show's producer; but a comparison he made to an interviewer from the *Southport Guardian* when *Florodora* arrived at the composer's birthplace in March 1901 is worth repeating. It reads, "In some respects it may be said to resemble a Savoy opera, but with all due respect to those really, in many cases beautiful creations, *Florodora* has considerably more 'go' than they have, whilst about its music, it has that peculiar charm that Stuart seems to have made so peculiarly his own. Take one instance. At the end of the first act, the tenor sings a farewell song with the refrain: 'Oh! my Dolores, Queen of the Eastern seas.' In both London and the provinces, frequently when this song is finished, the audience will sit absolutely silent for some seconds before breaking into applause."[55]

Altogether, Leslie Stuart was surely more adventurous than Sullivan in the way he set out to create effects, even if those effects did not always succeed in the way that Sullivan's painstaking settings of his lyricists' words did. While Stuart was tasting early success, such comparisons with Sullivan would hardly have bothered him; but later on he commented ruefully how composers for the musical theater were forever judged against the example of Gilbert and Sullivan: "We living composers either imitate—unpardonable sin—or do not imitate—which is worse."[16]

Chapter 8

From the West End to Broadway

London soon recognized *Florodora* as a triumphant success, and plans were made for a long run. Ada Reeve, committed to *Aladdin* in Bristol, relinquished her part for the pantomime season, while Evie Greene, having secured her release from pantomime, was forced by illness to hand her role over to her understudy for a while at the end of December. When she returned in early January it was not only with a new ballad, "The Queen of the Philippine Islands," written and composed by Paul Rubens, but with Sydney Barraclough as Abercoed instead of Melville Stewart.

At the premiere, Melville Stewart had received good notices: "a handsome, earnest, and manly Frank Abercoed [who] has a good voice, and sings his songs with admirable expressiveness," according to the *Era*. However, the more musically aware of the Lyric team were unhappy with his inability to sing consistently in tune. He had been engaged at £20 a week for the first eight weeks, rising to £25 thereafter until the end of the run; but, on December 23, Tom B. Davis gave him his notice. Stewart sued for wrongful dismissal.

The case came up in the Queen's Bench Division on May 18, 1900. Counsel for Stewart argued that he had previously played with De Wolf Hopper's company in *El Capitan* and had played his role in *Florodora* with the approval of the public and the musical press. The musical director of the De Wolf Hopper company spoke in Stewart's support, as did three members of the Albert Hall choir, who said they had several times heard Stewart sing in *Florodora* and that he never sang out of tune. For the defense, Tom B. Davis said that "when he heard him in private he sang very well . . . , [but] during performances he sang out of tune, not invariably, but so frequently that it seriously threw the orchestra out." Carl Kiefert, the musical director, confirmed that Stewart "sang so much out of tune that he interfered with the ensemble."

The most detailed evidence came from the composer, reported thus in the *Stage*:

> Mr. Barrett, professionally known as Leslie Stuart, the composer of the music, said he was present when the plaintiff was engaged, and was satisfied that he should be engaged. There was a marked difference in his singing, however, at the orchestra rehearsals. The plaintiff seemed uncomfortable, and his tone was erratic. The plaintiff himself attributed his false intonation to the difference of pitch between an English and American orchestra. He was accustomed to the latter, and the former was half a tone higher. He did not think his performance was satisfactory, and he thought he was uncomfortable. In the finale he invariably sang the solo out of tune in a very marked way. The management were very sore about it. On all occasions when the chorus finished the chord with him he was out of tune. The plaintiff was as disappointed as they were that he was not a great success. The most important song, "The Shade of the Palms [*sic*]," was cut out because he sang it so unsatisfactorily.

In the end, the jury found for the plaintiff to the tune of £300, equivalent to twelve weeks' pay. In Melville Stewart's defense it might be added that "The Shade of the Palm" is a very good example of Leslie Stuart's penchant for quite unpredictable turns in the vocal line. It is easy to see how it could defeat a singer who experienced no difficulty with more conventional composers. At the same time, it is clear why Stewart had to go.

Meanwhile, the show's success brought demands for new numbers to boost various artists' roles. Act 2, always something of a glorified variety show, was particularly susceptible to change. Stuart composed a duet, "We get up at 8 A.M.," for Leandro (Gilfain's farm overseer) and Valleda, the latter upgraded from head of a Florodorean farm to Lady Holyrood's maid. When the popular W. Louis Bradfield took over as Donegal in March, he did so with two extra songs, "He Didn't Like the Look of It at All" and a splendidly lively Stuart number, "I Want to Be a Military Man."

Thanks to its rousing rhythms and catchy melody, the latter was destined to become one of the show's outstanding successes. With a second verse extolling the virtues of the man in khaki, it became an anthem for Boer War patriotism. The war in South Africa between the British and the Dutch had begun in October 1899 with the expectation of an early resolution. However, the British suffered a series of reverses with the sieges of Ladysmith, Mafeking, and Kimberly. Among other things this dictated that a dance planned in celebration of the hundredth performance of *Florodora* in February 1900 be shelved. Although Kimberly and Ladysmith were relieved in February, the siege of Mafeking continued until May, at which time Willie Edouin was reported to be intending to introduce "a tableau, wherein he will appear, in quick change fashion, as four of the Generals now most talked of." Ultimately the Boer War dragged on until 1902.

Edouin's occasional absences from the cast were not the problem they might have been, because backer Ben Nathan was able to step into the role if required. For permanent departures of other principals, strong replacements were needed. When Evie Greene left the cast for good, she was replaced by Florence St. John—more than twice Miss Greene's age, but vastly celebrated. In his youth Stuart had worshipped her from the audience when he went on cheap trips to London to see her in comic opera, his great ambition being to wait outside the theater to catch a fleeting glimpse as she approached her carriage.[62] Now he wrote for her the reflective song "He Loves Me, He Loves Me Not," at the end of which he deftly wove in the "Flora! Florodora!" leitmotif. He got St. John's agreement that Lord Abercoed should enter on the last two bars, thereby depriving her of applause but greatly heightening the dramatic effect.[62] Stuart also provided St. John with a more conventional comic duet with Tweedlepunch for act 2, "When We Are on the Stage," while Ivan Caryll composed for her a solo, "The Island of Love." In addition, Stuart provided Kate Cutler, as Angela, with a new act 1 whistling song, "Willie Was a Gay Boy," a lyric that would never pass today. Kate Cutler's marriage to stage manager Sydney Ellison on April 12, 1900, served to heighten the sense of unity among the cast.

As early as the beginning of December 1899, Tom B. Davis had announced a provincial tour to begin in March 1900. This was immediately doing good business, with former Gaiety Theatre soubrette Amy Augarde as Dolores, her niece Adrienne Augarde as Angela, and Edward Lewis beginning a long touring career as Tweedlepunch. Both the show and its composer received an especially warm welcome when they touched down at the Theatre Royal, Manchester, on April 14, even if the *Manchester Guardian* felt the latter's earlier activities in the city had created rather higher expectations. It wrote, "When Mr Leslie Stuart entered the orchestra on Saturday evening he was received with quite an enthusiastic outburst of welcome, and the demonstration was renewed at the end of each act. Therefore it was that the right atmosphere was created for the success of a flimsy piece such as has been devised by Mr Owen Hall. One would have desired that Mr Stuart should have been better yoked in his first venture and that comic opera rather than musical farce should have been the vehicle chosen for his first venture in dramatic composition."

Having thus made his perspective clear, the reviewer at least conceded that *Florodora* contained something out of the ordinary for its genre, noting, "In *Florodora* something more ambitious has been attempted in the choruses and orchestrations than is usual in musical farce, and it must be said that the success of the work seems to depend chiefly on these choral and orchestral features. . . . A concerted piece sung by two groups of six secretaries and six young ladies, with the refrain "Are there any more at home like you?" is an amusing adaptation of what is known as a negro "cake-walk," and proved so much to the taste of the audience on Saturday that it was repeatedly encored. One or two of the sentimental songs, notably that allotted to the baritone lover in the first act, "Shade of the Palms [*sic*]," and "The Silver Star of Love," sung by the Spanish heroine, are likely to be heard on the concert platform."

Liverpool was no less keen to claim the new celebrity as its own when, on June 4, the show arrived at the Shakespeare Theatre, just around the corner from Stuart's boyhood home in Wilde Street. The composer conducted the first two performances, at which, according to the *Liverpool Daily Post*, he "had on several occasions to bow his acknowledgements to the audience." The report continued, "Previous to the opening of the performance an interesting little ceremony took place on the stage, when Mr. Stuart was made the recipient of a gold-mounted baton, subscribed to by members of the Old Xaverian Athletic Association, of

Program of Old Xaverians' Ladies Bohemian Concert, June 14, 1900 (author's collection)

which the composer of "Florodora" is a member. Mr. Austin Harford, C.C., made the presentation, as president of the association."

On June 14, moreover, Stuart was the star guest at a "ladies' Bohemian concert" held by the Old Xaverians Athletic Association at the Exchange Station Hotel and chaired by Councillor Harford. A caricature of Stuart, lighted cigarette in hand, adorns the front of the printed program, which he preserved in a scrapbook of his press cuttings and goodwill telegrams.[64]

When *Florodora* finally reached Stuart's birthplace, Southport, he broke off from his work on a successor show to conduct the opening at the Opera House in the Winter Gardens on March 4, 1901. The cast now included J. Robert Hale as Gilfain, Fanny Dango (one of the original Florodorean girls) as Angela, Amy Augarde as Dolores, Leonard Russell as Abercoed, and Fred Eastham (Willie Edouin's London understudy) as Tweedlepunch. The mayor and corporation were present, and the general manager of the Winter Gardens presented Stuart with an ivory baton. The *Southport Guardian*, having enquired about his birth, revealed no more than that "Birkdale has really the claim, and not Southport."[56]

Florodora, of course, was one of the first big musical theater successes of the sound-recording era, and it was perhaps inevitable that some of its music should find its way into London's Maiden Lane recording studio. Louis Bradfield started things off on September 27, 1900, with his hit number "I Want to Be a Military Man." Six days later he was back with other members of the cast and a skeleton chorus, with Leslie Stuart and Paul Rubens sharing the duty of accompanist. Rubens accompanied the section of the opening chorus, "Flora! Florodora!" together with "Tell Me, Pretty Maiden." Stuart then accompanied Bradfield in Gilfain's "Phrenology," as well as "She May Not Be That Sort of Girl," which Bradfield had introduced into *The Circus Girl* in 1897. Stuart also accompanied Florence St. John in "He Loves Me, He Loves Me Not," the only known recording of one of the leading ladies of nineteenth-century British musical theater.

Further recordings emerged from a burst of activity some two weeks later. On October 15 and 16, Bradfield recorded some eighteen miscellaneous sides, including cover versions of "The Lily of Laguna," "My Little Octoroon," and "Little Dolly Daydream." There was also a burlesque version of "Tell Me, Pretty Maiden," in which he sang the female parts falsetto. Four days later, Sydney Barraclough recorded "The Shade of the Palm," while, with Rubens at the piano, Ada Reeve recorded "Tact" and Rubens's own "The Queen of the Philippine Islands" and "I've an Inkling." Kate Cutler recorded both her original "Whistling" song (also by Rubens) and the Stuart song that replaced it, "Willie Was a Gay Boy," and she and Bradfield added their "Galloping" duet. For this final session, Rubens shared accompanist duties with Landon Ronald, who was the son of Henry Russell and was not only house accompanist for the Gramophone Company but also about to begin a stint as musical director of *Florodora*.

This was not quite the end of original cast *Florodora* recordings. Louis Bradfield made a further recording of "I Want to Be a Military Man" for Zonophone in 1903, and Evie Greene finally recorded Rubens's "The Queen of the Philippine Islands" with orchestra in 1911. In February 1901, Bradfield also recorded a substantial batch of Stuart's earlier songs. Altogether he was to prove himself a major interpreter of Leslie Stuart on gramophone records.[53]

That Willie Edouin took no part in the *Florodora* recordings may have reflected unease with the new medium—he never did make a recording—but more likely reflected the lack of an obvious hit number. He was also preparing to travel to New York, where—already an established name—he was to repeat his classic creation of Tweedlepunch. On October 26, 1900, he played the role in London for the last time, and the following day he set off across the Atlantic with Tom B. Davis and Walter Weil for the New York premiere.

Leslie Stuart later recalled with some glee that *Florodora* had been turned down by every prominent American manager. They said it was "too English, too refined, and it would die on its legs in a week if it were produced in New York." He added that eventually the play was leased for America by two men, "one John C. Fisher, who owned a theatre in San Diego, California, and Tom Ryley, a comedian in repertoire throughout the States. . . . Though Fisher and Ryley had never produced a play before, they came over to London and offered £500 on account of royalties, which we very gladly accepted."[62]

On October 6, 1900, the *New York Dramatic Mirror* announced the start of rehearsals for a first night at New York's Casino Theatre on November 12. It announced that the part of Cyrus W. Gilfain had been given to Robert E. Graham, who in 1881 had originated the leading light-comedy role opposite Minnie Palmer in William Gill's *My Sweetheart*, and in 1886 the role of General Knickerbocker in Willard Spenser's *The Little Tycoon*.[8] Subsequently the paper reported on the various other performers converging on New York. Guelma Lawrence Baker came from California to play Valleda, Lady Holyrood's maid. Mabel Barrison, later to be one of the babes in Victor Herbert's *Babes in Toyland* and later still the wife of performer-songwriter Joe Howard, came in as another Florodorean girl. There was also news of the recruitment of Lewis Hooper to play one of Gilfain's clerks, and of an English *première danseuse* named Beanie Galletley, of whom no more seems to have been heard.

On October 20, "after a flying trip to Europe," Edna Wallace Hopper—former wife of De Wolf Hopper—arrived to play Lady Holyrood, along with May Edouin, who was to play Angela. From Europe, too, came Cyril Scott, who had appeared in the London production of *The Casino Girl* and was now to take the role of Abercoed. Finally, on November 3, Willie Edouin arrived with producer Tom B. Davis and backer Walter Weil.

It was on Edouin, more than anyone else, that hopes for *Florodora* in America rested. Born in Brighton, England, on New Year's Day, 1846, he had already been on the stage for half a century as a member of a theatrical family that had settled in Australia in 1856. At the age of twenty, he went to America, and was later leading comic of Lydia Thompson's burlesque company in both America and Britain. It was there that he met his American wife, Alice Atherton, with whom, after performing in America for some years more, he settled in Britain in 1883.[28] Edouin's portrayal of Anthony Tweedlepunch in *Florodora* in London had proved such a triumph that it was only natural that he should be enlisted to launch the show on Broadway. It was also an opportunity for him to further the career of his daughter, May Edouin, who had gained coast-to-coast celebrity in America before her third birthday as the subject of an angelic portrait called "Angela" that sold over 20,000 copies.[28]

There were considerable doubts and alarms before the work reached the stage; as the composer recalled, "In the preparation for the production the funds behind the enterprising partners became exhausted. In the cast was a certain lady who was not without means, and Fisher and Ryley offered her half share in the profits if she would put up two thousand five hundred dollars (£500). The actress appeared to share the opinion of the general body of American theater magnates regarding the destiny of *Florodora* as she would not even consider the proposal. However, seeing that she was in the cast, she said she would grant Fisher and Ryley a *loan* of the sum on the undertaking that it was repaid out of the *first week's takings*. These, or any other conditions for that matter, they were glad to accept so long as they got the money that was direly necessary."[62]

Produced by John W. Dunne, Thomas Ryley and John C. Fisher at the Casino Theatre, New York, 10 November 1900

FLORODORA

English Musical Comedy in Two Acts, Three Scenes.

Book by Owen Hall, revised for America by Frank Pixley.

Lyrics by Ernest Boyd-Jones, Paul Rubens and Leslie Stuart.

Music by Leslie Stuart.

Cyrus W. Gilfain, proprietor of the island and the perfume of Florodora
Mr. R. E. Graham

Captain Arthur Donegal, Fourth Royal Life Guards, Lady Holyrood's brother
Mr. Cyril Scott

Frank Abercoed, Manager for Mr. Gilfain of the island of Florodora
Mr. Bertram Godfrey

Leandro			Mr. Nace Bonville
Tennyson Sims	|	|	Mr. George De Long
Ernest Pym	|	|	Mr. Lewis Hooper
Max Aepfelbaum	|	Gilfain's clerks	|	Mr. Edward Gore
Reginald Langdale	|	|	Mr. Joseph Welsh
Paul Crogan	|	|	Mr. Thomas A. Kiernan
John Scott	|	|	Mr. Joseph S. Colt

Anthony Tweedlepunch, showman, phrenologist, hypnotist, palmist
Mr. Willie Edouin

Dolores			Miss Fannie Johnston
Valleda, maid to Lady Holyrood			Miss Guelma L. Baker
Inez	|	|	Miss Elaine Van Selover
Jose	|	|	Miss Sadie Lauer
Juanita	|	Florodorean girls,	|	Miss Adelaide Phillips
		heads of the various farms		
Violante	|	|	Miss Aline Potter
Calista	|	|	Miss Mabel Barrison
Angela Gilfain			Miss May Edouin
Daisy Chain			Miss Margaret Walker
Mamie Rowe			Miss Vaughn Texsmith
Lucy Ling			Miss Marie L. Wilson
Cynthia Belmont			Miss Marjorie Relyea
Lottie Chatmore			Miss Agnes Wayburn
Clare Fitzclarence			Miss Daisy Greene
Lady Holyrood			Edna Wallace-Hopper

Florodorean Farmers, Laborers, Flower Girls, Welsh Peasants, etc.

Act I: The Island of Florodora in the Philippines.

Act II, Scene I: Abercoed Castle, Wales. Act II, Scene II: Grand Ball-room in the Castle.

Staged by Lewis Hooper, under the personal supervision of Willie Edouin.

Musical Director: Arthur Weld.   Scenery: Moses & Hamilton

The New York press greeted *Florodora* with qualified warmth. The *New York Herald* had the headline "The Comedian Is Applauded, but the Musical Comedy Is Not Always Amusing." It declared that "with much that was applauded, there were long wastes which tried the patience of the audience and which, it was the general opinion in the lobbies between the acts, should be cut." On the other hand, the *New York Times* reported "a pronounced and instantaneous hit":

> The music was tuneful, sensuous, and as a whole so completely above the music of the average Casino productions of recent years as to put it to a class wholly by itself among them. It belongs with the brightest and best of the recent operettas and its honest reception last night would seem to augur as long a run as the managers of the theatre care to give it.
>
> Aside from its decided merit as a musical production, it has a story that has continuity and some sense and that can certainly be followed to an intelligible conclusion. It has exceptional brilliancy in costuming, pretty groupings, and a constant life and jingle that keep both eye and ear pleasantly occupied.

The same report also praised the musical numbers, noting, "The song which will attain the greatest vogue is 'I Want to be a Military Man,' sung by Cyril Scott and the chorus. It is full of snap and go and more martial than anything we have had since 'Oh, Listen to the Band' of *The Runaway Girl*. Another catching solo and chorus was the syncopated 'Tell Me, Pretty Maiden,' a rag-time air, sung by a well-trained, well-dressed, and good-looking chorus, and the crowd was unwilling to stop the staging. A galloping duet by Cyril Scott and May Edouin was a decided hit."

The *Herald* focused even more firmly on the double sextet, noting, "a chorus for six girls and six men, in the second act, had six encores—made the hit of the evening, in fact. . . . The six maidens were in becoming pink costumes, with black picture hats, and the six men in gray frock suits and high 'tiles.' The singers' chic nods at the audience as they walked off the stage in pairs caught the house's fancy as much as the well turned tune."

Two days later, the same paper returned to *Florodora* to welcome back Willie Edouin and analyze his performance in perceptive detail:

> Willie Edouin has returned to New York after an absence of sixteen years. It was considerably longer ago than sixteen years that he made his first hit here as the Heathen Chinee in the burlesque of *Blue Beard*. In this he carried a rifle with a revolving barrel. He would threateningly aim the rifle at one of his associates, and the barrel would then turn around toward his head, while, in a well-simulated fit of comic bewilderment, he would try to avoid the muzzle by stepping backward in a circle, never changing the relative position of the preposterous gun at all. If you go to the Casino to hear the tunes in *Florodora* and see the remarkably pretty ballroom scene, with its dainty suggestion of the cotillion, you will be delighted, if you are an old stager, to see Willie Edouin doing his same old backward circling. There is no trick gun now, but the personage the comedian is utter-ing his wheezes to keeps moving out of the way and the bewildered talker is trying to keep him in focus. These old burlesque comedians cling fondly to all the old "business" that used to be laughed at. Edouin, all through *Florodora*, is like an echo of the sixties. He leans his elbow carelessly on nothing at all and falls on the floor, he wears a different shockingly bad hat in each scene, and he plays a property fiddle until it falls to pieces like the one Charles Ross used to play in the first "musical act" he and Mabel Fenton ever did, when Tony Pastor was still a young man. He "mugs" incessantly. Sweet memories of childhood!

However, that same writer declared that Edouin's daughter May "hardly seems to have inherited her mother's talent," and, in closing, seized the opportunity to offer a gratuitous dig at the show as a whole. "It is a pity about *Florodora*," it read. "The lyrics are gracefully written, and much of the music is unusually tuneful. But the singing is generally bad. The chorus is numerous and capable, and contains many pretty women. Much money has been expended on dresses, and the expenditure has been guided by good taste. But the 'book' is quite beneath contempt."

Nor was that writer alone. The *New York Dramatic Mirror* had a woman columnist, The Matinee Girl, whose mission was evidently to be smart and provocative. She felt she had found ample material in *Floro-dora* and wrote, in the issue of December 15,

> It was long ago in the beautiful dead summertime that the Matinee Girl first heard some of the prettiest songs and music in *Florodora* and began to look forward eagerly to its New York production. . . . And now that *Florodora* is here and I have seen it—whew! It's about the most impossible sort of thing a long-suffering Matinee Girl was ever up against.
>
> Of course it is a Casino success. Anything put on the Casino stage with enough girls in it is sure to be a success. . . . People have the habit of dropping in at the Casino, for there never was known to be anything on there with sufficient plot to be non-understandable at nine, or even at ten o'clock in the evening. . . . But there is something so pathetically English about *Florodora*. There are parts of it almost too sad to write about, and this in spite of its many tuneful songs, opulent scenery and Cyril Scott, who cleverly does nothing for he has nothing to do, but he does it in his usual brisk, lively way. If any rising young actor wishes to learn how artistically and seriously one can do nothing, he has but to watch this estimable young man capering about valiantly, as earnestly as if he were a great comic opera star with tumbling specialities. . . .
>
> Then there is the scene where Willie Edouin tears his coat up the back. There is always a delicious touch of droll comedy in a coat torn up the back. And when the actor buttons it and reverses it you almost expect another comedian to come on with a stuffed club or a plank and beat him about the stage and jump on him. And there are times when you almost wish this would happen.

The Matinee Girl particularly dug her claws into one musical number:

> In *Florodora* there is one song which none of the critics seem to have perceived in which the actors give imitations of horses, their arms doing duty as fore-feet. In this they must stamp, snort and do all but neigh. . . . At the end of the song Miss Edouin ejects two red ribbons from her bodice and Mr. Scott takes these as reins and they go trotting off the stage as though they were in a cotillion. Then they come back—they must come back to get in the next delightful touch—and at the climax two more ribbons are exuded and they romp off again. . . . They have a pretty song which they sing for this, the words of which as I remember them go:

Miss Edouin: So we go galloping, galloping, galloping.

Mr. Scott: Galloping, galloping, galloping.

Both: Yes, we go galloping, galloping, galloping.

At least the reviewer exempted "The Shade of the Palm" and "Tell Me, Pretty Maiden" from adverse criticism, considering the latter "the one dainty little bit of blue china verse in *Florodora*." But then she returned to the attack, writing, "Edna Wallace Hopper has one song to sing in which she repeats that she has an "ink-ling, ink-ling, ink-ling." If you just try to say that three times in time to music you will realise that it is almost as difficult a feat to perform as to say "She stood at the door welcoming and beckoning him in" three times quickly in succession without having a fit. This is something the Songsters' Union should protest against. This and having to give an imitation of a horse, singing all the while, and at the same time go galloping, galloping, galloping. . . ."

Overall the reaction was mixed. However, the press agents had by now been set to work. As Rudolf Aronson, proprietor of the Casino Theatre, recalled, "[When] *Florodora* was produced at the Casino . . . its business for the first few weeks was very mediocre, but the quick and persistent work of the press agent, the heralding of the tuneful, original and catchy sextette, helped *Florodora* to develop into one of the greatest artistic and financial successes of a decade. . . ."[3]

It was not only the tunefulness and catchiness of the sextet that press agents were able to highlight so much as the attractions of the female members. The *Florodora* girls were described in the press as "goddesses" and "the most beautiful women on the stage." The girls played up to it and took part in all sorts of publicity stunts. They would smile and wink at some man in the audience as they exited, which in turn encouraged the men about town to crowd the theater nightly and lavish expensive gifts on them. Reputedly some men bought seats at the front on a regular basis, came into the theater in time to see the double sextet, and left straight after the last encore.

Thus, by the time W. J. Ferguson took over as Tweedlepunch in January 1901 to enable Willie Edouin to return to England, *Florodora* had established its New York raison d'être through the double sextet. Its continuing success thereafter was such that the *New York Dramatic Mirror* could report on June 1, 1901, that Edna Wallace Hopper was buying all the seats in the theater so that everyone could go to the races. The Matinee Girl added that "the girls are clubbing together to buy the

The *Florodora* sextet, Casino Theatre, New York (courtesy Gerald Bordman)

musical director a pair of diamond suspender buckles, and the press agent's salary has been raised."

Not everything in the garden was harmonious, though. In June 1901, the Supreme Court heard a suit against Thomas W. Ryley and John C. Fisher by John W. Dunne, whose name had appeared with theirs as New York producer. According to Dunne, *Florodora* had made a great deal of money for its producers, and he had not received a cent of it. He claimed he had an agreement with Ryley and Fisher "to bring out the production of *Florodora* on a share-and-share-alike basis." He understood the profits already amounted to $125,000, and he claimed a quarter share to date and over the next six years. Fisher's reply was that Dunne never had, and never would have, a financial interest in the production and had not contributed one cent to the finances. The judge appointed Ryley and Fisher receivers pending a judicial settlement. Dunne was seemingly pacified out of court.

Meanwhile, the readiness with which the *Florodora* girls found a better existence outside the theater meant there was a fair turnover, as Rudolf Aronson recalled:

Upon every hand you heard nothing but stories about the piece, . . . of the enormous fortunes made by the different chorus girls in Wall Street speculations, of their various matrimonial affairs, and as for the famous sextette, their names and reputed exploits were to be found in the public prints at least seven days a week. . . .

For five years after the first night of *Florodora*, at least nine-tenths of the chorus damsels in the world, young and old, fat and slender, blond and brunette, each and every one made the claim "Oh I was in the original Florodora sextette."

In a literal compilation of various girls identified with the sextette at one time or another, the number is some seventy odd, and of these only three achieved anything like lasting success, one of whom soon gave up her stage position for the greater security of matrimony. . . .

Had Miss Frances Belmont remained on the stage there is no telling what she might have achieved, for she seemed well started upon a most promising career. . . . Then somewhat abruptly she gave up the stage and went to Paris to live. The next thing heard of her was the information that she had married into one of England's most exclusive titled families. On February 19th, 1906, she became the wife of Francis Denzil Edward Baring, the fifth Baron Ashburton and holder of the oldest of the four peerages held by the Baring family, the ceremony being performed at the English Church at Passy, France.[3]

The original New York sextet had comprised Margaret Walker, Vaughn Texsmith, Marie L. Wilson, Marjorie Relyea, Agnes Wayburn, and Daisy Greene, who achieved a cachet that had never attached to the original London sextet of Edith Housley, Jane May, Nora Moore, Beryl Somerset, Nellie Harcourt, and Nina Sevening. Of all the New York *Florodora* girls, however, perhaps ultimately the most celebrated was Evelyn Nesbit, the daughter of a Pittsburgh lawyer whose death threw his family into poverty. Her mother took the family to Philadelphia, where Evelyn's good looks made her an artist's model at the age of fifteen. In New York she posed for Frederick S. Church, a prominent magazine illustrator, while Charles Dana Gibson, famous for his "Gibson Girl," sketched her with her hair streaming down to form a question mark, calling it "The Eternal Question."

These illustrations brought her to the attention of Stanford White, architect of many important New York edifices, including the Washington Square arch and the first incarnation of the magnificent sports garden at Madison Square. A regular Broadway first-nighter, White took Nesbit and her mother under his wing and used his contacts with theater managers to find her a position in *Florodora*. In his late forties and married, he had a secret hideaway in the Madison Square Garden complex on West 24th Street. Evelyn was persuaded to go there, and she rode on the red velvet swing he had installed. White plied her with drink and seduced her.

When White turned his attention elsewhere, Harry K. Thaw, millionaire son of a coal and railroad baron from Evelyn's native Pittsburgh, came onto the scene. On April 4, 1905, he and Evelyn were married. Thaw then discovered how Stanford White had seduced Evelyn, and his hatred grew. On June 25, 1906, White and the Thaws were by chance at nearby tables for the first night of the musical comedy *Mamzelle Champagne* at the open air Madison Square Garden roof theater. Thaw approached White's table and shot him between the eyes. The subsequent trial was one of the most sensational of the century, and Evelyn Nesbit's notoriety was perpetuated by Hollywood in the 1955 film *The Girl on the Red Velvet Swing*. She was also a leading character in E. L. Doctorow's 1975 novel *Ragtime*, its 1981 film version, and its 1998 adaptation as a stage musical.

If the *Florodora* chorus line attracted most gossip, the show's music also soon entered the American consciousness. As Rudolf Aronson noted, "[You] simply could not escape it, no matter how hard you might try. First thing when you arose in the morning someone in your neighborhood would be playing 'The Shade of the Palm.' Later when being served with your eggs at the breakfast, your otherwise irreproachable and irreplaceable maid would be quietly humming 'I've an Inkling.' Then all day long, in either business or residential section of New York, the good old hurdy-gurdies would grind out one tune after another, the favorite in this repertoire being 'Tell Me, Pretty Maiden.' Indeed, one had to have patience and fortitude during the *Florodora* fad."[3]

Chapter 9

The Silver Slipper

While *Florodora* was running in London and New York, Stuart continued to provide new material for Eugene Stratton. The year 1900 saw the appearance of two new songs: "I Don't Know Nobody" and "The Banshee." For the former, Richard Morton provided the words, but "The Banshee" was another in the sequence of Stratton songs for which Stuart provided both words and music. Stratton launched it on November 12, 1900, when he divided his evening between the Oxford, the Tivoli, and the London Pavilion, which was celebrating its grand reopening after five months of refurbishment.

The number was different again from its predecessors, much of its appeal being due to the special scenery painted by John Watson and the involvement of a number of children. Not least it was notable as an "Irish coon song," as described by H. Chance Newton, who wrote in the *New York Dramatic Mirror,* "In this scena Stratton represents a coon who has been wrecked on the Irish coast and since become regarded by the local peasantry as a banshee or midnight fairy. It is a quaint if not particularly striking piece of work, its chief effect being caused by the beautiful Irish scene provided for it and by a group of little colleens hovering around Stratton with little candles which from time to time go out and relight themselves when necessary."

A portion of its verse gives a further idea of its content:

The ship went down with ev'ry soul but me,
I was washed ashore on the rocks of Donegal.
When it thundered down the night was black as me,
And the folks on shore, when they took me up and look'd me in the face,
They were scared.
So what could I do when they all began to sing,
"Me black and tan, you are me fairy man."

Two days after the launch of "The Banshee" and four days after the New York premiere of *Florodora*, the latter enjoyed a special first-anniversary performance in London, with Florence St. John as Dolores, Decima Moore as Angela, Harry Monkhouse as Tweedlepunch, and Ada Reeve as Lady Holyrood. To mark the occasion, every member of the audience was presented with a copy of the vocal score. The show was also still touring Britain with success, and on December 15, 1900, an Australian production opened at Her Majesty's Theatre, Melbourne, "as full of good things as a pudding is of plums," according to the *Argus*. Heading the cast were Grace Palotta as Lady Holyrood, Carrie Moore as Dolores, Charles Kenningham as Donegal, George Lauri as Tweedle-punch, Maud Chetwynd as Angela, Wallace Brownlow as Abercoed, and H. J. Ward as Gilfain. Kenningham had been a soloist at Leslie Stuart's Manchester concerts before creating the roles of Captain Fitzbattleaxe in *Utopia Limited* and Ernest Dummkopf in *The Grand Duke* for Gilbert and Sullivan. In March 1901, the Salvation Army's pioneering Lime-light film production department filmed highlights of the show, and these were then used to advertise the production.[37] When the Australian production reached Brisbane, the mayor and his family were invited to attend. In the party was, of course, the mayor's daughter, whose tantrum had originally provoked the composer's question "Are there any more at home like you?"[62]

Even before *Florodora* set off around the world, Stuart had left the house in Battersea for a grand new residence. The Priory—later more mundanely numbered 194 Goldhurst Terrace—was imposingly situated on the corner of Goldhurst Terrace and Aberdare Gardens in West Hampstead. He took with him the treasured mementos of his Manchester concerts, as well as the American organ at which he would sit for hours on end, cigarette or pipe in mouth, composing his songs. The house in Battersea was later occupied by the writer Rafael Sabatini, author of *The Sea Hawk*, *Scaramouche*, and *Captain Blood*.[66]

Stuart's fame inevitably brought him to the attention of magazine feature writers. Soon after the opening of *Florodora*, for instance, *M.A.P.* wrote, "The composer is a slight, pale young man of medium height with flaxen hair that is almost white, worn rather long. He is an impulsive man, and leans forward when talking to one, fixing his eyes upon one's centre stud, and talking very quickly and volubly, in a low, persuasive voice, with a very pronounced Manchester 'burr' in it. He is a thorough provincial, and has only been a few years in London. Directly he speaks, one says 'Lancashire!' He has the dogged pertinacity of his countrymen, and that accounts for his so quickly coming to the front.[39]

For another feature in June 1901, the *World* visited him at his new home and wrote, "[The] fact that Mr. Leslie Stuart hails from Lancashire is unmistakable as he welcomes you in his delightful study. This room, forming an angle of the picturesque villa which Mr. Leslie Stuart built for himself about three years ago in the still fairly open district between Hampstead and Kilburn, is not only charming in its colours, harmonies and appointments, but . . . almost every object seems in some way or another suggestively reminiscent of Mr. Leslie Stuart's musical career. . . ."[77]

The article noted many of Stuart's prized possessions, including "the little organ placed below a life-size portrait of the late Sir Arthur Sullivan, which is flanked by beautiful photographs of Wagner and Liszt." It also commented on "the little piano . . . now used for trying over his compositions from time to time, and placed under a most interesting reproduction of an original photograph of Beethoven." It described the photographs of great artists who had assisted at his concerts: "Here are Albani, Melba, Zélie de Lussan, Fanny Moody, Lady Hallé, Piatti, Paderewski, Foli, Popper, Ysaye, and others. . . ."[77]

Another interviewer, from the *Royal Magazine*, noted an old silver matchbox that Paderewski had given after his first successful engagement in England, as well as other notable souvenirs elsewhere in the house: "The drawing-room is stocked with original scores and rare old editions of the great operas. Sundry mementoes from many of the famous singers and songstresses who sang at her husband's concerts in Manchester can be seen on Mrs. Stuart's treasure table. But the most valued of all Leslie Stuart's numerous gifts is a curiously wrought gold

Leslie Stuart composing at his American organ (Mander and Mitchenson Theatre Collection)

Maltese cross, the Order of St. John of Jerusalem, presented to him when he was organist to Cardinal Vaughan, at Salford Cathedral."[51]

The article described how Stuart created his music:

Leslie Stuart's method of composing is almost as original as his music. His invariable plan is to think of a catching title, and then to write a song up to it. He has a large notebook, full of suggested titles, which he jots down as they occur to him from time to time. What a valuable possession this book would prove to a writer of short stories! . . .

Leslie Stuart does not belong to that school of musicians who make a point of composing as far away as possible from a musical instrument of any sort. Having hit on his title, and written the words . . . , his next move is to the organ, which, together with a small piano, forms the main portion of the furniture in his "composing" room.[51]

The interviewer from the *World* ended his feature by referring first to the many batons Stuart had received for his conducting, and then noted, "no sketch of Mr. Leslie Stuart at home would be complete without the mention of another kind of playing—that of billiards; for he wields a cue with the same dexterity and precision as his conducting stick. Indeed, it has been said that what he does not know of either game is not worth learning."[77] A further feature in the *Illustrated Mail* in January 1901 pictured Stuart, pipe in mouth, first working at his American organ, and then in his billiard room, "umpiring" a game between his own son and Florence St. John's son.[36] A hundred years later, one can still make out the single-story extension that housed the billiard room, although the house is now almost completely hidden from the road by mature trees.

During this time, Stuart had been working on a successor to *Florodora*, which ultimately closed in London on March 30, 1901. Its total of 455 performances fell well short of the London theater record of 931 performances for Alfred Cellier's *Dorothy*, as well as the runs of various shows at Daly's, the Gaiety, and the Savoy. Yet it still qualified as among the greatest hits of the London musical theater.

The Silver Slipper, which was to follow it at the Lyric Theatre, was very obviously designed to echo the formula that had already worked so spectacularly well. The book was once again the work of Owen Hall; but instead of Ernest Boyd-Jones (who was to die in 1904 at the early age of thirty-four) the principal lyricist was this time W. H. Risque. Sharing Mancunian links with Stuart, he had already worked with Owen Hall on the 1895 Frederick Rosse musical *All Abroad*. Willie Edouin and Louis Bradfield remained from the *Florodora* principals.

Of the newcomers, Coralie Blythe was the elder sister of Vernon Blythe, who later became the male half of the celebrated dance team Vernon and Irene Castle. In supporting roles were handsome Frenchman Henri Leoni as a French student, and comedy actress Connie Ediss as a housekeeper. Like Ada Reeve's role in *Florodora*, Connie Ediss's in *The Silver Slipper* was somewhat peripheral, designed primarily to suit the performer. Just past the age of thirty, plump Connie Ediss's performances in Gaiety musical comedies had made her one of those artists who were always welcome, in her case for a walk that was "not a waddle exactly, but a comfortable roll."

Produced by Tom B. Davis at the Lyric Theatre, London, on 1 June 1901

THE SILVER SLIPPER

A New Modern Extravaganza in 2 Acts.

Book by Owen Hall. Lyrics by W. H. Risque.

Music by Leslie Stuart.

MORTALS.

Sir Victor Shallamar	An Astronomer	Mr. E. Dagnall
Louis Tiraupigeon		Mr. Henri Leoni
Douglas Wharton	|	| Mr. Charles S. Kitts
Harry Hepworth	|	| Mr. Roy Horniman
Roland Western	| Students at Shallamar Hall	| Mr. Sydney Mannering
Claud Croucher	|	| Mr. Harry B. Burcher
Fred Rawlins	|	| Mr. Frank Walsh
Noel Gaisford	|	| Mr Murri Moncrieff
Berkeley Shallamar	Nephew of Sir Victor	Mr. W. Louis Bradfield
Snax		Mr. William Cheesman
Crushall		Mr. Frank Holt
Samuel Twanks	An Ex-Riding Master	Mr. Willie Edouin
Wrenne		Miss Coralie Blythe
Brenda Shallamar	Niece of Sir Victor	Miss Nancy Girling
Miss Bella Jimper		Miss Connie Ediss
Cynthia Grey	|	| Miss Edith Housley
Ella Hatfield	|	| Miss Lydia West
Maisie Rhodes	| Students at Shallamar Hall	| Miss Dora Nelson
Jenny Vereker	|	| Miss Nellie Harcourt
Mary Astell	|	| Miss Nina Sevening
Minnie Lomas	|	| Miss Nora Moore
Millicent Ward		Miss Fanny Dango
Suzette		Miss Edith Neville

Dancers. Misses Fanny Dango, Beatrice Grenville, Lucy Murray, Madge Greet, Dora Dent, Lilian Brendall.

IMMORTALS.

Judicia	Miss Agnes Delaporte
Gillian	Miss Mollie Lowell
Avoria	Miss Augusta Walters
Queen of Venus	Miss Mimi Margotine
Curia	Miss Grace Evelyn
Echo	Miss Edith Lofthouse
Foreman of the Jury	Miss Lena Maitland
Usher	Miss Nellie Pryce
Minna	Miss Dora Langroyd
Stella	Miss Winifred Hare

ACT I—Shallamar Hall and the Court of Justice on the Planet Venus.

ACT II.—Scene 1.—Neuilly Fair.
Scene 2.—The Turkey Room in the Art Club, Paris.

Production by Sydney Ellison.

Musical Director: Landon Ronald.

A curious aspect of the new work was its description as "a modern extravaganza." As in *Florodora*, such plot as there was unfolded largely in act 1, with act 2 essentially a sequence of incidental numbers. Act 1 opens in Shallamar Hall, a college run by Sir Victor Shallamar, an enthusiastic and vain astronomer. Sir Victor has notions that the planets are inhabited, and in the grounds of his college he has constructed a gigantic telescope through which he can see everything taking place on the surface of Venus. His interests are not shared by his household of nephew Berkeley Shallamar, niece Brenda Shallamar, her French boyfriend Louis Tiraupigeon, and faithful housekeeper Bella Jimper.

Twenty-five years earlier, Sir Victor disowned his daughter for marrying a disreputable riding master, Samuel Twanks, who is now a bookmaker and card sharper and has come to see what money he can make out of the hall's residents. His wife, Sir Victor's daughter, is dead, leaving Twanks to bring up a daughter, Wrenne, whom Sir Victor has never seen. When the students bring in an intruder they have found in the grounds, it turns out to be Wrenne in the male clothing she wears to accompany her father to racecourses. She wins sympathy for her plight, and Berkeley is especially taken by her. While passing through the grounds, Wrenne has found a mysterious silver slipper, which she claims has fallen from the sky. When Sir Victor gathers everyone around his telescope, he sees strange things happening on Venus.

The second scene is in the Court of Justice on the planet Venus, which is inhabited only by females. Watched over by the Queen of Venus, the court is passing judgment on the fair Stella, who has peered over the edge of a cloud at planet Earth and, in a fit of overeagerness, kicked her slipper off the planet. She vainly protests that she only caught a glimpse, and her announcement of the existence on Earth of another type of being likewise cuts no ice. She is sentenced to descend to Earth to recover the slipper.

The third scene takes us back to Shallamar Hall, where the students are playing "Hunt the Slipper" when Stella suddenly appears among them. Her ignorance of the ways of the world causes much confusion, as does her attempt to fall in love with every man she sees. Sir Victor welcomes her as someone sent from the stars to prove the truth of his theories, but the others are unwilling to believe that Stella has come from Venus until a group of maidens arrive from Venus to lend her support. The unscrupulous Twanks considers the Venusians a ready source of income and grabs the slipper to further his plan.

Act 2 opens at Neuilly Fair, with Wrenne now in female garb and Twanks a showman, doing a splendid business with some of Stella's companions from Venus. Actually Twanks's show is a sham, as the girls from Venus have run off with members of the public, and Twanks is forced to persuade Miss Jimper to dress up as a goddess. Sir Victor is furious with Twanks for robbing him of his Venusian discoveries, but Miss Jimper, Brenda, and Berkeley manage to pack him off home. Berkeley arranges to take Stella to the Artists' Ball in Paris and, when Wrenne confesses her love for Berkeley, Twanks sells his booth in order to take his daughter to the ball too.

Act 2, scene 2, unfolds in the Turkey Room in the Art Club in Paris, at whose fancy dress ball Stella is so much in demand that she finds herself spoilt for choice. This does nothing to endear her to Berkeley, and altogether she makes such a nuisance of herself that everyone is happy for her to return to Venus. Twanks thereupon produces her slipper on condition that she will reconcile Sir Victor to his granddaughter. This is promptly achieved, leaving Wrenne and Berkeley happily in each other's arms.

Leslie Stuart preserved in a scrapbook the telegrams of best wishes that came to him for the show's first night on June 1, 1901. They included messages from family and friends; theatrical folk such as Amy Augarde, Evie Greene, Florence St. John, and Kate Cutler; music-hall artists such as George Robey and Eugene Stratton; songwriters; and *Florodora* lyricist Ernest Boyd-Jones. Stratton's enigmatic message was, "Now you know what to do, it's all right. See you Trocadero. No good me giving wishes, you know. Gene." From Morecambe, Leslie Stuart's brother Steve and wife Hettie wished "Success to Silver Slipper and good old Tom."[64]

For that first night, Sir Henry Irving was in a box on one side of the house, with Florence St. John and actress Lillie Langtry's daughter in boxes on the other. Stuart himself conducted act 1. He entered the pit to warm applause and received another ovation at the final curtain, Landon Ronald having taken over to conduct act 2. Willie Edouin, speaking his opening lines offstage, received a huge burst of cheering when his voice was recognized. He was welcomed as "once again a plausible, weirdly dressed, sentimental, colossally conceited, and highly amusing adventurer." However, the evening was at best a qualified success, and boos mingled with the applause at the final curtain. The biggest problem lay in the way both acts overran. Even though encores were rigidly refused and the interval limited to ten minutes, the show ran from 8:00 until 11:30 P.M.

Not all reviews gave even a pretense of polite acceptance. *Candid Friend* opined that "Mr Leslie Stuart and Mr Owen Hall . . . had a good idea [but] didn't know how to develop it." Of Winifred Hare, the same critic declared that she "entirely misunderstood and vulgarised the role of Stella." As for Nancy Girling as Sir Victor Shallamar's niece Brenda, she "has been given a part entirely beyond her powers of acting or singing [and] severely handicapped Mr Leoni in his duet with her." Although Leoni was praised for his singing of "Two Eyes of Blue," his character had no greater relevance to the story than those of Connie Ediss and Nancy Girling. The *Gravesend Standard* wrote, "I can quite imagine that he has been engaged for the sole purpose of singing his one song 'Blue Eyes,' which, for all the bearing it has on the story, might have been sung by anyone else in the company. It is perfectly true that it is . . . sung in a delicate and effective style, but . . . for the rest of the evening one is irritated constantly by Mr Leoni aimlessly walking in and out from the wings, saying nothing, doing nothing, and looking like a man who has strayed on casually."

One aspect of the production that won almost unbounded praise was the staging. *M.A P.* was especially enthusiastic, writing, "The curtain rises

Willie Edouin as Samuel Twanks in *The Silver Slipper*, London (author's collection)

on a scene of lilac and laburnum. In the foreground there are great bushes of full-blown flowers, and in the far distance a long stretch of purple and yellow blossoms beneath a sunny sky. In the midst of all this fragrance the students of astronomy at Shallamar Hall, a brilliant throng in their caps and gowns of all the faint colours of the rainbow, start the story...." As for the transformation to act 1, scene 2, "The pale blue light in the sky slowly changes into rosy red; a cloud palace, with faintly outlined dome and towers, glows like a great ruby. From one side of the stage to the other stretches a flight of wide, opal steps, scattered with scarlet roses. The Queen of Venus sits on her throne beneath a tangle of gleaming, bell-shaped flowers. The inhabitants of the planet are draped in the palest blue dresses. Stella is in white, glittering with stars."

A puppet scene that introduced act 2 was also praised, and the costumes throughout were considered among the most beautiful ever seen. *Onlooker* expressed a general sentiment when suggesting that Sydney Ellison was "the cleverest stage manager in London for this sort of piece. His dances are wonderfully ingenious in their arrangement, his groupings are intricate and often beautiful. But his great feat lies in his making of all the bodies and faces of his singers and dancers gay." The *Sunday Sun* made special mention of his "Danse Parisienne" in act 2, scene 1: "One clever invention is that of the waiters bringing the young ladies their *apéritif*, and then dancing off with them, tables, glasses and all."

The musical numbers that succeeded most included several that were clear equivalents of the hit numbers in *Florodora*. Instead of Lady Holyrood's "I've an Inkling" there was Stella's "A Glimpse-impse-impse." Instead of "The Shade of the Palm," the baritone had "Two Eyes of Blue," sung "in French chansonette style." For Ada Reeve's song about "Tact, tact, tact," there was Connie Ediss at the Art Ball singing of "Class, class, class." Just as "Tact" had contained a verse about racing at Goodwood, so Berkeley's song "She Didn't Know Enough About the Game" referred to cricket at Lord's. There was also the double sextet "Come, Little Girl, and Tell Me Truly," an obvious attempt to repeat the success of "Tell Me, Pretty Maiden." As if that was not enough, the familiar Stuart dotted rhythms were to be heard again in "Four and Twenty Little Men," sung by Stella and the male chorus at the Art Ball in act 2, scene 2.

This very obvious attempt to capitalize upon the success of *Florodora* caused repeated comment. The *People* summed up Stuart's musical contribution as follows:

> As a writer of lilting melody, as one who can fascinate the ear with the grace of his musical themes and the distinctive charm of his orchestration, Mr Leslie Stuart has won for himself an enviable position among those who love the light and the bright in music. No one would deny that Mr Stuart has a musical mannerism, but his melodies have always been fresh and engaging, if in his treatment of them his style is unmistakable. Call it mannerism or what you will,

the public have shown their liking for it, and, judging from the applause which greeted the various musical numbers last night, there is not the slightest indication of their being yet tired of it. To be candid, there is nothing very new in his contributions to *The Silver Slipper*, and Mr Stuart so far repeats himself as to give us another double sextette. This time it is "Come Little Girl and Tell Me Truly," but it has not the novelty and entrain of the now familiar "Tell Me, Pretty Maiden."

The *Daily Telegraph*, too, questioned Stuart's repetitions and mannerisms:

> The composer of *The Silver Slipper* draws upon his unquestioned melodic gift with a free hand. His tunes romp merrily along, sometimes even giving the ear a hard task to keep pace with their tricks and turns. These latter characteristics, indeed, belong closely to Mr Leslie Stuart's style. He has little love for a direct simple rhythm that finds its appointed end at the place where ninety-nine composers in a hundred would have ended it. On the other hand, he revels in a complicated measure, and a "prolonged cadence" is to him as the breath of life. These things all give individuality, and among those who pen the popular tunes of London to-day Mr Stuart is, perhaps, the one most easily identified by his work. At the same time, a personal characteristic may be carried too far.

The *World* mixed the same charge of repetition with an interesting comparison between Stuart and Lionel Monckton, whose rich vein of melody had lit up the London theater in shows such as *The Circus Girl, A Runaway Girl,* and *The Messenger Boy.* It wrote, "Mr. Leslie Stuart is not infrequently a delightful composer. He has the gift of writing tune which can be recognised as his, and this recognition does not result from what are loosely called 'mannerisms' or tricks of style, but from his possession of an individual fancy different from that we call 'distinction.' Not a cleverer musical-phrasemaker than Mr. Monckton, he surpasses that admirable person in scope of design and colouring, being, I take it, a better equipped musician, and thinking with not less elegance than brightness. But, if he will forgive me for saying so, he does not sufficiently vary his landscapes. . . ."

The *Referee* considered that in one number "Mr Stuart rises to a height he never reached before." This was the ambitious "Invocation to Venus" at

The Champagne Dance, *The Silver Slipper*, London (author's collection)

the start of the second scene. Beginning with a sixty-nine-bar prelude that gave rich scope for orchestral expansion, it is followed by a three-part female chorus and soprano solo for the Queen of Venus. The *Sunday Special* was struck that the scene of the Court of Justice in Venus "reminds one strangely of the opening scenes of *Tannhäuser*." It would indeed be strange if Leslie Stuart had not thought back to the times when he had conducted Wagner's *Tannhäuser* overture at his Manchester concerts.

Cuts were quickly made, and two numbers mentioned in reviews were eliminated: "My Studio" for Louis Bradfield as Berkeley, and a quartet, "Toys," both of which survive in early copyright deposits at the British Library. The dialogue was also heavily pruned, shedding an ill-conceived attempt to add some pathos to the part of Twanks, and some ill-judged quips. One of the latter was about the supposed brashness of American entertainment, another about French justice, referring to the Dreyfus affair, in which a Jewish officer was accused of spying and committed to Devil's Island penal colony before being pardoned.

This quick surgery seemed to do the trick. *The Silver Slipper* may have disappointed those whom *Florodora* had caused to expect too much, but its attractions were very real, and it was soon drawing capacity audiences as new numbers were introduced to keep the work fresh. There was a trio for Brenda and two showmen, Snax and Crushall, in the Neuilly scene, and a new number, "If You Must Sigh," for Stella. Louis Bradfield earned two solos, "The Detrimental Man" and "Fun on a Motor," the latter composed by Landon Ronald. Bradfield also had a new duet with Coralie Blythe, "Ping Pong," composed by Ivan Caryll.

The Silver Slipper settled in to such an extent that, when a new monthly magazine *The Playgoer* started publication in October 1901, it singled out the show for special review and referred to it—overoptimistically, no doubt—as an "even greater success" than *Florodora*. The most encored vocal number remained Connie Ediss's waltz song "Class," but attention had now shifted to the "Danse Parisienne" sequence, featuring six waiters and six handpicked lady dancers in frilly dresses. This was scarcely noticed by the first-night critics; but the *Playgoer* described it as "one of the smartest and most original ballet movements ever presented."

It was perhaps most successfully in this "Danse Parisienne," alias "Champagne Dance," together with Wrenne's "If I Were a Girl Instead," that Stuart seemed to give his rhythmic predilections even greater scope than in *Florodora*. Of the other numbers, Bella Jimper's "Class" catered admirably to the tastes of the time, with its topical lyric and attractive waltz melody. If neither the show's concept nor its musical numbers had quite the freshness of their predecessors in *Florodora*, audiences derived much of the same uncomplicated fun and enjoyment.

Moreover, just as bottles of scent had served to promote *Florodora*, so this new work had its marketing gimmick. The *Era* recorded in August 1901 how Francis, Day and Hunter were promoting the vocal score at their Charing Cross Road premises, writing, "A great attraction to passers by is a number of beautifully modelled silver slippers displayed by Messrs Francis, Day & Hunter in their window, which serve to draw attention to the music, vocal and instrumental, of Mr Leslie Stuart's latest musical play now on sale. The slippers have been designed and cast by Mr Robert Coan, the well-known worker in aluminium, at his Clerkenwell foundries, and are splendid examples of the metal-worker's craft."

Touring companies were also soon presenting the show around Britain to encouraging business, and productions were to follow not only around the British Empire and the United States but also in continental Europe. The performing rights of *The Silver Slipper* for Germany were soon sold to José Ferenczy, director of the Central Theater, Berlin, who planned to produce the work as early as December 1901. Francis, Day and Hunter had arranged for the German publisher Bote and Bock to act as agency for the music in Berlin and for Fred Day to go out to the firm for twelve months to learn the business in Germany. Hopes for another great international success were high.

Chapter 10

Across America

While *The Silver Slipper* found its feet at London's Lyric Theatre, *Florodora* continued its sensational run on Broadway. An eastern touring company was launched in August with a water polo match, one side featuring the six "pretty maidens" of the company, the other those of the Casino Theatre. It was, of course, a publicity stunt, offering the opportunity to photograph the girls in bathing costumes. The eastern tour duly opened at the Montauk Theatre, Brooklyn, on September 15, 1901, moving to the Chestnut Theatre, Philadelphia, for six weeks from September 23. Isadora Rush was Lady Holyrood, Alf C. Whelan was Tweedlepunch, Bertha Waltzinger was Dolores, and William G. Stewart was Abercoed. The western company began tryout performances at Parsons' Opera House, Hartford, Connecticut, on September 2, the *New York Dramatic Mirror* reporting "two packed houses that were much pleased" and a company that "may be compared favourably with the original cast."

Stuart was meanwhile hard at work not only on further songs for *The Silver Slipper* but also on a new "coon" song for Eugene Stratton. This time it was a Mexican cowboy ditty, which it was announced Stratton would perform on his return to London in October. Stuart was also preparing to travel to America in conjunction with the first anniversary of *Florodora*'s opening in New York. On September 25, 1901, he and his wife Kitty were given a splendid send-off on the midday express train from Euston Station to Liverpool to join the *SS Majestic* for New York. David Day was at Euston, having just returned from Germany with an invitation from the Berlin management for Stuart to conduct *The Silver Slipper* at the first performance there.

Preparations for his U.S. trip had been overshadowed by the assassination of President William McKinley. On September 6, a deranged anarchist, Leon Czolgosz, walked up to McKinley at the Buffalo Pan-American Exposition and shot him. McKinley died eight days later, and Stuart remembered the enthusiasm the former president had expressed for "Louisiana Lou" in an interview he gave in New York, reported in the *Era*: "I was pained beyond measure to learn of the death of President McKinley, for I was looking forward to a meeting with him. He had expressed a desire to see the manner of man who was responsible for 'Louisiana Lou,' which I have been gratified to hear was one of his favourite airs. I do know that he said he would like to the meet the man who wrote it. This is in itself a seal of recommendation—if I may say so."

The *Era* reported that everywhere Stuart went in New York he was given celebrity treatment: "He has been elected a member of every prominent club in New York, and on several occasions he has been fêted and lionised at Delmonico's." Like many before and after, Stuart felt bewildered at the grandness and speed of so much in the New World. He commented, "You have so many things here that are a source of wonder to me.... For instance, I discovered so many new and delightful drinks on the steamer coming over. You Americans are marvellous at that sort of thing. I understand you have several hundred different drinks. Now in England we have but seven or eight. I do not want to say I will try all your concoctions, but I would certainly like to try a few. You have, too, a certain habit of doing things on a lavish scale. At the hotel where I am lodging I have seen some things I never would have thought of. You fellows look out for comfort, certainly. I almost wish I lived here."

His bewilderment of the speed of everything American extended not least to the interpretation of his music at the Casino Theatre. "Of course, your American manner of doing things is somewhat of an astonishment to me," he noted. "I did write the music, but the tempo in which it is conducted here would never go in London. I do not know that I am against it, but it is a different atmosphere entirely. Things seem to move so much faster here."

Despite this, Stuart had agreed to conduct the opening night of *Florodora*'s transfer to the New York Theatre. On October 12, it closed at the Casino, reopening at the larger theater two nights later, with a larger orchestra, a chorus almost doubled, and prices raised. Smoking was prohibited in the New York Theatre, and the ticket speculators who traditionally operated outside it were outlawed. "Messrs Fisher and Ryley had wisely insisted on the previous sidewalk policy of the house being abandoned and free trade at the box office re-established," reported the *New York Herald,* adding that the audience "were stricken dumb at the absence of the old time crowd of ticket speculators." The paper reported that the composer "received a warm welcome when he took the conductor's chair and was frequently applauded during the evening." As at the London first night, the audience was presented with souvenir bottles of perfume.

Then Stuart and Kitty crossed the continent to join the western company. This had traveled from Saratoga, New York, to Omaha, Nebraska, followed by Denver and Salt Lake City, for a three-week season at the Columbia Theater, San Francisco, from September 30 to October 19. Before the opening night there, the *San Francisco Chronicle* wrote about the operation that had gone into the tour, "Not only is the aggregation equipped with its own orchestra from the New York Casino but the managers have provided a special train of seven Pullman coaches to make certain the comfort of the company during the journeyings from city to city all the way from New York to San Francisco and back East by the way of Los Angeles, San Diego and New Orleans. It is one of the most expensive theatrical ventures ever undertaken in this country. The train is named the Florodora special, bearing the entire company of 100 members, the business staff, a specially selected staff of expert electricians, stage workers and scenery handlers, and the servants of the principal members of the company."

Featuring English-born William T. Carleton as Gilfain, Philip H. Ryley as Tweedlepunch, Grace Dudley as Lady Holyrood, and Laura Millard as Dolores, the three-week San Francisco visit was rated "one of the successes of the season." After its first night, the *San Francisco Chronicle* reviewer sized up the work as well as anyone, writing, "*Florodora* at the Columbia Theater bids fair to equal the success of *The Geisha*.

It is a development of the same kind of musical comedy, and, although the music of the other is of better quality, the new piece has an incessant movement, more action and is even a brighter series of stage pictures all the time. It is a gay, vivacious, kaleidoscopic show; there are few moments when the colors are not flashing, and there is hardly a musical number without its accompaniment of movement or dancing."

From San Francisco, Stuart and his wife traveled with the company on the Florodora special. They called first at San Diego, and then at Los Angeles for a further four performances from October 24. Everywhere the show's reputation preceded it. The Los Angeles Theater was not unusual in reporting a phenomenal sale of reserved seats for a show described as "clean, wholesome and beautiful." The *Los Angeles Daily Times* reported that the house was "packed with the eager and animated atoms left of the crowds who tried to squeeze in through the one narrow entrance.... *Florodora* is a brilliant spectacle, a musical kaleidoscope in its ever-changing form and color."

The same paper featured an interview in which the composer said, "Ever since I was a boy I had wished to see this great country, and especially California." Seemingly ignoring the revision of the *Florodora* libretto by Frank Pixley, he claimed that the secret of John C. Fisher's success with the show was "that he has produced it here in its exact English version, instead of trying to change it to make it sound American." He noted that there were currently twelve companies performing the work: one in Melbourne on a sixteen weeks' engagement, one playing for six weeks in Cape Town, one in Bombay, one in New Zealand, five in Great Britain, and three in the United States.

The paper also reported comments that in those days were evidently deemed safe to make halfway round the world, to wit, "Mr Stuart makes enormous earnings out of his productions, as he controls all the royalties on the music that is for sale, and gets a big lump out of each company that is on the road. It has been said that his income is $4000 a month. Last night he said that he would rather not be quoted as making this statement, as he feared that when he got back to England he would be assessed so hard on the income-tax proposition that it would break him up; but he did not deny that these figures are very close to the truth."

From Los Angeles the company moved to El Paso, San Antonio, and Austin; on to Waco (November 1); Fort Worth (November 2); Galveston (November 6); Houston (November 7 and 8), and Beaumont, Texas (November 9). The Stuarts seemingly left the tour to see something of Mexico, but were evidently with it in Galveston fourteen months after the city had been almost completely destroyed by a hurricane that cost 6,000 lives. The *Era* reported back to British readers that Stuart "speaks in enthusiastic terms of the kindness he has met with everywhere."

On Sunday, November 10, the company opened in New Orleans to "the biggest business in the history of the Tulane." The reporter of the *Daily Picayune* fell under *Florodora's* spell no less than anyone else:

> Girls so pretty that the usual wholesale exposure of charms is unnecessary to the achievement of ample recognition. Dresses which are dreams. Ravishing airs from opening chorus to finale, with a solo and double sextette snatched from the genuine soul of music—stage settings of the costliest—constantly shifting scenes, flashing in brilliant colors, harmoniously set, and displayed to strains of catchy melodies, symphonically strong—that is *Florodora,* as *Florodora* was presented last night at the Tulane Theatre before one of the largest audiences of the season. . . . Success here had been predicated by the unbroken stream of success which had been poured upon the production elsewhere, but even those who had hoped most for the engagement were hardly prepared for encores so frequently persistent as to stretch a show built for two hours and a half into three hours and a quarter.

The New Orleans success was sufficient for an extra performance to be staged on Sunday, November 17, in place of a scheduled appearance by Helena Modjeska, who, according to the *Daily Picayune,* "never plays on Sundays." In New Orleans, Stuart and Kitty left the tour to travel up the Mississippi River so that he could conduct the first anniversary performance of *Florodora* at the New York Theatre on November 12.

Meanwhile, the eastern company had moved on from Philadelphia to Washington, Baltimore, Pittsburgh, and other major cities. Among those who absorbed the music in Baltimore was seventeen-year-old Eubie Blake, future composer not only of "Memories of You" and "I'm Just Wild about Harry" but also a piece entitled "Florodora Girls." In those days, blacks were generally restricted to no more than a special section of the gallery; but, in an interview a few years before his death in 1983 at the age of one hundred, Blake stressed how much the music of *Florodora* meant to him. "Leslie Stuart is the cause—*direct* cause—of me becoming a composer," he said. "I liked his style. He wrote a number called "Tell Me, Pretty Maiden" from *Florodora.* It was 1900 when it first came out over here and they played it at Fords' Theatre in Baltimore. . . . "The Shade of the Palm"—I love that tune; and I said "If I could write tunes like that . . . !"[59]

For all Leslie Stuart's enthusiastic reception in the United States, the issue of having composed "coon" songs without direct contact with American blacks constantly recurred. In its issue of November 30, 1901, the *Era* reported one exchange that also produced some new information: "Being chaffed as to his non-acquaintance with the real darkie and coon, Mr Stuart said, in the true American way, 'See here! I'm going South at once to learn something, because I am writing a new opera on American lines, with an American author as the writer of the libretto!'" The paper noted that Stuart had entered into a contract with Charles Frohman for a musical play with Paul Potter for production in New York in October 1902. Potter was actually British by birth, his stage adaptation of *Trilby* having inspired Stuart's early song "Trilby Will Be True." The report described Stuart as the first English composer to be commissioned by an American manager to write for the American stage.

Leslie and Kitty Stuart finally sailed for England on the White Star liner *Majestic* on December 4, laden with presents for the family.[65] They left behind the New York company and the two touring companies still presenting *Florodora* to huge acclaim. From New Orleans the western company had visited such cities as Mobile, Montgomery, Atlanta, Birmingham, Chattanooga, Knoxville, Lexington, and Louisville, followed by Minneapolis (December 15) and St. Paul (December 19–22). After swaps between the western and eastern companies at St. Louis and Cincinnati, crowded houses followed in Iowa: Des Moines, January 1, 1902; Cedar Rapids, January 2; Clinton, January 3; and Dubuque, January 4. Then came Illinois: Rockford, January 7; Aurora, January 8; Joliet, January 9; Bloomington, January 10; Decatur, January 11; Peoria, January 14; and Galesburg. From Davenport, Iowa, the tour moved down the Mississippi via Quincy and Cairo, Illinois, to Paducah, Kentucky, and onward.

In New York, the production clocked up a further 120-odd performances at the New York Theatre to add to over 380 at the Casino. It closed on January 25, 1902, after a grand total of 505 performances, having become the third-longest running show in New York theater history. Only the burlesque *Adonis* (603 performances at the Bijou Theatre in 1884–86), and the musical comedy *A Trip to Chinatown* (656 performances at the Madison-Square Theatre in 1891–93) had run longer.

Still it was not finished. A further production immediately opened at the Winter Garden Theatre, above the New York Theatre. Sydney Barraclough repeated his London role of Abercoed, Dorothy Morton was Dolores, Thomas Q. Seabrooke played Tweedlepunch, and Donald Brian, Broadway's future Danilo in Franz Lehár's *The Merry Widow*, was Donegal. This production clocked up a further forty-eight performances. Even without them, the New York run outstripped London's 455 performances, breaking the usual pattern in much the same way as *The Belle of New York* had done in reverse by becoming a far greater success in London than in New York.

Throughout the United States, in short, the show was a sensation, becoming a landmark in the history of the American musical theater. If "Louisiana Lou" was the favorite song of President McKinley, *Florodora* had a later president among its fans. On November 28, 1911, Harry Truman wrote to his childhood sweetheart and future wife Bess Wallace, contrasting the *Florodora* sextet with a rather different operatic sextet: "Do you think you could stand some Grand Opera? What? I have a desire to hear *Lucia di Lammermoor* or to see it, whichever is proper. Would you go? I don't believe that just one yelling match would be unenjoyable. I have never seen *Lucia* and I am curious to know how much torture one has to endure to get to hear the sextet. I hope not any more than *Florodora*. The whole works could be endured in that. . . ."[73]

Everywhere, indeed, the *Florodora* girls and the double sextet were at the center of its appeal. As William O. Inglis summarized in 1926, "Do you know anything in the wide world of music more sumptuous, sensuous, intoxicating than the orchestration that went with 'Tell Me, Pretty Maiden'? That, and the dancing and the come-hither winks under the flapping hats, rather than the words, made this *Florodora* sextette song the most popular musical comedy feature that ever swept America."[68]

As Stuart and his wife sailed back across the Atlantic, *Florodora* was also achieving another landmark with its first continental European performance at the Magyar Színház (Hungarian Theatre) in Budapest on December 5, 1901. However, they arrived home to find *The Silver Slipper* in the last few days of its London run, which ended on December 14, 1901. The total of 197 performances was clearly disappointing by comparison with its predecessor, though *The Silver Slipper* had already begun to convert its London run into a solid touring history. Moreover, following the precedent already established with *Florodora*, Louis Bradfield and Connie Ediss had been into the Maiden Lane studio to record excerpts from the show. In November 1901, Bradfield recorded "The Detrimental Man" and a number entitled "A Happy Day." The following month Connie Ediss recorded "Good Behaviour" and "Class," and in March 1902, Albert Pearce added the baritone aria "Two Eyes of Blue."

Meanwhile, Eugene Stratton's introduction of the Mexican scena that Leslie Stuart had composed before his trip to America had been delayed. Stuart's absence may have been a reason, but an event of personal significance to Stratton could have been another. Over Christmas 1900, Stratton had visited his mother back in Buffalo; but, in November 1901, she died shortly after Leslie Stuart had visited her in Buffalo during his American trip: "She died in my arms, in Buffalo, practically, where I called to see her there. Her last words to me were 'My love to 'Gene.'"[62]

In the end it was at the London Pavilion at Christmas 1901 that Stratton created what was arguably the very finest of his Leslie Stuart creations, albeit one that lacked the immediate upbeat appeal of "Little Dolly Daydream" or "Lily of Laguna." It was a heartfelt dramatic scena, about which the *Era* reported, "Mr. Eugene Stratton ... appears as a Texan horse thief. The 'boys' are after him, and a reward is offered for his apprehension. Notwithstanding this, he is inspired by Cupid to serenade his 'gal,' and follows his song with a dance. Naturally enough, he is captured by the cowboys. He takes a tender farewell of his inamorata, and the curtain falls as he is led away."

W. Macqueen-Pope described the number more vividly:

The whole song was drama, it had an urge, a breathlessness of words and music admirably suited to the situation. You could hear and understand the gasping prayer of the hard-pressed desperate man in every note and syllable. Stratton's very eyes were hunted, his figure tense and taut, as he stood before the cabin of his loved one and stammered out his plea.

He might be crazy, but he loved her, he gasped—he would do and dare anything—he might be shady, but he adored her—so would she not come out and bid him "Good-bye"—because—he might not— see her any more. . . . The music matched the tensely gripping drama and the mad, violent hopeless dance of abandon which followed was a very miracle, all the more for its silence. It ended with the posse, pistols in hand, dragging him away, as he wrenched himself round in their grasp to give one last despairing glance of dumb, stricken grief at the house of his loved one and throw out his arms in a mute appeal. . . . Great actors have played scenes less skillfully and with less art than this music hall artist showed.[38]

In both words and music, Leslie Stuart perhaps reached his apogee with the emotional emphasis on the final climax of the refrain.

Another who saw Eugene Stratton perform the number was music critic Neville Cardus, who as a starstruck fourteen-year-old sold chocolates during Stratton's three-month season as Pete the page boy in the pantomime *Cinderella* at the Comedy Theatre, Manchester, over Christmas 1902. Cardus described how Stratton "stood with his slouch hat hanging down from his right hand, looking at the bedroom window of the shack where his lady-love dwelt; he lifted himself slightly on tip-toe to get his high notes."[13] He described Stratton as "dancing as though with no weight on him, feet only brushing the boards of the stage."[12] He also recalled being spoken to once by Stratton—"a little man with a careworn but kindly face [who] had about him a strange odour of limelight and Havana cigar."[13]

"I May Be Crazy" was to prove as profitable as any of Stuart's songs to the sheet music pirates, who still flourished. In his first speech to Parliament in 1901, King Edward VII had announced a bill to amend copyright; but the congested state of parliamentary business delayed its introduction. In October 1901, the Attorney General received a deputation pressing for the prosecution of anonymous publishers and distributors of pirated musical copyright, but in January 1902 decided to take no action.

Publishers and composers were understandably reaching the end of their tether. Against legal advice, David Day of Francis, Day and Hunter decided once more to take the law into his own hands. As the *Era* reported, "For weeks Mr Day dived down dirty courts into noisome cellars where thousands of copies of pirated works were being printed, and took them away. At all hours of the night and day he raided illicit printing houses, and, after the most dangerous experiences with men who threatened his life, he had the courage to bring them into court, with the inevitable result—an injunction. Vehicles were stopped in the street, and their cargo lifted."

Day's efforts led to the February 1902 formation of the Musical Copyright Association, with Day at its head and an organized corps of ex-police officers and other strong men to raid the street vendors, leaving cards with the name and address of the association, and inviting them to take steps against it if they felt they had a grievance.[1] Within fourteen weeks of the association's foundation, a bill for the Suppression of Piracies of Musical Copyright passed through Parliament and received royal assent. On October 1, 1902, it became law, and the following month a dinner was held in honor of David Day's efforts. Leslie Stuart presented him with a specially commissioned portrait and assured him that the work of the testimonial committee was a "labour of love made exceedingly pleasant by the unanimity and liberality of the donors."

However, it was soon apparent that the law as enacted was ineffective. In passing through Parliament it had encountered particularly strong opposition from James Caldwell, member of Parliament for one of the Glasgow divisions, and along the way it lost the crucial provision of making it a criminal offense to print or sell pirated music. Caldwell had made his fortune out of copyright patterns on calico, but apparently he saw it as an absurdity that a mere writer of songs should be similarly remunerated for his work. Lester Barrett, who two or three years earlier had abandoned his performing career for the greater security of a job as manager of Francis, Day and Hunter's professional department, was quoted as describing Caldwell as "a bit of a Socialist and a Scotchman."

The new Copyright Bill required a publisher to go through a wholly unrealistic rigmarole. His agent carried around printed forms, claiming copyright in specified songs. When he found pirated copies on sale in the streets, he was required to find a police constable and hand the signed form to him to authorize seizure. By the time this was done, the pirate had probably made his way to another location.

The anomalous British position on musical copyright was highlighted particularly when foreign musicians found themselves affected by it. John Philip Sousa, for instance, visited Britain with his band in 1900, 1901, 1903, and 1905. On the 1901 visit, he arranged a patrol called *The Rose, Shamrock and Thistle,* which combined melodies representing England, Ireland, and Scotland. Ireland was represented by "The Minstrel Boy" and Scotland by "Where Is Your Highland Laddie Gone?" and "Comin' Thro' the Rye." And England? Besides Sullivan's "He Is an Englishman," what else but "Soldiers of the Queen"? During his 1903 visit, the piracy problem hit Sousa, and he was moved to write to the *Times,* saying, "We have a tradition in America that English law is a model to be emulated by all peoples. You can imagine my astonishment therefore, on arriving in London, to find that pirated editions of my compositions were being sold broadcast in your city!"[14] Another astonished visitor was André Messager, who arrived from France to supervise the production of his *Véronique* and found songs from it being hawked outside the theater. In France, an English composer in such a situation could have the hawker promptly arrested.

Meanwhile, *The Silver Slipper* had finally made it to Berlin, albeit on a rather less grand scale and somewhat later than originally predicted. It was on Tuesday, July 1, 1902, adapted by Wilhelm Mannstädt and as part of a summer season, that the German premiere of *Der silberne Pantoffel* took place at the Neues Königliche Opern-Theater (New Royal Opera Theater). It provided novelty interest in repertory with two Viennese operetta classics, Carl Millöcker's *Der Bettelstudent* and Johann Strauss's *Der Zigeunerbaron.* According to continental custom, the work was performed in three acts, with a ballet interpolated into act 3. Mia Weber, who had previously triumphed in Berlin in the title role of Sidney Jones's *The Geisha,* took the leading female role.

Not until October 1902 did *The Silver Slipper* finally reach the United States, in a production by John C. Fisher for which Clay M. Greene rearranged the book. Greene's work mostly involved adapting the humor of the Willie Edouin and Connie Ediss roles for their American performers. Samuel Twanks was transformed into Henry Bismark Henschs for English-born dialect comedian Sam Bernard, famous for his "Dutch" low comedy characters at the Weber and Fields Music Hall.

Other changes in the U.S. production were made to divert attention away from potentially adverse comparisons with *Florodora.* Unflattering comment on the new double sextet "Come, Little Girl, and Tell Me Truly" was partially forestalled by concentrating attention instead on the act 3 "Champagne Dance," with six female dancers brought over from London for the purpose. An attempt was also made to build upon the success of the "Invitation to Venus" in act 1 by recruiting French soprano Mai de Villiers. By sending the Queen of Venus down to Earth with Stella, her role was prolonged into act 2, with Leslie Stuart composing for her an additional number, "Mademoiselle Éternelle," in the ballroom scene. She also took part in a duet written by Arthur Weld, who directed the forty-two-piece American orchestra with a luminous-tipped baton during the dark scene changes.

Further changes included reducing the third scene of act 1, whose "Hunt the Slipper" ensemble had been considered somewhat tiresome at the London premiere. Bella Jimper's "Good Behavio(u)r" was moved to the first scene, as was "Two Eyes of Blue," sung now not by a Frenchman but by a man in uniform, with Louis Tiraupigeon becoming Donald Gregor of the Royal Navy. The New York opening was preceded by a brief tryout of four performances at the Hyperion Theatre, New Haven, Connecticut.

Produced by John C. Fisher at the Broadway Theatre, New York,
27 October 1902

THE SILVER SLIPPER

A Musical Comedy in 2 Acts and 5 Scenes.

Book by Owen Hall, rearranged for America by Clay M. Greene.

Music by Leslie Stuart.

Lyrics by W. H. Risque.

HENRY BISMARK HENSCHS, riding master, showman, card sharp and all round fakir	SAM BERNARD
Sir Victor Shallamar, an Astronomer	Snitz Edwards
Berkeley Shallamar, of the Household Brigade, Nephew of Sir Victor	Cyril Scott
Donald Gregor, of the Royal Navy	Mackenzie Gordon
Roland Western	Harry B. Burcher
Duval	J. Ardisonne
The Queen of Venus	Mai de Villiers
Belle Jimper, servant of Sir Victor	Josie Sadler
Stella, the girl from Venus	Helen Royton
Brenda, niece of Sir Victor	Susan Drake
Judicia	Daisy Greene
Susette	Clarita Vidal

and

EDNA WALLACE-HOPPER, AS "WRENNE."

Cleo				Gertrude Douglas
Dione				Margaret Walker
Ira		Venus Girls		Marie Allen
Astria				Alice Toland
Lydia				Marjorie Relyea

Cynthia Grey		Edith Blair
Minnie Lomas		Francis Hill
Mary Estelle		Clarita Vidal
Jenny Vercker		Sadie Hollister
Maisie Brooks		Louise Lonsdale
Ella Hatfield	Students of Shallamar College	Maud Thomas
Harry Power		Jack Taylor
Algernon Hepworth		Benjamin H. Burt
Claud Coucher		Fred Walsh
Fred Rollins		W. H. Pringle
Douglas Wharton		Atherton B. Furlong

English Dancing Girls: Sallie Lomas, Dollie Corke, Beatrice Grenville, Rose Martin, Maggie Taylor and Lillie Lawton.

Student boys and girls, Flower girls, Nurse girls, Soldiers, Gendarmes, Troubadours, Waiters, Attendants.

ACT I Scene I.   The Gardens of the College of Sir Victor Shallamar.

Scene II. Hall of Justice on the Planet Venus.   Scene III. Same as Scene I.

ACT II. Scene I. Neuilly Fair, France.
Scene II. Ball Room of the Art Club, Paris.

Production staged by Mr. James Francis, of the Lyric Theatre, London, assisted by Mr. Harry B. Burcher.

Orchestra under the direction of Mr. Arthur Weld.

Scenery by Ernest Albert. Costumes by Charles Alias.

Leslie Stuart was kept informed of the reception by transatlantic cable. From the New Haven tryout on October 21 came the message, "New Haven audience pronounces Slipper big success. Congratulations." A day later, after matinee and evening performances, came confirmation from John C. Fisher: "LATE CABLING WAITED FOR VERDICT OF PRESS & PUBLIC ENDORSED BY BOTH THREE HUNDRED POUNDS YESTERDAY FIVE TODAY SLIPPER HOWLING SUCCESS." Nor did Mai de Villiers beat about the bush in her own transatlantic cablegram: "SILVER SLIPPER GREAT SUCCESS I ALSO."[64]

On Monday, October 27, the New York first-night audience gathered at the Fourteenth Street Theatre. Alas, they were kept waiting; as the *New York Herald* explained, "One thing that rather spoiled the pleasure of the audience last night was the long delay in raising the curtain. Eight o'clock was the hour set and it was nearly a quarter of nine before the overture began. By way of explanation the management said that Mr Cyril Scott's uniform hadn't arrived. He went on finally in mufti, and it is a pity he didn't do that earlier.

Critics greeted the two stars as familiar friends. Sam Bernard was, well, Sam Bernard—described as "funny in the same old way." The *World* considered his Henry Bismark Henschs "the most legitimate comic role of his career." Edna Wallace Hopper was deemed "a nice little thing to look at.... Her voice was as small as her person, yet she made it reach to the back of the big house." The *Morning Telegraph* felt that she "gave the artistic performance of her life" and "should in the future taboo all skirts for stage purposes."

As for Mai de Villiers, at least one critic seemed to agree with her own assessment. He commented that she "sang ... far better than is usual in comic opera" and recognized that she had been engaged "so that justice would be done to Mr Stuart's 'Invocation to Mars' [*sic*], a dramatic composition far superior in serious worth to anything in *Florodora*." Other critics had very different views. The *New York Daily News* stated bluntly that "Mai de Villiers, as Venus, was fine to see, as long as she did not walk or sing." In the *New York American,* Alan Dale elaborated, "The 'Invocation to Venus' in the second scene of the first act was murdered. Miss Mai de Villiers was the 'Queen of Venus'—a nice-looking queen, but oh! that invocation. The nocturnal miaulings of enraged tabbies were harmony compared with it. If they sing like that in Venus, let us take a tumble to earth again."

Memories of *Florodora* also affected critics' minds. In William Randolph Hearst's *New York Evening Journal,* under the heading "'Silver Slipper' Show Is all Sextet," James Montague penned his own words to the *Florodora* sextet:

Tell us "Florodora" are there any shows abroad like you?
    There is a new one due,
    But none, it's true, just like you.
"The Silver Slipper" which is from the tuneful pen of Leslie Stu-
    Art, will not do
    Compared with you.
And though that sextette da-de-da-da-dah runs through every song,
And people sing by sixes, and by sixes stroll along,

Edna Wallace Hopper as Wrenne in *The Silver Slipper*, New York (author's collection)

A bunch of six
In all the mix-
Ups, dances, songs, side-steps and kicks,
Don't make a show
Always a go.
And so we know
The reason why "The Silver Slipper's" show,
'Tis sad, but Oh!
'Tis so.

The *New York Evening Journal*'s case was that the show had "suggestions of the sextette music in every song, and with sixes and multiples of sixes appearing and reappearing with dread certainty." The *New York*

Times was even more forceful, writing, "The moral of *The Silver Slipper* ... is that you cannot achieve success a second time by doing over again the things that have once been successful. You must have something more than the method and the formula. *The Silver Slipper* ... has a sextet, with all the stage manoeuvring that helped to make the *Florodora* sextet; it has the same turns of melody, the same pattering rhythms, the same brisk, vaulting methods of chorus writing. Now *Florodora* is not a remarkable production judged by any fair standards of operetta; but it is a towering masterpiece compared with *The Silver Slipper.*"

As it was, the sextet that took the plaudits was not the innocuous "Come, Little Girl, and Tell Me Truly," but the "Champagne Dance." The *Evening Sun* reported that the show "was fast slumping into a spectacular failure when just at 11 o'clock six English dancing girls, clad in yellow, accompanied by half a dozen men dressed as waiters, came on and indulged in a 'champagne dance.' ... The effect was electrical, the tribute spontaneous." The following Sunday's *Sun* described it in more detail:

> We were crushed. Then a few bars of gay music burst forth, and six girls were before us. ... We wouldn't look twice at them on the street, but on the stage they quickly fired our attention by kicking, whirling and fairly dancing their clothes off in mad gayety. And such pretty clothes they were—all flaming yellow. The six creatures danced about in French deviltry until six men joined them with a sympathetic skip of agile friskiness. They were not half as animated as the [vocal] sextet men—in fact they were waiters, in unpicturesque little black coats and white aprons; but we liked them much better. They were as animated as jumping jacks, and the fact that each carried a little table did not interfere a little bit with their agility. When the men finally put the tables on the ground, the girls took their feet up. They rested their legs on the table, and when the waiters went away from them they touched the bells gracefully with their toes to call them back. After that they danced some more, and kicked the bells again, and kept the whole thing up everlastingly, not because their gayety was insatiable, but because the audience wouldn't let them go. They lost hats and underskirts and still the spectators yelled for more. The success of *The Silver Slipper* was made in that dance.

The critic of the *Sun* noted that "it took a month for the sextet in *Florodora* to become the talk of the town; the day after the production of *The Silver Slipper* everybody was chattering about the champagne dance."

Even so, further changes were deemed necessary. During November the Venus scene, which had been the play's second scene, was moved to become the prologue, and a further new song, "The Love Star," by the show's musical director, was added for Mackenzie Gordon as Donald Gregor. Other changes to the musical content followed as *The Silver Slipper* ultimately managed a very creditable five-month run before going on the road to further acclaim.

Chapter 11

The School Girl

With *The Silver Slipper* running smoothly in America, Leslie Stuart could enjoy the next significant step in the spread of his music, when *Florodora* received a French production at the Théâtre des Bouffes-Parisiens, Paris, on January 27, 1903. Jacques Offenbach's old theater was in dire financial straits at the time, and it was a somewhat desperate measure for its managers to look to a British work. The production starred Paulette Darty as Dolores, Albert Piccaluga as Abercoed, Simon-Max as Plum-Quick (= Tweedlepunch), and Gabrièle Dziri as Lady Holyrood. Sydney Ellison went over to direct and to teach a song-and-dance musical comedy style that was unfamiliar to the French.

Paris scarcely knew what to make of it. The impression of ceaseless dance numbers flouted all French conventions of soundly constructed libretti and integrated scores. In *Le Petit Journal*, Léon Kerst declared that he would have "to begin his theatrical education all over again to comprehend the idiotic gestures of such vertiginous puppets, who talk when they ought to be silent, sing when they ought to talk, and dance in the right or wrong place—always, always, always the perpetual jig before and after each couplet, replacing wit which is kept purposely absent."

On the other hand, Félix Duquesnel in *Le Gaulois* declared that the piece "is not wearisome, because it is different—something to which we are quite unaccustomed—and ... at length one is taken with the St Vitus's dance and music, carried away by an irresistible whirl." *Le Petit Parisien* considered Leslie Stuart's music "delicious." Edmond Stoullig summed up the general reaction when he wrote in his *Annales du Théâtre et de la Musique* that "the strangeness and the madness win you over, in spite of oneself." To French taste or not, the six-week run put money in the theater's coffers and prepared the ground for the Théâtre du Moulin-Rouge to look across the Atlantic and create its hugely successful staging of *The Belle of New York*.

During the run of *Florodora* at the Bouffes-Parisiens, Stuart had the proud honor to take the baton himself in the theater where, forty years earlier, Offenbach had presided.[62] It was probably also on that trip that he went to Monte Carlo and experienced an event that had a strong impact on him. Every day, a little Italian boy came and sang in the gardens of his hotel there, playing a mandolin and collecting money in a battered hat. An old man was always hovering near him, and one day Leslie Stuart began talking to him. The old man confided that the little boy was really a girl. The situation had in it shades of Wrenne in *The Silver Slipper*, and in due course it was to provide the basis of his musical play *Nina*.

For the present, Stuart was at work on the collaboration with British-born, American-based Paul Potter for which he had contracted during his New York stay in the autumn of 1901. With Tom B. Davis looking elsewhere for a show for the Lyric Theatre after *The Silver Slipper*, Stuart's return to the West End with *The School Girl* would be a joint production of London's leading exponent of musical comedy, George Edwardes, and American producer Charles Frohman. The latter was increasing his operations in the West End, with a view to obtaining works for New York. Production on both sides of the Atlantic was thus planned for *The School Girl* right from the start.

The book's authorship was shared between Potter and Henry Hamilton. Neither was associated primarily with the musical theater, though several songs with lyrics by Hamilton had found their way into George Edwardes's productions. Potter's stage adaptation of *Trilby* had fuelled the Trilby craze on both sides of the Atlantic in 1895, and he had also written half a dozen farce comedies and extravaganzas. The lyricist chosen for *The School Girl* was Charles H. Taylor, yet another who had proved his abilities in Manchester's Prince's Theatre pantomimes, and who had also received considerable praise for some contributions to *The Silver Slipper*.

The combined resources of Edwardes and Frohman brought together a cast that was far stronger than for *The Silver Slipper*. In the leading role was Edna May, a native of Syracuse, New York, who had made her name on both sides of the Atlantic—but more especially in Britain—as *The Belle of New York*. Her sister Jane had been one of London's original *Florodora* sextet. Supporting Edna May was soubrette Marie Studholme, a picture postcard beauty with more than ten years in leading roles in musical shows in London and the provinces. The leading man was Reginald Somerville, who was not only an actor but also a composer who in 1909 would provide the score for a comic opera, *The Mountaineers*. However, the main strength of the male side of the cast lay in the comedy roles. G. P. Huntley had recently achieved stardom in Paul Rubens's *Three Little Maids*; George Graves had graduated through Robert Courtneidge's Manchester pantomime school; and James Blakeley also had served time in pantomime as well as seaside pierrot shows.

Making a cameo appearance was Violet Cameron. She was a niece of burlesque performer Lydia Thompson and during the 1880s had starred in British productions of many native and French comic operas before retiring. As with Florence St. John, Stuart had worshipped her from the audience in his youth. Now he got George Edwardes to introduce her to him and persuaded her to sing a solo he had written specially for her. Her solo spot was timed for 8:10 P.M., after which she could go straight home and be in bed by 9:00![62]

Produced by George Edwardes and Charles Frohman at the Prince of Wales Theatre, London, 9 May 1903

THE SCHOOL GIRL

A Musical Play.

Book by Henry Hamilton and Paul Potter.

Lyrics by Chas. H. Taylor. Music by Leslie Stuart.

Lillian Leigh	Miss Edna May.
Mother Superior	Miss Violet Cameron.

Marianne (a French Bonne)			Miss Marianne Caldwell.
Norma Rochester			Miss Norma Whalley.
Mamie Reckfeller			Miss Billie Burke.
Yolande	(American Girls)		Miss Pauline Chase.
Violette			Miss Maude Percival.
Mimi			Miss Ethel Negretti.
Fifine			Miss Mamie Stuart.
Saaefrada (a Model)			Miss Clarita Vidal.
Kate Medhurst			Miss Mildred Baker.
Jessie Campbell			Miss Mary Fraser.
Evelyn Somers	(School Girls)		Miss Evelyn Bond.
Mabel Kingston			Miss Alice Coleman.
Miss Yost (the Typewriter)			Miss Lulu Valli.
Mrs. Marchmont			Miss Barbara Huntley.
Cicely Marchmont (her Daughter)			Miss Marie Studholme.
Sir Ormesby St. Leger			Mr. G. P. Huntley.
General Marchmont			Mr. George Graves.
Peter Overend (of the Open Stock Exchange)			Mr. J. A. Warden.
Corner (his Clerk)			Mr. Gilbert Porteous.
Jacques de Crevert (Clerk)			Mr. Frank Walsh.
Tubby Bedford			Mr. James Blakeley.
George Sylvester			Mr. Charles Hampden.
Adolphe Delapois	(Artists)		Mr. Murri Moncrieff.
Jack Merrion			Mr. Talleur Andrews.
Edgar Verney			Mr. Reginald Somerville.

Mesdames C. Marsden, Ada Webster, M. Graham, Hilda Scott, Ida Worseley, A. Dawson, M. Harvey, Stella de Marney, &c., &c.

Messrs. Edgar Wolseley, F. Hatton, G. Gotto, E. Williams, Bourne, H. Borrett, H. Goodwin, F. Garton, &c. &c.

Act I., Scene I.—The Convent Lawn Scene II.—The Open Stock Exchange

Act II.—Edgar Verney's Studio

Musical Director: Leslie Stuart.

Dances arranged by Willie Warde.

Scenery by Hawes Craven (Act I) and Joseph Harker (Act II).

The plot of *The School Girl* was slight and improbable even by the standards of the day, with act 2 substantially a sequence of novelty numbers dependent on visual appeal. Act 1, scene 1 is set on the lawn of a French convent school. Cicely Marchmont, a senior pupil, is shortly to leave, because her parents have arranged for her to marry middle-aged man-about-town Sir Ormesby St. Leger, whom she has scarcely met. Her friend Lillian Leigh discovers that Cicely is really in love with Edgar Verney, a young painter. Their discussion is interrupted by the arrival of the grave and saintly Mother Superior; but, when news arrives that Cicely must prepare for an early departure, Lillian suddenly decides to go to Paris in search of Edgar.

Act 1, scene 2, transports us to the bustling Open Stock Exchange in Paris, run by the unsavory Peter Overend. Also present are two of his clients, Sir Ormesby ("Nunky") St. Leger and genial but gullible "Tubby" Bedford, whose prime interest seems to be to buy chocolates, jewels, and lunches for some American young ladies who are in attendance on them. Another arrival is Edgar Verney, who is finding difficulty obtaining payment for a picture he has painted for Overend.

Arriving in search of him, Lillian is mistaken for an eagerly awaited new typist. Being given confidential letters to type, she becomes party to the worthlessness of the "Jumping Jack" shares that Overend is planting on his clients, among whom are not only "Nunky" and "Tubby" but her own father and Cicely's. She discloses the scam and persuades them to sell rather than buy, thereby ruining Overend. Having also discovered that "Nunky" is somewhat ambivalent about marrying Cicely, she makes her escape before the arrival of the real typist.

Act 2 unfolds in Edgar Verney's studio, where students in workaday garb are at their easels, painting from models. However, the studio very soon undergoes a remarkable transformation to house a fancy dress ball, with the dingy walls gorgeously tapestried, chandeliers suspended, and a throne raised for the queen of the ball. Among the costumed guests is the group of American girls, with a young lady called Mamie Reckfeller at their head. Lillian is also there, intent on sorting matters out for Cicely and Verney. Cicely's mother and father arrive, the latter in the costume of a doge. When Lillian finds him in the embrace of a shapely female model, she turns the situation to good use in gaining consent for Cicely's marriage to Edgar. Cicely and Lillian only too readily coax "Nunky" into dropping his own plan to marry Cicely.

The press was quick to point out the story's limitations, the *Playgoer* stating that "no doubt the authors ... had excellent reasons for putting the whole of their plot into the first act." The *Times* commented particularly on the improbabilities of a convent school girl "giving tips on the 'Open Stock Exchange' which the most experienced financiers of Paris act on instantly." The *Times* reviewer advised seeing the show on a full stomach, writing, "You must have dined well, and rather fully than sparsely; if the advice may be hazarded, just one more glass than usual would be valuable, because it is quite necessary that you reach the theatre in that comfortable state (with just a touch of rosiness in it) to which everything appears probable and nearly everything appears pleasant.

Reviewers singled out Marie Studholme as particularly bewitching in her song "The Honeymoon Girl," and felt that too little was seen of her. Edna May was praised for her "delightful simplicity and fascinating grace," her catchy "Call Round Again" sung at the Paris Stock Exchange, and her song about "Clytie" in the ball scene. Violet Cameron was welcomed back and lauded for her ease and repose in "When I Was a Girl Like You," a "pensive ballad [delivered] in a manner which makes the pathos doubly delicate and affecting."

Of the three comedians, James Blakeley had the best songs, in "Looking for a Needle in a Haystack" and "One Girl Too Many," though G. P. Huntley provided sufficient "business" to make a hit with "Belinda on the Line." Indeed, the *Times* felt his comedy the major attraction: "Were it right to talk of the acting in such productions as this, we should be tempted to say that Mr Huntley was first and the rest were nowhere."

The *Times* correspondent also made particular reference to the act 2 ballroom sequence. He noted in the handsome chorus "a not very tall lady with clematis in her hair—whose performance in the second act is really worth studying as an example of the *afflatus*, the frenzy of dancing, not very often seen in England." This was Billie Burke, later Mrs. Florenz Ziegfeld and a star of stage and film, here making her musical comedy debut. "A huge success was gained by Miss Billie Burke and a party of American ladies, for their 'Cake Walk' was taken up by the gallery, who whistled the tune at once and insisted upon one of the few encores granted," reported the *Graphic*.

Billie Burke had what was to prove the undisputed hit song of the show in a coon song entitled "My Little Canoe." "[It] has a swing and go that won insistent encores and set the gallery whistling the refrain," reported the *Stage*. Leslie Stuart told later how, seeking someone with the necessary charm for the number, he consulted his brother Lester

Andrew Lamb
150

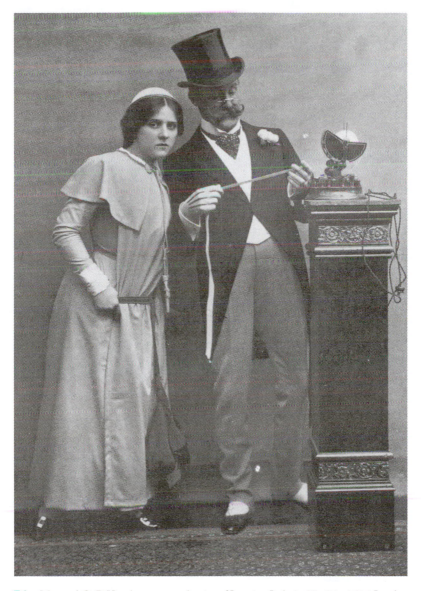

Edna May and G. P. Huntley measure the rise of Jumping Jacks in *The School Girl*, London
(author's collection)

Barrett, who recommended that he see Billie Burke performing in variety at the London Pavilion. He recalled, "She was on about 7-30 and received but meagre applause, such as the first turns in variety theatres generally get. I went to her dressing-room immediately afterwards, and she tells the story herself that the prospect of having a special number in

Billie Burke, James Blakeley, and Maude Percival in *The School Girl*, London
(author's collection)

a West End production took her breath away. She came to my house next day. I coached her in the song, introduced her to Edwardes, and advocated her very strongly, but I impressed on her the necessity of keeping secret the song I had allotted to her."[62]

Billie Burke recalled that it was her mother who snapped up Stuart's offer, even though the salary was only £3 per week compared with the £10 she was receiving at the London Pavilion. She added, "I did not know at the beginning why there was a mystery about my little song in this production. Show-wise Frohman and Edwardes knew, of course, that the "Canoe Song" was unusual; the game was not to let either Miss May or Miss Studholme know that the best song in the show had been given to an unknown girl. I was not allowed to sing it until the dress rehearsal. . . . Both threatened to resign immediately, sulking in their dressing rooms like offended queens. . . . Still, Edwardes and Stuart won out and the show opened the next night."[11]

In *The School Girl*, Stuart took the trouble not to imitate his previous stage scores so closely, and the word "sextet" is scarcely to be found in the press reviews. Yet his musical characteristics are still readily apparent. Two successive comedy numbers in act 1—Sir Ormesby's "Belinda on the Line" and Tubby's "Looking for a Needle in a Haystack"—have his trademark dotted rhythms, even though the latter is described as based on an old Norwegian air. "Clytie," in act 2, sounds at one point as though it is about to burst into "Little Dolly Daydream." The standout number is very obviously "My Little Canoe," whose chorus is a cakewalk pure and simple—and a thoroughly exhilarating one. There is also another cakewalk to conclude the ballroom dance sequence that also features a polonaise and a waltz in which it is easy to believe the composer was recalling his youthful Chopin performances. At the start of act 2, Stuart supplied a typically elegant orchestral introduction and uplifting chorus.

Opening night reviewers mentioned Verney's ballad, sung by Reginald Somerville, "acting the part with grace and ease." The earliest printed score in the British Library shows this as "From Skies to Earth Again," published originally in 1898. Soon Somerville was succeeded by J. Edgar Fraser, and the ballad was replaced by a revised version of "An English Girl," which had served previously in *The Ballet Girl*. For Verney's duet with Lillian in act 2, Stuart also reused the refrain of "Just the Tale by Night and Day" from five years earlier. There may even have been a further reworking in Lillian's "Call Round Again," as Phil Herman quotes a song of that title as among Stuart's earliest compositions. When W. Talleur Andrews later combined his minor role of artist Jack Merrion with the leading role of Verney, he introduced a new number, "Oh, Woman! In Days of Romance." Stuart also composed a new trio for act 2.

This was Leslie Stuart's first full score for George Edwardes, and the two reportedly got on well together. Edwardes valued Stuart's musical advice, and the two would also play cards well into the night. Their wives socialized together, too.[10] For all their familiarity, however, Edwardes subjected Stuart to his renowned habit of calling people by the wrong name. "Many times he has greeted me with "Hello, Sidney," as though confusing me with Sidney Jones, the composer of 'The Geisha,'" recalled Stuart. "Jones was always 'Leslie' to Edwardes."[62]

In June 1903, Stuart was with Edwardes when the latter had a visit from New York's English-born critic Alan Dale, who had been so critical of Mai de Villiers in *The Silver Slipper*. Dale was ostensibly interviewing Edwardes for the *New York American*, but Dale had fun with the way that Stuart seemed to agree with everything that Edwardes said. Stuart did break in momentarily to express diplomatic admiration for the American press, commenting that it was far easier to meet them and form a bond of sympathy than was the case in London. As Dale was leaving, Edwardes asked Stuart to sing the "Canoe Song" from *The School Girl*, which he dutifully did, with Edwardes and Dale joining in the chorus.[64]

Dale's article made reference to the difficulty Edna May had learning her parts. However, her virginal charm was lost on neither her fellow members of the cast nor the men in the audience. Billie Burke recollected how, in the show's early days, the Maharajah of Cooch Behar came "nightly through the fog in an elegant electric brougham, with a cluster of jewels on his great white turban and his hands full of gems as he paid court to Edna May."[11] Later, when G. P. Huntley had given way first to George Grossmith Jr. and then Arthur Roberts, the latter recalled that the pianist Mark Hambourg was one of Edna May's most devoted admirers. "But she remained unspoilt by all this private and public adulation," recalled Roberts. "Night after night wonderful bouquets would be sent to various hospitals and two or three times every week Edna would plead a sudden headache to escape an all-night party or dance."[50]

Roberts also highlighted what he perceived as May's lack of a sense of humor, an attribute on which Billie Burke and a colleague sought to capitalize: "We used to take orange peels, slice them into crescents to represent teeth, and when our chance came, turn our backs to the audience, stick them in our mouths and grin foolishly at Edna May while she sang her song."[11]

Roberts claimed he had been playing his role for a month or so when, hurrying into the theater for his entrance in the second scene, he was greeted by "a very stately and handsome lady." He eventually recognized her as Violet Cameron, with whom he had appeared on stage years before. She had to explain that she had been playing the Mother Superior in the show's opening since the start of the run without Roberts apparently ever troubling to find out that she was in the cast.

According to another of Roberts's recollections, when he entered the stage door of the Prince of Wales Theatre for the first time during the run of *The School Girl* he was solemnly handed a sealed letter containing a document. He elaborated, "This took the form of a burlesque will and started off in strict legal phraseology as the last Will and Testament of George Grossmith, Junior, as Ormesby St. Leger. In this he said: 'I hereby will and bequeath to Arthur Roberts an uncomfortable dressing-room, some dirty grease-paints and a part out of which I could never make anything.' He also left me his deepest sympathy."[50]

Roberts clearly regarded the bequest as license to do what he wished with the part. His changes included introducing a whole burlesque section on David Belasco and John Luther Long's play *The Darling of the Gods*, enabling him to cavort around in Japanese costume in the ball scene. "Quite whether these 'improvements' were responsible for the show's survival or hastened its end is open to doubt," theater historian Kurt Gänzl has observed.[27]

For much of Roberts's time in the cast, Leslie Stuart himself was conducting. The two had known each other since early 1879, when Roberts was making his first appearance at the Theatre Royal, Manchester, in a piece called *The Yellow Dwarf*. Having a fortnight without engagements at the end of that run, Roberts and other members of the cast arranged a series of concerts at the Free Trade Hall, Manchester, and in various halls around Manchester. Leslie Stuart—still T. A. Barrett at the time—had been the accompanist. The Free Trade Hall appearance drew a packed house; but Roberts's fame had not permeated to remoter districts. In Radcliffe, some seven miles from Manchester, there was an audience of twenty who received the first half of the show in silence, became aggressive during the second, and ended up demanding their money back. Despite police being called, the performers' horse bus was stoned before they finally made their getaway. Ever after, whenever Roberts and Stuart met, the former put on a Lancashire accent to open the conversation with, "Does tha know a place called Radcliffe?"[62]

George Grossmith and Arthur Roberts were both in generous agreement over the significance of George Graves in making *The School Girl* such a success. Grossmith doubted if he was ever much funnier, while Roberts declared that Graves made the character a priceless comic cameo, playing the small part of the irascible, liverish, and gouty old colonel to perfection. Graves in turn paid tribute to Roberts's friendliness and readiness to help him along, but was rather less impressed with what Roberts did to the show. He considered that "the whole show was pulled about and a good deal of what had proved excellent material went by the board."[31]

Graves, too, had known Leslie Stuart in Manchester, even before George Edwardes saw him appearing in pantomime there:

> When I was appearing in my first Manchester pantomime, a musician then known by his family name of Tom Barrett was conducting a series of concerts. . . . One night some years after, when I was playing in another show, his brother, Lester Barrett, came round to see me, bringing with him a quiet, kindly man whose name I missed in the rather informal introduction. The newcomer chatted with me and reminded me of my performance of some years before, which he said made him prophesy a conspicuous stage career for me. He congratulated me with a simple sincerity that encouraged me much more than the fulsome flattery which is so often the portion of the young pro. . . . What was my surprise and delight to learn that my well-wisher was Leslie Stuart, formerly known as Tom Barrett. . . . Stuart was then at the height of his fame, but his unobtrusiveness and self-effacement made an impression on my youthful mind and taught me a lesson in the gentleness of true genius which I hope I have never forgotten.[31]

The School Girl was something of an in-between score, a transition from *Florodora* and the imitative *The Silver Slipper* toward something more consistently different. When the London production ended on April 4, 1904, it completed a highly successful run of 333 performances. It left behind no original cast recordings, though the faithful Louis Bradfield recorded various numbers in June and July 1903. These comprised Lillian's "Clytie," Tubby's "One Girl too Many" and "Looking for a Needle in a Haystack" (the former recording rejected), and Mamie's "My Little Canoe." In addition, R. Lloyd Morgan recorded Sir Ormesby's "Belinda on the Line."[53]

Although designed with American production very much in mind, the latter did not follow until some months after the London closure. It opened at Boston's Colonial Theatre in August 1904, prior to a run at Daly's Theatre, New York. The delay was evidently to allow the producers to bring over to New York as many of the London cast as possible. Besides Edna May, Mildred Baker came over in the role of the Mother Superior she had understudied in London. Edna May's sister Jane retained the minor role of Norma Rochester that she had taken over in

London, as did W. Talleur Andrews the major role of Edgar. Of the comedians, James Blakeley repeated his performance as Tubby, and George Grossmith Jr. that of Sir Ormesby St Leger. The major replacements were for Cicely Marchmont, played now by Constance Hyem, and General Marchmont, played by Fred Wright Jr., a member of a celebrated British theatrical family who also later took over as Sir Ormesby.

Produced by Charles Frohman at Daly's Theatre, New York,
1 September 1904.

THE SCHOOL GIRL

A Musical Play in 2 Acts, 3 Scenes.

Book by Paul M. Potter and Henry Hamilton.

Lyrics by Chas. H. Taylor. Music by Leslie Stuart.

Lillian Leigh			Edna May.
Mother Superior			Mildred Baker.
Marianne, a French Bonne			Clara Braithwaite.
Mamie Reckfeller			Lulu Valli.
Norma Rochester			Jane May.
Yolande		American Girls	Vivian Vowles.
Violette			Ivy Louise.
Mimi			Dorothy Dunbar.
Louise			Barbara Dunbar.
Margot			Madge Greet.
Saaefrada, a Model			Lakme Darcier.
Miss Yost, the typist			Virginia Staunton.
Mrs. Marchmont			Mrs. Watt Tanner.
Cicely Marchmont, her daughter			Constance Hyem.
Kate Medhurst			Jeannette Patterson.
Mabel			Joyce Thorn.
Jesse Campbell			Queena Sanford.
Evelyn Somers			Ethel Kelly.
Waitress			Adele Carson.
Edgar Verney, an artist			W. Talleur Andrews.
Gen. Marchmont			Fred Wright, Jr.
Tubby Bedford			James Blakeley.

Peter Overend, of the Stock Exchange				Robert Minster.
Corner, his clerk				W. R. Shirley.
George Sylvester	|	Artists	|	Harry Hudson.
Adolphe Delapois	|		|	Murri Moncrieff.
Sir Ormesby St. Leger				George Grossmith, Jr.

Act I., Scene I.—The Convent Lawn   Scene II.—The Open Stock Exchange.

Act II.—Edgar Verney's Studio.

Directed by J. A. E. Malone.

Musical Director: William T. Francis.

For all the continuity between London and New York in the cast, there was rather less of it in the score. Billie Burke wanted to go with the show to New York and sing "My Little Canoe," but dropped out on learning that Charles Frohman and Edna May had already agreed that the latter would perform it. It again proved the big hit in New York, alongside various interpolated numbers. Besides several by Paul Rubens, George Grossmith had John W. Bratton's "My Cosey Corner Girl," and later substitutions included Albert von Tilzer's "Lonesome" for Edna May, and "Sweet Sana-oo," composed for W. Talleur Andrews by musical director W. T. Francis.

The *New York Times* wrote about the show, "The secret of the charm of these English importations . . . is first refinement and then modulation. The scenes are in a simple way, richly beautiful, the costumes modish and well worn, the dances lightly graceful and seemly. The wit and horseplay are never cheap, and are always such as one can give way to without parting with the finer and dearer risibilities."

The reviewer added that "the music of Mr Leslie Stuart (eked out by Mr Paul Rubens) is a little more scintillant [*sic*] [than the book]; but the main responsibility for the evening's enjoyment rests with the actors." Of these, the male comedians seemed to get his vote. Of Edna May, whose mother, father, and little sister were in the audience, he felt that "it can hardly be said that she took the house by storm, and [she] will probably always enjoy her most genuine successes in London."

After 54 performances, the show transferred on October 24, 1904, to the Herald Square Theatre, running for a further 66 performances to December 24, an impressive enough total of 120 performances prior to the inevitable tour.

Chapter 12

Fruits of Success

While *The School Girl* was running successfully in London, *Florodora* followed its Paris production with a German version at the Stadttheater, Leipzig, on November 21, 1903. The review in the *Illustrirte Zeitung* suggested that the audience was pleased, even if the critics were somewhat sniffy:

> The new English dance-operetta *Florodora* by Leslie Stuart (text by Owen Hall, German by J. Burg and C. Wenck) achieved strong outward success at the Old Theater in Leipzig. Most suitable for variety stages, the piece is on the whole reminiscent of the style and manner of the Sidney Jones operetta *The Geisha*, and contains many tiresome comic exaggerations and repetitions but not much humor and wit. The music is distinguished particularly by rhythmic liveliness, is pleasing and appealing, but without originality; the many imitations of *The Mikado*, *The Geisha* and Viennese operettas are striking. Some smart solos, duets, trios and choral pieces aroused lively approval and had in part to be repeated. From the glorious success of the staging

and acting, the most careful preparation of the operetta could be recognised. The splendid outfits and the dances succeeded extremely well.

That same month saw the third and fourth anniversaries, respectively, of *Florodora*'s New York and London productions. In America, being a *Florodora* girl had such distinction that those who achieved it held a reunion to mark the occasion. It was organized by Daisy Greene, one of the genuine original New York sextetters, who was also in *The Silver Slipper* and was to reappear in later Stuart shows. In November 1903 she was in Washington in the out-of-town tryout of *Winsome Winnie*, whose original score by Londoner Edward Jakobowski was progressively replaced on the road by numbers by Gustave Kerker. It was to Washington that she invited all Florodora girls:

> Three Years Ago This Coming Sunday
> Almost to a day
> "Florodora"
> Was Produced at the New York Casino
> And 10,000 Pretty Maidens
> Were Made Famous
> As Members of the Original Sextette.
>
> Washington, D. C. Also Won Fame as
> The Town the Pretty Maidens Come From.
>
> At the Hotel Raleigh, Washington, a
> Graduate From the Ranks
> Bids You to a Reunion.
>
> To be followed by a box party at the
> Performance of "Winsome Winnie" Monday evening.
>
> Bring your "Florodora" wink, nod and smile.
> Daisy Greene.
> R. S. V. P.   Four o'clock.
> In Hotel Stafford, Baltimore

The continuing thirst for *Florodora* in America was such that John C. Fisher and Thomas Ryley brought it back to the Broadway Theatre, New York, in March 1905 for a month, with Cyril Scott repeating the role of Donegal. In 1907 it was produced in Italian in Milan. *The Silver Slipper*, too, continued to thrive. Following its German production in 1902, it was produced in Hungarian at the Népszínház (National Theatre) in Budapest on January 8, 1904, with popular Hungarian musical star Klára Küry in the lead. In America it continued to tour with immense success. On March 12, 1904, for example, the *New York Dramatic Mirror* printed a rave review from Denver, describing the show as a "glittering, vivifying, scintillating success." The report commented of the Champagne Dance that "never was its equal seen in Denver," and the costumes (most particularly Stella's pink hat) were enthusiastically hailed. In April 1907 John C. Fisher's company played both *Florodora* and *The Silver Slipper* in Mexico City, along with Victor Herbert's *The Wizard of the Nile* and *The Idol's Eye*.

Success brought Leslie Stuart all the trappings of fame. There were bazaars to open, such as the Florodora Bazaar at the Drill Hall in Sunderland in aid of St. Benet's Church, Monkwearmouth, in November 1903. Stuart traveled there with his daughter May, now almost seventeen, and in his opening speech he recalled assisting in the management of many similar events.[64] Most particularly, *Florodora* brought in a ready stream of income, which alas went out as quickly as it came in. "Father never let his money hang idle in his hands," his daughter May recalled. "He would arrive back from a jaunt in the West End, with a taxi full of expensive pictures, bought by the dozen. He lavished jewellery on Mother—and as much on me as Mother would allow." For the younger children there were less exotic extravagances. "Whenever we made an excursion into Town we would raid the toyshops, ride on the buses, and finally burst into Gatti's restaurant, consume these enormous ices, and tell the waiter to put them on father's account. Poor father, he never kept accounts—he wasn't the saving type."[66]

It had always been thus. May recalled her father being really cross only once during her childhood, when "[s]omebody gave us a money box—a black Sambo money box. One put a penny in his hand, pulled a lever at the back, and he swallowed it. Father found it on the nursery mantelpiece. He raised the roof. 'Money,' he said, 'was meant to be spent. . . .' He took poor old Sambo out and smashed it."[65] Nor did his extravagance stop at the family. Ada Reeve recalled that she once stayed with the family for a week and "had a lovely time, though it was a little strenuous having to drink champagne at breakfast."[49]

The most detailed account of life in the Stuart household comes from Hilda Brighten, née Cohen. Her father Edgar Cohen worked to promote various leading London stores and also introduced motorized taxicabs to London. At the Cohen home in Hall Road in St. John's Wood there was much informal music making by visitors who included Enrico Caruso, John McCormack, and Leslie Stuart, "playing *Florodora*, or what he called 'trying it on the dog' with his half-composed latest composition."[10]

Leslie Stuart fondly remembered one evening spent at the Cohens' with the famous Italian singer. As he later recalled, "We met one night at dinner at the house of a mutual friend who resided in St. John's Wood. The occasion was a birthday party. In order to attend that friendly party, Caruso had declined an enormous sum offered to him to sing at the house of one of London's millionaire aristocrats. I had the unique experience of accompanying Caruso in the famous *Pagliacci* aria whilst the gramophone was also playing the rendering he had been paid a staggering fee to register. I therefore had the novel delight of playing as it were to two Carusos at the one time. The volume produced by Caruso in the flesh and the mechanical Caruso made the piano sound like ten cents in a Rockefeller safe. It was truly equal to a grand opera chorus of 100 voices."[62]

Hilda Brighten recalled equally lavish gatherings at the Stuart household:

> Their Sunday afternoons and evenings vied with ours in number. Wine flowed, supplies of food could not always bear the strain of extraneous guests. In the Priory Road dining-room more and more chairs would be wedged around the table. There would be a quick consultation just before the meal, Katherine Stuart indicating which dishes were unlikely to stay the course, and we arranged that signals would tell us when it was desirable that the youngsters of both families should practise denial.
>
> Food did not greatly matter; it was all such fun. Leslie sat at the head of the table, and was invariably unsympathetic to many of the guests. We were always an exception. So on either side of our host Mother and I were placed—to hold the peace. There was always good conversation and laughter. The Sunday backbone of the invited was invariably Evie Greene, Ruth Vincent, George Egerton and her husband, Goulding Bright, Guy d'Hardelot and Jimmy Waters, editor of the *Daily Mail*. . . . The Stuarts, husband and wife, had not infrequent heated altercations. When this happened Leslie would

turn to Mother and say, "Please forgive me, Ada, but I intend to be Leslie Stuart in my own house."[10]

A frequent Sunday visitor to the Stuart home was Israel Zangwill, the Jewish author who was an ardent supporter of the Zionist movement and who lived close by in West Hampstead.[62] Another welcome visitor was Edward Morton, columnist of the journal *The Referee* and book author of Sidney Jones's *San Toy*. While Morton passed hours in ardent conversation with Leslie Stuart at dinner, his son spent time with Stuart's son "Chap," who was of similar age. Morton's son, recalled Stuart's daughter May, was "a freckle-faced boy with an air of complete bewilderment—no doubt he was staggered by the strange collection of mad dogs, wild children and eccentric butlers at the Leslie Stuarts'."[66] She claimed that it was at these times that young J. B. Morton conceived the comic characters such as "Dr Strabismus (whom God preserve) of Utrecht," whom he later made hugely popular when writing as Beachcomber for the *Daily Express*.[66]

The dogs were part of wife Kitty's excesses. May told of what her father called "the Dynasty of Unspeakable Dogs," which had apparently begun with Gyp, a large collie whom Kitty insisted on taking on their honeymoon. When Gyp died his coat was made into a rug. Then came Tommy, a vicious Yorkshire terrier, followed in turn by a mongrel named Zaza. When a man arrived to see Leslie Stuart about income tax, he somehow managed to sell Kitty a Pomeranian called Peter. Kitty particularly loved Peter and had a large sable muff made with a pocket inside it for Peter, whom she even took to Covent Garden in it. Birds, cats, parrots, and rabbits were also welcome, along with two chameleons called Clarence and George. "All this," May added, "was on top of a household that included five young children, usually sliding down banisters or playing cowboys and Indians, plus three or four servants, a cook, and an eccentric butler named William, who never smiled."[66]

Of Stuart's lavish spending outside the home, John Abbott of Francis, Day and Hunter recalled that "no one whom he knew appealed to him in vain, and there was a standing order at the Savoy, that any friend could have a meal at his expense."[1] Stuart's youngest daughter Lola likewise recalled that he "spent the proceeds on five-star meals at the Savoy Hotel for out-of-work musicians."[17] Hilda Brighten, too, recalled his generosity: "Even in those days of extravagance his profligate spending of money was extraordinary. During rehearsals of his plays any

Leslie Stuart and his wife, Kitty (courtesy Ross and Barbara de Havilland)

or all of the cast lunched, dined and supped with him at the Savoy or Romanos. If Leslie was not present himself he told his guests to sign his name to their bills."[10]

Stuart's interest in horse racing was a particular extravagance. His daughter May recalled, "One day Mother and I were driving over Putney Common, and I pointed to the glittering white, flower-decked, expensive-looking houses. 'Who,' I asked, 'live in those houses that look like wedding cakes?' Mother replied: 'Bookmakers, darling. Your father built most of them.'" [66] Tennis, fly fishing, and shooting were other interests, as was cricket. W. Macqueen-Pope recorded that "out of his love for cricket he appointed himself the host of visiting teams and gave them a royal time."[38] There were Australian touring parties in England in 1902 and 1905.

Besides his London home, Stuart also rented a summer home, Sunningdale, complete with tennis court, backing on to the sea in West Worthing, on the Sussex coast. "Every week-end," recalled May, "we had large parties down there, with tennis and croquet, at both of which father excelled himself. And he took it all so seriously. On many a summer's evening games of croquet went on till midnight, and he used to stick candles on the hoops, so that he could make his shots in the darkness."[66]

There was also another house, called Priory Ford on the River Thames, near Cookham in Berkshire. May remembered it as "a lovely place on the river at Bourne End—tennis courts, boats on the river, strawberries and cream."[66] There, too, Leslie Stuart worked and entertained, with the Cohen family among the guests:

> It was always crammed with people. Leslie did much composing down at the river. One knew when the mood was upon him, for he would appear distrait and dressed in a very tight bandsman's braided jacket. It was a significant hint, and those of us who appreciated the fact kept well out of the way. There was, however, one insensitive young man who, ignoring the fact that his host was not only a great composer, but a fine pianist and organist, would come downstairs and both before and after breakfast play for hours, with painful reiteration, a horrid tune called "Poppies" [composed by Neil Moret, 1904].
>
> Leslie, distraught, would rush to the tennis-court for solace, seizing as he went a racquet. When he returned to the house some time later, the same dreary tune was still being strummed out with monotonous persistence.

The atmosphere once became so sulphurous that the young man was hastily hustled from the house on to the London-bound train.[10]

Eugene Stratton was also among the visitors to Bourne End, their artistic relationship producing a number that resulted from London acquiring its largest purpose-built theater. This was the London Coliseum, designed by the great theater architect Frank Matcham. The opening ceremony was fixed originally for December 19, 1904, but had to be postponed because of a London "pea-souper" fog. Eventually it took place with a star-studded program on Christmas Eve, December 24, 1904, Eugene Stratton singing not only the old favorite "The Lily of Laguna" but also another new Leslie Stuart creation, "My Little Black Pearl."

Meanwhile, for all his affluence, the loss to Leslie Stuart through pirated editions of his work remained an irritant. There had been widespread agreement that the music publishers should shoulder some of the blame for the unsatisfactory situation since they refused to reduce prices to meet the public demand for cheap editions. Finally, in September 1903, Francis, Day and Hunter announced their decision to introduce a Sixpenny Edition. The *Musical Opinion and Music Trade Review* commented that the new departure was practically a result of the pirates and "an enormous new market for cheap music created by the rapid multiplication of pianos in working class homes." Again "The Soldiers of the Queen" was used by way of example, the pirates having reportedly sold a million copies in a few months while its rightful owner and publisher, in the same period, sold an additional 100,000. Stuart was quoted as seeing sixpenny editions "as an admission of the claims made by the defenders of the pirates that publishers have been robbing the public."[14]

As the issue rumbled on, publishers used various ruses to implement the existing legislation. The biggest ever haul of pirated editions occurred on Christmas Eve 1903, an event dramatized in the 1945 Gainsborough Pictures film *I'll Be Your Sweetheart*, starring Margaret Lockwood. Frustratingly, new bills introduced into Parliament in 1903 and 1904 were talked out by calico-millionaire member of Parliament James Caldwell, and in the latter year the Home Secretary appointed a departmental committee to enquire further into the matter. There emerged a strong majority report to the effect that fresh powers were necessary; but Caldwell submitted a minority report maintaining that copyright in music was artificial ownership brought about by legislation, not natural justice.[14]

Caldwell thereby raised the wrath of publisher William Boosey of

Chappell and Company. Boosey not only set out a detailed exposé of the glaring errors in Caldwell's report but addressed a "Great Protest Meeting" at Queen's Hall on 4 July 1904 organized by a newly formed Musical Defence League of publishers and composers. The league's acting committee included such composers as Hubert Parry, Alexander Mackenzie, Charles Stanford, André Messager, Paolo Tosti, Edward Elgar, Frederic Cowen, Hamish MacCunn, Stephen Adams, Ivan Caryll, Edward German, Lionel Monckton, Paul Rubens, Sidney Jones, and Leslie Stuart. At the protest meeting, William Boosey asked why Caldwell considered it wicked to make money by printing music on paper but not wicked to print patterns on calico. If Caldwell believed cheap music was a necessity for the poorer classes, should he not consider cheap, or even free, calico for them too? The league also organized a petition to Parliament, containing hundreds of signatures from not only composers and publishers, but also actresses, singers, playwrights, and authors.[7]

By 1905 the situation had deteriorated further. The issue was taken up with Gerald Balfour, president of the Board of Trade and brother of the Prime Minister, A. J. Balfour. Someone hit on the notion of issuing a pirated cheap edition of a treatise entitled *Economic Notes on Insular Free Trade* published by A. J. Balfour in 1903. When the original publisher sought help from the music publishers, the response was that, as they had not yet discovered a means of protecting their music, they could hardly suggest any means of protecting Balfour's publication.

By this time, however, a new approach had been suggested. Early in 1905 a lawyer introduced by composer Hermann Löhr suggested to William Boosey that proceedings might be taken under existing conspiracy law.[7] Selling pirated music alone and without outside help was a civil offence, but if it could be proved that two or more people had worked together they could be charged with conspiracy and, on conviction, be subject to imprisonment. After taking counsel's opinion, warrants were applied for at Bow Street for the arrest of James Frederick Willetts (the "King of the Pirates"), together with a printer, a wholesaler, and one or two hawkers. After a hearing lasting eight days, convictions were recorded in January 1906, and Willetts was sentenced to nine months' imprisonment.

This was at last a significant breakthrough, because the risk of imprisonment was not something that appealed to the pirates. However, it remained a cumbersome and expensive deterrent, and Leslie Stuart for one was unconvinced that the result was advantageous. "I am afraid," he noted, "that this case will not act as a deterrent against music pirates because they are all so familiar with every phase of the copyright law. It is my opinion that this conviction will only show them that they need only now avoid the charge of conspiracy to keep themselves within the pale of the law. . . . I fear that the result of the Old Bailey trial will damp the enthusiasm of our supporters in the House of Commons, as it may appear to them that we have now ample means of restitution."[24]

The death of composer George Le Brunn in December 1905 at the age of forty-two had served to strengthen Stuart's outrage. Le Brunn had composed many hugely popular music hall songs such as "Oh! Mr Porter," "The Dandy Coloured Coon," "If It Wasn't for the 'Ouses in Between," "It's a Great Big Shame," and "Everything in the Garden's Lovely." Now his wife and family were left penniless, and a benefit matinee was organized for the Oxford Music Hall on January 22. But the discovery that Le Brunn's income from Francis, Day and Hunter for the previous twelve months amounted to no more than one pound and seven pence—less than £50 even in year 2000 terms—added fuel to Stuart's fire.

With a general election imminent, he wrote a letter to the *Daily Mail* that the paper published on January 9, 1906. In it he expressed himself as appalled at the remuneration received by Le Brunn, and he laid the blame firmly at the door of Caldwell and his associates. His argument was illogical to the extent that the basic problem lay in an out-dated remuneration system based on printed music, but the letter demonstrated the strength of his feeling and produced some interesting information on his own remuneration from printed music:

> One pound and sevenpence has George Le Brunn left to his widow as the inheritance of his genius. Meanwhile the pirate-thief remains unchallenged and grows affluent.
>
> All this is due to the scandalous procedure of Mr Caldwell and his Radical followers who are at present seeking re-election in the Radical interest. I appeal to those—a hundred thousand at least— who are dependent and directly interested in the musical output of this country to record their parliamentary votes, uncompromisingly and uninfluenced by promises, against the party claiming as a member, prominent, powerful and trusted, the Radical champion and protector of this iniquitous trade.
>
> To emphasise my plea I also forward to you my own latest royalty statements covering the period, more remunerative than any other

part of the year, January 1 to June 30 (six months). In this you will perceive that "The Soldiers of the Queen" yields me the sum of 4s. 1d. [£0.20]; "Little Dolly Daydream," 16s. 11d. [£0.85]; "Lily of Laguna," £2 1s 3d. [£2.06]; "I May Be Crazy," £1 17s. [£1.85]; the entire proceeds of the music of "Florodora," £33; and "The School Girl," £14 2s. 3d. [£14.11]; my sum total received from all sources in Great Britain in six months amounting to £63 10s. 7d. [£63.53]. I have not yet received my return from July 1 to December 31, but I am prepared to dispose of my royalty claims on all my compositions for £50. I am willing to present this amount to anyone who can prove that my income from my compositions—all bearing royalty—have exceeded £5 a week for the past three years.

This is the wage Mr Caldwell insists shall be mine for my labour of many years. The consciences of those who have for so many years been purchasers of pirated music and who uphold the pirate trade as a boon may inspire some redress to the dead composer and his widow by assisting towards the success of a benefit matinée arranged for January 22 at the Oxford Music-Hall. Every member of renown in the variety and many of the theatrical world will appear—those not engaged in London will travel from various parts of the provinces to pay a tribute to the memory of the man who helped them to renown, and, further, to protest against the legalised plunder that has made the appeal necessary.

LESLIE STUART[60]

The fund for Le Brunn's widow was generously supported. Marie Lloyd led the way with a donation of £100 (over £4,000 in year 2000 terms), as well as acting as a program seller at the Oxford Music Hall matinee performance. As for Leslie Stuart's offer to dispose of his royalty claims on all his compositions for the period from July to December 1905 for £50 (just over £2,000 in today's money), it was reported that it had promptly been accepted by an enterprising speculator.

Composers continued to take the law into their own hands, and in June 1906 Walter Slaughter, musical director at the Coliseum and composer of the ballad "The Dear Homeland," was reported to have decided to seize music of his that was being hawked in the street. He duly captured two dozen copies in Upper Street, Islington. Herman Finck, musical director at the Palace Theatre, described how he, Leslie Stuart, and Slaughter had "several times enlisted the services of two 'chuckers-out' from the Empire and the Palace and of some fighting members of the National Sporting Club and of the Eccentric Club, and descended in a band upon the 'pirates.'"[26]

Happily the battle against printed music piracy in Britain was finally approaching some sort of resolution. Music publishers now had the crucial support of T. P. O'Connor, father of the House of Commons, founding editor of *M.A.P.*, and a champion of justice. In June 1906 he introduced his Musical Copyright Bill of three short clauses. Although it was only a private bill, he induced the Government to give it full support. It still required determined effort and some *legerdemain* to force it through, and it only passed its third reading on the very last night of the parliamentary session. A special sitting of the House of Lords was called to pass it without amendment, and the following morning it was on the table of the House of Commons to receive royal assent. On August 4, 1906, it became law. It was finally a criminal offense to produce, sell, or possess pirated copies or plates for making them, and the police were given rights of entry and search.[14]

Thus was the curtain effectively brought down on the matter. Sheet music piracy ceased to be a significant issue, though other manifestations of the problem reared their heads. In June 1908, for instance, a trader appeared at Bow Street Court charged with "offering for sale pirated copies of a musical work, namely, a perforated music-roll and a talking-machine disc, each being a reproduction of the pianoforte accompaniment of a song called 'The Bandolero.'" The head of steam that had been worked up finally led to the foundation of the Performing Right Society in Britain in 1914 and the American Society of Composers and Publishers (now better known as ASCAP) in America in 1916, and Leslie Stuart was an ardent supporter of both. He would never forget how, when his fame was at its height, the music pirates had skimmed off part of the benefits.

Chapter 13

The Belle of Mayfair

Music piracy was just one of the subjects that caused Leslie Stuart to take newspaper space to express his views. Another of his personal hobbyhorses that we have already encountered was the academic musician's hypocrisy regarding popularity in music. He returned to the subject in a letter to impresario Thomas W. Ryley that was published in a New York newspaper around 1906. He suggested that it was ten times more difficult to compose a haunting melody than a sonata and that there was more cant and hypocrisy in music than in religion.[64]

Another subject on which he held strong views was the practice whereby performers interpolated into musical plays extraneous songs that they thought would enhance their performance. He had established himself with interpolations into the musical comedies of others, and had then been subjected to it with *Florodora* and, to a lesser extent, *The Silver Slipper*. With *The School Girl*, he had managed to resist the fashion in Britain, even if not in America. He shared his antipathy with the likes of Victor Herbert and Sidney Jones, but he was more inclined to express it publicly, as in an interview published on May 15, 1906, in the *Daily Mail*.

One might imagine that his sentiments would not endear him to theater managers:

> In comic opera the song has to be deftly "worked up to"; in musical comedy, plunges are made into the numbers without remorse and without apology. That is the explanation of the inferiority of many musical comedies. How many managers have the smallest musical knowledge? A German improvisatore was engaging a company over here recently who could sit down and play anything Mr Lionel Monckton or I, or any other popular composer had ever published. How many of our managers could?
>
> Music is only one of the parts of a modern musical production. Managers often spend £10,000 staging a modern play, and naturally enough have their own way in the direction of it. The result is that the poor composer often finds his pet number cut out without the smallest pretext, and something totally alien to the whole spirit of the music interpolated.
>
> Oh for the good old days of Offenbach, Hervé, and the others. Our managers would be shot stone dead—assassinated at sight by those men were they to display their musical ignorance of their works or to place the caprice of artistes before the wish of the composer.[16]

For the time being, at least, Stuart was powerful enough to be able to ban interpolations in his London works. This was the case with his next musical comedy, which was composed for the management of Charles Frohman, in partnership with A. and S. Gatti, proprietors of London's Vaudeville Theatre. Production was delayed until Edna May was again available for the leading role. Since going back to New York in 1904 with *The School Girl*, she had been on tour in the United States. Because of the demand for her reappearance in London, Charles Frohman had then canceled projected Californian engagements. The British press noted that, had that tour gone ahead, she would have been in San Francisco around the time of the April 1906 earthquake.

The Belle of Mayfair was announced as a modern-dress version of *Romeo and Juliet*, with the heads of the rival houses of Montague and Capulet becoming the Earl of Mount Highgate and Sir John Chaldicott. Romeo and Juliet became the Honorable Raymond Finchley and Julia Chaldicott. Of the rest, Mercutio became Hugh Meredith, Paris became the Comte de Perrier, and Friar Laurence was transformed into Dr. Marmaduke Lawrence, Bishop of Brighton. However, little of William

Shakespeare's play remained beyond the basic concept of love between warring houses.

The opening night was fixed for Wednesday, April 11, 1906, and the telegrams of good wishes were dutifully pasted into Leslie Stuart's scrapbook along with the press cuttings. Charles Frohman sent the message, "All I ask is that they appreciate what you have done as I do. Charles Frohman." Another came from the Essex resort of Clacton-on-Sea from a young man of twenty-one who had recently become a familiar figure in London's theaterland, having come over from America under Frohman's auspices to gain experience of writing numbers for interpolation into American productions of European shows: "Sincere good wishes for big sure fire hit. Jerome D. Kern." Eugene Stratton belatedly sent a telegram from Birmingham: "Sorry did not know you produced last night. Pleased to see criticisms Mail and Telegraph. Best of good wishes, Gene." Telegrams came from farther afield, too. Ahead of the premiere, the impresario Adolf Philipp sent a message from Vienna wishing "Long Life and Success to the Belle," and he followed it from Budapest with a brief "Bravo. Wonderful notices."[64]

Produced by A. & S. Gatti and Charles Frohman at the Vaudeville Theatre, London, 11 April 1906

THE BELLE OF MAYFAIR

A Musical Comedy

Book by Basil Hood and Chas. H. E. Brookfield.

Music by Leslie Stuart.

The Earl of Mount Highgate		Mr. Sam Walsh.
Honourable Raymond Finchley (his Son)		Mr. Farren Soutar.
Sir John Chaldicott, Bart., M.P.		Mr. Arthur Williams.
Hugh Meredith		Mr. Courtice Pounds.
Comte de Perrier		Mr. Charles Angelo.
Doctor Marmaduke Lawrence (Bishop of Brighton)		Mr. Charles Troode.
Captain Theobald	| (Friends of Raymond) |	Mr. Mervyn Dene.
Charlie Goodyear	|	| Mr. Philip Desborough.
Bandmaster		Mr. T. A. Shale.
Simpson	| (Footmen to Sir John | Chaldicott)	Mr. W. Pringle.
Gregory	|	| Mr. Norman Ridley.
François		Mr. Murri Moncrieff.

Bramley (Footman to Lord Mount Highgate)		Mr. C. A. Cameron.
Bagstock (Gardener to Sir John Chaldicott)		Mr. John Blankley.
H.S.H. Princess Carl of Ehrenbreitstein		Miss Louie Pounds.
The Countess of Mount Highgate		Miss Irene Desmond.
Lady Chaldicott		Miss Maud Boyd.
Lady Rosaline Rockesly		Miss Ruby Ray.
Lady Violet Gussop		Miss Jane May.
The Duchess of Dunmow		Miss Camille Clifford.
Lady Jay		Miss Hilda Hammerton.
Lady Paquin		Miss Kitty Harold.
Lady Louise		Miss Dora Glennie.
Lady Lucille	(Débutantes)	Miss May Hobson.
Lady Peter Robinson		Miss Kitty Dale.
Lady Hayward		Miss Florence Randle.
Lady Swan		Miss Ivy Desmond.
Lady Edgar		Miss Helen Colville.
Pincott (Julia's Maid)		Miss Lillian Digges.
Sophie		Miss Stella de Marney.
Miss Corrie Fay		Miss Vivien Vowles.

AND

Julia Chaldicott	Miss Edna May.

Stall-holders.—Misses Margaret Long, Agnes Marchant, Gladys Anderson, Connie Ross, Lily Maynier, Munro Ross, Florence Manton, Ethel Leigh, Daisy De Levante, Alice M. Cox, Dora Denton, Winifred Godard, Vera Chrichton, Nessie Walker.

The Chippy Girls—Misses Dorothy Monkman, Marjorie Villis, Dorothy Brunt, Phyllis Monkman, Rose Gibbons, Winifred Hall.

Guests.—Messrs. Mendy Wigley, Cecil Tresilian, Michael Henry, J. Martin, Pearce Robinson, H. Wescombe-Penney, Blair Headsworth, E. Crampton Bryant.

ACT I.—Bazaar in a Private Park.

ACT II.—Drawing-room in Sir John Chaldicott's House.

Directed by Herbert Cottesmore. Musical Director: Edward Jones.

Dances arranged by Fred Farren.

The press had difficulty identifying any real plot, but the *Yorkshire Post* provided what looked like the beginnings of one:

Julia's father, Sir John Chaldicott, Bart., M.P., enjoys an income of £95,000 per annum, made through the manufacture of boot protectors; he is described as a "protectionist"—a "boot protectionist"—and consequently he can indulge his pretty daughter's slightest whim. There is one important thing lacking to the happiness of Julia—her father's consent to her marriage with the Hon. Raymond Finchley, the son of the impecunious Earl of Mount Highgate. Sir John . . . is obdurate in refusing his sanction to the union, and goes to the length of engaging her to the Comte de Perrier, a hard-up nobleman from the Continent, who consents to a nominal engagement for a monetary consideration and immediately begins to make extravagant love to Julia in the approved stage manner of foreign Counts.

Beyond that, the further plot summary in the *Daily Telegraph* should suffice. It reads, "At an aristocratic bazaar the young lovers exchange their vows, parental anger notwithstanding; and these vows are duly renewed in the principal saloon of Sir John Chaldicott's town mansion. There is an echo of the famous balcony scene, and a plan for elopement in young Raymond's motor-car, which is snorting outside the front door. For this extreme step, however, there is finally no need. Nor is it necessary for the lovers to throw themselves upon the amiable chaperonage of the kindly Bishop. In short, 'Papa' gives way, as 'Papa' generally does in musical comedy, and Romeo and Juliet will have an orthodox society wedding after all."

The *Daily Telegraph* added that Shakespeare's plot had been "twisted into a brilliant variety entertainment." The *Times* picked up the same cue and described the evening as if it were a series of variety turns, quoting the time of each, and, with tongue in cheek, concluding, "There is, perhaps, a little sameness about the programme as a whole. There are no equilibrists, no performing animals, no biograph. And we noticed rather too much similarity of subject in the songs. Nearly all of them concern love, marriage, girls or hearts. There was no sameness in the music. Though it was all the work of one composer, its variety had the effect of keeping the mind constantly alert to see whether he would in each coming number do his best or worst. His best is full of spirit and pleasant and original melody."

The *Daily Mail* did something similar to the *Times*, but kept one eye on the composer in the pit:

The scene of the first act is laid at "a bazaar in a private park." After the usual opening, enter Mr Arthur Williams (Sir John). He, with the help of others, contrives to explain the situation and to get a laugh or two at the same time. Song—Lord Highgate: "I am a military man." Very spirited, and the dance is encored. Mr Stuart, however, who is conducting, shakes his head. Enter Miss Camille Clifford in a terrific hat. A rocking-horse is put up to auction, and Miss Edna May (off) buys it for a fabulous sum. Enter Edna. Cheers as aforesaid. Song—Edna: "In Gay Mayfair." Encored. Mr Stuart consents. Enter Mr Farren Soutar, as Romeo—in a white hat with a pink ribbon. Song—Mr Soutar: "What makes a Woman?" The woman is dressed (more or less) on the stage, and that makes her. Mr Stuart shakes his head. Enter the Comte de Perrier—natural and sparkling. A "chorus," and Miss Louie Pounds arrives. She sings very daintily a dainty song: "Said I to Myself." Mr Stuart shakes his head.

Are we all here now? No. There is Mr Courtice Pounds to come. The audience receive him with a roar of delight, and encore his fine ballad, "What Will the World Say?" Mr Stuart consents. Mr Pounds parodies the "Queen Mab" speech with "Marriage is a Motor-Omnibus." A clever piece of writing, admirably delivered. The act closes with a jolly quartette, sung by Miss Pounds, Miss May, Mr Soutar and Mr Pounds, "Come to St George's." Mr Stuart consents. This will be on "all the organs."

The scene changes to the drawing-room in Sir John's house. Several energetic young people "decorate the room with roses." Mr W. Pringle (a clever young comedian) and Miss Lillian Digges dance nimbly. Mr Stuart shakes his head. Miss Camille Clifford, despite a 14in. waist, just manages to sing "I'm a Duchess." Display of dresses. Mr Pounds sings a delicious little number, "Hello! Come Along, Girls," and follows it with a wonderfully light dance. Mr Stuart consents.

Enter Miss May—straight from Court. A pretty quintette, "We've come from Court." Raymond, in beautiful boots, comes over the balcony. Miss May sings "Play the Game." Mr Stuart consents. Miss Pounds sings a plaintive little story-ballad, "And the Weeping Willow Wept." Mr Stuart consents. Follow another song from Miss May, "In Montezuma," and a quartette, "I know a girl." The lovers are made happy and the curtain falls.

The *Times* was not alone in praising the composer. Reviewers were at pains to note that, while Stuart's individuality remained, he was not simply repeating himself as he had in *The Silver Slipper* or, to a lesser extent, *The School Girl*. The *Daily News* commented that, for all the book's tameness, it had inspired the composer "to write some of the prettiest and freshest music which has been heard on the musical comedy stage since *Véronique* first visited us." It continued:

> I do not mean that Mr Stuart's score can be compared in exquisite grace and sparkle to M. Messager's, but one naturally thinks of the French operetta rather than of the hackneyed musical comedy of commerce. Mr Stuart has indeed written some numbers which are at once tuneful and ingenious in their device. He has learnt something from all kinds of compositions, but has well assimilated his knowledge. His treatment of the chorus is remarkable for having broken away from the conventional manner of musical comedy. This was especially noticeable in the "Debutante's Song," "Hail! Her Serenity," and the finale of the first act. Then his concerted music has a deftness which set one thinking of the glories of the Gilbert and Sullivan days. "Come to St George's," a quartet, with a quaint folk-song refrain, was quite one of the successes of the evening. . . .

The *Star* was another that considered the best number to be "Come to St. George's," but was probably alone in noting "its reminiscence of *Carmen*." Other papers to detail the musical merits included the *Sunday Times*, whose critic likewise cited Messager and noted that the score was distinctly above the norm for the musical theater of the day, writing, "Unlike many writers of musical comedy, Mr Leslie Stuart is a trained musician. He does not merely compose his songs on the piano and afterwards present them with an orchestration of tum tum, ta ta, or boom boom, but he has great technical skill, as is shown in the overture and most particularly in the finale of the first act, which in its way is equal to rank with that very fine piece of orchestration, the finale of the second act of Messager's *Véronique*. If the latter expresses the gaiety of the *ville lumière*, the former quite pictures in melody the whirl of Bohemian London."

Although Edna May's reappearance had drawn the crowds to *The Belle of Mayfair*, she did not earn the major acclaim. If anyone challenged Leslie Stuart as the star of the evening, that person was to be found elsewhere. Courtice Pounds, who had created the roles of Colonel Fairfax in Gilbert and Sullivan's *The Yeomen of the Guard* and Marco in *The Gondoliers*, was in *The Belle of Mayfair* the somewhat plump portrayer of

Hugh Meredith. His younger sister Louie Pounds played the minor role of Princess Carl of Ehrenbreitstein, and it was she who especially gained mention from reviewer upon reviewer. "Her song, 'The Weeping Willow,' is one you ought to learn before your milk-boy anticipates you," advised the *Glasgow Evening Citizen*. The extent and unexpectedness of her success can be gauged from events at the final curtain, as recorded by the *Sunday Times*:

> At the close of the performance the pit and gallery were enthusiastically eruptive. They rightly cheered the composer, Mr Leslie Stuart. They judiciously declined to name or call the authors of the feeblest of librettos. They received Miss Edna May with the cordiality due to the memory of her pristine appearance in *The Belle of New York*. But when in response to continuous applause and cheers, Miss Edna May appeared again and again, there fell a spoonful of tar into the honey cask. "Louie!" roared the house. "Louie"!! "Pounds"!! thrice repeated. After that time the stalls and balcony had cleared, save one or two lingerers; and yet the earnest first-nighters in pit and gallery clamoured for justice. It lasted fully twenty minutes, but at length patience was rewarded. Miss Louie Pounds appeared, and for herself and her brother received vociferous felicitations. That was *vox populi* indeed. For if *The Belle of Mayfair* succeeded, it is solely due to the composer, and Courtice Pounds and his sister. They bore the burden of the play, and they carried it to victory.

The feebleness of the libretto was something on which reviewers repeatedly commented. On the first night it was credited to Basil Hood and Charles H. E. Brookfield, the former of whom was a capable writer whose work included collaboration with Arthur Sullivan on *The Rose of Persia*, and with Edward German on *Merrie England*. However, his comic opera structures were less appropriate for a musical comedy, and Leslie Stuart for one had evidently been unhappy. His daughter May recalled,

> One day, after a more than bitter passage at arms, father came home and wrote a letter to Captain Basil Hood, telling him exactly what he thought of him and his libretto. It was my mother who saved this situation. She said that as she and I were going shopping in the Strand we would deliver the letter to Captain Hood. I remember it so clearly—my mother standing there in the foyer with almost a wink in her eye. "Oh, Captain Hood, how are you? What a delightful day!

May and I were just passing the theatre, and we thought we would bring you this letter from my husband." He took the letter gingerly, as if it were a charge of dynamite, which in fact it was. Then mother took his hand, and pressed it, and put on the purr in her voice which could charm birds off trees. "You know, Captain Hood, I want you to understand that Leslie cannot express himself as well as you do. . . ." The result of this was that the gallant captain sent a huge box of cigars round to father that evening, and all was well.[66]

Stuart evidently tipped off the *Daily Mail*, whose reviewer specifically hinted that the book had been "edited" at rehearsal. Directly after the premiere, Hood had his name removed from the credits. That of Cosmo Hamilton was substituted, Hood's name remaining only as author of a number of the lyrics. Hamilton had been involved with Charles Frohman's previous Vaudeville Theatre show, *The Catch of the Season*, and he explained in his autobiography how Frohman called on him again to sort out a little local difficulty with *The Belle of Mayfair*:

Edna May, the star of the play, was popularly supposed to have flung her part on the stage and trampled it under her feet. In other and less dramatic words she expressed her disapproval of the lines with which she had been provided and drove away to lunch, leaving a large and expensive company in chaos and amaze. With a Napoleonic gesture, therefore, and with a view to speed, Frohman gave the first act to Charles Brookfield to write all over again and the second to me. Brookfield and I never met to discuss the thing and decide on a plan of campaign, and so he had no notion of what I was going to do and I hadn't the remotest idea of his line of thought. All that either of us had to go upon was a rough sketch of the plot as it was told to us by Frohman in the fewest of words. We both wrote against time in different parts of London, while the company, in a strange, uncertain frame of mind, rehearsed the numbers, all of which had, of course to be "worked in" by the independent collaborators. At the end of a week both acts were finished and in rehearsal. Edna May was pleased and the clouds had lifted.[33]

According to Hamilton, neither he nor his coauthor actually managed to see the whole of *The Belle of Mayfair*:

Busy with other pressing jobs, Brookfield and I were unable to put in an appearance or to see the play until it had been running for weeks. We met, for the first time, when Leslie Stuart invited us to lunch at the "Savoy" on a matinée day, and he was so astonished to be told that we had never seen the result of our disunited efforts that he telephoned to the theatre in order to reserve two seats. But the house was sold out, and so Brookfield and I strolled over to the theatre together to stand at the back of the dress circle. It so happened, however, that I was caught in the foyer by an interviewer and was only able to join the sardonic Brookfield as the curtain was descending on the act that was his. My apology was accepted, and we talked until the curtain was about to rise on the act that was mine. Then Brookfield, with the obvious purpose of creating a story to add to his magnificent collection, begged to be excused and hurried away. I do not believe that he ever did see my act and I'm perfectly certain that I never saw his.[33]

Considering the flimsiness of the book, it is a tribute to the music and the "variety" elements that the show settled in for an extended run. The attractions included, of course, Camille Clifford of the wasp waist that had won her fame as the personification of "The Gibson Girl" conceived by Charles Dana Gibson in New York. Having paraded her talents in New York and London in *The Prince of Pilsen* without uttering a word, she had remained in London and had to do rather more to justify her continued existence. Comments on her musical contribution to *The Belle of Mayfair* were at best tactful acceptance. In the *Morning Advertiser* B. W. Findon drew the line not for her fourteen-inch waist, but for her even thinner voice: "Why on earth any composer or stage manager, after having heard Miss Camille Clifford—of Gibson girl and illustrated picture paper fame—once sing 'I'm a Duchess' at rehearsal, should have had the mistaken kindness of allowing her to sing it in public, belongs to the things which Lord Dundreary used to say 'no man can understand.'"

Clifford was sent for singing lessons to the distinguished singing teacher Madame Clara Novello Davies in Maida Vale. There she would often arrive in riding togs, finding the most convenient time for her lessons to be after her evening ride.[20] Her lessons proved a godsend to Madame Novello Davies's fourteen-year-old son, who recalled invading her dressing room and demanding seats she had promised for himself and two school friends.[11] That stagestruck teenager later became famous as actor-playwright-composer Ivor Novello.

It was Camille Clifford who inspired the first major ripples on *The Belle of Mayfair*'s tide of success. Having received innumerable proposals of marriage, she finally found one sufficiently aristocratic and attractive enough to accept from the Honorable Henry Lyndhurst Bruce, heir to

American sheet music front of "Why Do They Call Me the Gibson Girl?"
from *The Belle of Mayfair*

Lord Aberdare. She sent the management her resignation, threatening what, as Leslie Stuart recognized, was a publicist's godsend: "It was agreed by Miss Clifford and her husband-to-be that she would see the run out if I composed a special number and to give her also special publicity. . . . The result was the song that became immensely popular in England and particularly America, entitled 'Why Do They Call Me a Gibson Girl?'"[62]

The audiences that had turned up to gaze on her as the Gibson Girl were nothing compared with those eager to see what Lord Aberdare's heir was getting for his money. Finally the Gatti brothers took the variety show idea to its ultimate extreme by posting an announcement outside the theater that "Miss Clifford will appear tonight positively at 10:10." Edna May, nominal star, decided that enough was enough. Although Charles Frohman took her side, the Gattis refused to back down. The Frohman/Gatti agreement came to an end, and May left the cast.

More trouble was to follow, though no doubt its publicity value was again considerable. Edna May's part was taken initially by her understudy, Ethel Newman. However, the management wanted a bigger attraction as leading lady and came up with beautiful sixteen-year-old Phyllis Dare, who had hit the headlines when she went straight from school into the previous Frohman/Gatti production *The Catch of the Season*. Now she was taken from her convent again to be leading lady of *The Belle of Mayfair*, complete with the almost obligatory new song, "I'll Wait for You, Little Girlie." Understudy Ethel Newman did not take kindly to Phyllis Dare's arrival. Having played the part for over a month, she felt she deserved it permanently, and she sued. Initially she was awarded damages, but the decision was reversed on appeal.

By then a British provincial production was happily touring, and an American production was in preparation under the management of Thomas W. Ryley. Alas, he found that some of the music had reached the New York stage rather earlier than the official opening, according to a newspaper report following the opening on September 20, 1906, of *My Lady's Maid*, the American version of Paul Rubens's *Lady Madcap*:

> Thomas W. Ryley, the theatrical manager, was among those present at the opening performance of *My Lady's Maid* at the Casino last night. He took languid interest in the proceedings until the orchestra struck up the opening bars of a song that appeared on the programme as "Flirtation."
>
> Before the first verse was over Mr Ryley was beating it up the aisle like a volunteer fireman on his way to the engine-house. By the time the chorus was finished Mr Ryley had corralled all the Shuberts, the Shubert managers, the Shubert press agents and Shubert lawyers in the lobby and was reading them an improved version of the riot act.
>
> "Robbery!" shouted Mr Ryley. "Piracy! Assistance! Help! Murder! Thieves! Grafters! You stole that song.

"That is the song hit of *The Belle of Mayfair*, now running with Edna May at the Vaudeville, London, and I own the rights for the United States and Canada. In *The Belle of Mayfair* the song is called 'Hanover Square.' Your bum authors have swiped the music and words bodily. All you've changed is the title. Nothing so cruel and inhuman has happened since the kidnapping of Charlie Ross. Here is me coming into Daly's with *The Belle of Mayfair* in two months and you abduct the song hit of my piece that I pay good money for."

The Shuberts acted as though they were from Missouri, instead of from Syracuse. They wanted to be shown. Mr Ryley offered to sing the rest of the song to prove that he knew it, but happily this was averted. However, Mr Ryley was unable to convince the Shuberts that "Flirtation" was "Hanover Square." Mr Ryley got busy to-day. Through his counsel, Judge E. P. Coyne, he got an injunction restraining the Shuberts from allowing their performers to sing "Flirtation" to-night or any other night. The injunction will be served to-day if Mr Ryley can find any of the Shuberts.

Ryley need not have worried too much, since *My Lady's Maid* closed within six weeks. By then he was putting the finishing touches to his production of *The Belle of Mayfair*, which played Washington, Baltimore, and Boston before New York. Harry B. Burcher came over from London to play the Earl of Mount Highgate, and the cameo role of Princess Carl was entrusted to Irene Bentley, who had recently married Harry B. Smith, Broadway's most prolific librettist. The problem of replacing Camille Clifford was solved one evening when the producer saw a beautiful young woman walk down a New York City hotel staircase in a backless gown. She was Valeska Suratt, from Terre Haute, Indiana, who went on to appear as a femme fatale in Broadway comedies as well as in silent films.

Produced by Thomas W. Ryley at Daly's Theatre, New York,
3 December 1906

THE BELLE OF MAYFAIR

A Musical Comedy

Book by Charles H. E. Brookfield and Cosmo Hamilton.

Music by Leslie Stuart.

The Earl of Mount Highgate	Mr. Harry B. Burcher.
Honourable Raymond Finchley (his Son)	Mr. Van Rensselaer Wheeler.
Sir John Chaldicott, Bart., M.P.	Mr. Richard F. Carroll.

Comte de Perrier	Mr. Ignacio Martinetti.
Hugh Meredith	Mr. Jack Gardner.
Sir George Cheatham	Mr. J. Louis Mintz.
Charlie Goodyear (Friend of Raymond)	Mr. Cyril Offage.
Bandmaster	Mr. J. Costellanos.
Simpson (Footman to Sir John Chaldicott)	Mr. Frank W. Shea.
Bramley (Footman to Lord Mount Highgate)	Mr. W. Freeman.
H.S.H. Princess Carl of Ehrenbreitstein	Miss Irene Bentley.
Countess of Mount Highgate	Miss Honore Franch.
Lady Chaldicott	Miss Jennie Opie.
Julia	Miss Christie MacDonald.
Pincott (Julia's Maid)	Miss Bessie Clayton.
Duchess of Dunmow	Miss Valeska Suratt.
Lady Violet Gussop	Miss Annabelle Whitford.
Lady Jay	Miss May Hobson.
Lady Paquin	Miss Elinora Pendleton.
Lady Louise	Miss Margaret Rutledge.
Lady Lucille (Débutantes)	Miss Hattie Forsythe.
Lady Peter Robinson	Miss Stella Beardsley.
Lady Hayward	Miss Clare Cascelles.
Lady Swan	Miss Elizabeth Whitney.
Lady Edgar	Miss Rose Beatrice Winter.
Sophie	Miss Helen Cullinan.

Stall-holders.—Misses Florence Gardener, Eula Mannering, Beaula Martin, Caroline Lee, Palmyre Monnett, Lillian Earle, Beatrix Tuite-Dalton, Sadie Milner, Bessie Penn, Alice Tallant, Alice Knowlton, Myrtle Lawton, Florence Saville, Viola Bowers, Gene Cole, Maud Falkland.

Little Buds.—Misses Dorothy Hutchinson, Edith Barr, Effie Wheeler, Ethel Davis, Grace Russell, Rose Eaton, Ethel Vivian.

Guests.—Messrs. Joseph Parsons, Pierre Young, Harry Husk, Walter Grover, William Griffin, Arthur Nestor, Trestell Ayres, J. Sidney, Richard Davis, Harry Hoffman, J. Nelson.

ACT I.—Bazaar in a Private Park.

ACT II.—Drawing-room in Sir John Chaldicott's House.

Musical Director: Mr. A. de Novellis.

In both Boston and New York, the press reception was enthusiastic. Even the book seemed perfectly acceptable. For instance, Philip Hale stated, in the *Boston Herald*,

When this musical comedy was first produced in London last season there was much talk about the flatness of the text. . . . Whether the book has changed materially, whether the lines have been fattened since the first performance either by the authors or in the passage across the Atlantic, is of little moment. It is enough to say that, while the music is still superior to the play, the latter is much better than the run of the librettos now in fashion. . . .

This Mr Stuart has more than a pretty melodic gift. He writes light music that has something more than the jingle and the blare that keep the heavily fed and the cocktail heated from snoring in their seats. His music appeals to the people at large and it interests musicians. It has charm and distinction. In the best numbers in *The Belle of Mayfair* there is well defined and long continued melody, piquant harmonies, agreeable instrumentation and a knowledge of stage requirements.

The New York audience and critics were no less enthusiastic. Valeska Suratt was given six encores for her "Gibson Girl" song, and the gentlemen three for "I Know a Girl." But, commented the *World*, "there was nothing to equal 'Come to St George's,' a romping melody that would start a gouty old bachelor on a dead run to the altar." "It's going to be THE song of the season," added the *Evening Mail*, quoting lyricist William Jerome that never before had he heard so many splendid tunes strung together.

Valeska Suratt and the girls of *The Belle of Mayfair*, New York (author's collection)

In the *New York Daily News,* Roland Burke Hennessy again used André Messager's *Véronique* as the touchstone: "Not since another composer waved his magic baton and showed us the glowing musical qualities of the score of *Véronique* a couple of seasons ago had we been more regaled by the numbers of a production than we were last evening at Daly's Theater when *The Belle of Mayfair* made its initial bow to a metropolitan audience."

By Christmas 1906, *The Belle of Mayfair* was running successfully in both London and New York. Phyllis Dare, though, had left the London cast to take up a prearranged pantomime engagement, and Leslie Stuart again sent for Billie Burke from the variety theater.[62] Having reworked the show for Dare, the writers now rejigged it again, with the further novelty of a Harlequinade, described thus by the *Daily Graphic* when Burke introduced it on the afternoon of December 22: "She goes to sleep towards the end of the second act, dreaming and hoping that the intervention of the fairies may help her in eloping with her lover. The stage then grows dark, and Miss Louie Pounds then enters as a charming fairy Queen. In a trice she introduces the whole Christmas crowd.... One and all enter into the spirit of the thing, as though they had played naught but pantomime all their lives."

Later, on February 8, the London show received a further major relaunch with yet more new numbers, enabling the production to survive until April 13, 1907, for a handsome total of 416 performances. On Broadway, meanwhile, it had closed after four months and 140 performances. Although not up to the number of performances of *The Silver Slipper* and well behind *Florodora*, it was a genuine success by the Broadway standards of the time.

Examined today, *The Belle of Mayfair* stands out as a significant step forward for Leslie Stuart, who kept his personal idiosyncrasies in check and produced a much more balanced and varied score. "Come to St. George's" is the obvious showstopper for its buoyancy and liveliness. Striking, too, is Lord Mount Highgate's "I Am a Military Man," and there is another obvious hit in "Hello! Come Along, Girls" for Meredith in act 2. Arguably most delightful of all, and by way of stark contrast, is the beautifully reflective waltz number, "What Will the World Say?" It surely deserves a place alongside those other outstanding numbers created by Courtice Pounds, "Is Life a Boon?" from *The Yeomen of the Guard* and "Take a Pair of Sparkling Eyes" from *The Gondoliers.*

Chapter 14

Havana

Like most theater composers, Leslie Stuart received many propositions for collaborations. One was to work with George Bernard Shaw, which would doubtless have excited Stuart as much for Shaw's Irish nationality as for his eminence as a playwright and wit. Stuart explained that this occurred around 1904, when Harley Granville Barker was producing Shaw's works at London's Court Theatre:

> In the beginning of his season at the Court Theatre, London, where he was producing his remarkable plays, he complained to his agent, Goldenbright, of the short runs his plays were having at the time. Goldenbright was, incidentally, also my agent. . . . Shaw asked Goldenbright why it was that his plays should not have long runs as compared with musical comedy. He could not understand why the public taste should be thus absorbed. . . . Goldenbright said to Shaw: "Well, now, why not write a musical comedy in collaboration with, say, Leslie Stuart?" Shaw replied, "That's a good idea." Goldenbright said he would arrange a luncheon for Shaw and myself to meet and talk the proposition over.

Goldenbright put the matter to me, and I said I would be very happy to meet Shaw at luncheon . . . , and I agreed to a date. Goldenbright then wrote to Shaw asking him about the date, and he received the following reply: "Dear Goldenbright, I will be very glad indeed to collaborate with Leslie Stuart, but only on condition that I write the music."[62]

Stuart admired the response not only for its wit but also for the way Shaw had delayed it until he had a suitable retort.

A proposition of a different kind came in a letter dated January 24, 1907 from William Lincoln Balch of Boston, Massachusetts. Annexing a recent news clipping as his excuse for requesting a reading of the book and lyrics of an English comic opera, which he mailed under a separate cover, Balch expressed the hope that Stuart would consider composing the score. He continued, "I have a strong hope that the romantic environment and the wealth of legend and history associated with the picturesque island of Malta will inspire you as it did me when I selected that locale for the setting of my story. I ask your attention particularly to the effectiveness obtainable in the ballet music of the second act, culminating in a semi-military, semi-monastic climax to the weird passages preceding."[64]

A Maltese setting would certainly have been a novelty for comic opera; but the proposal came to nothing.

Stuart's next work, written for George Edwardes, did have an island setting, but it was Cuba rather than Malta. The *Era* announcement on July 20, 1907, suggested that Stuart was then working on not just one work but two. It read, "Mr Leslie Stuart has contracted to write the score of a new musical play for Mr George Edwardes, who will supply the book. The piece will be ready for production early next year. Mr Stuart has also signed with Mr Charles Frohman to write an opera in two acts, the scene of the first being in Monte Carlo and of the second in England. Mr Stuart will furnish the libretto, and the work will probably be produced in America."

The second of these two works was almost certainly *Nina*, whose idea had come to Stuart in Monte Carlo around 1903, and which was to occupy him on and off for the last twenty-five years of his life. He was to work extensively on it with Cosmo Hamilton, with whom he had been associated on *The Belle of Mayfair*. In his memoirs, Hamilton also mentioned what seems to have been yet another proposed collaboration around this time, writing, "Several years before the war I had spent a few days with Leslie Stuart at his delightful house on the Thames at Cookham, and had mapped out in elaborate detail the plot of a play to be called *The Little Governess*, in which we were to collaborate—his music, my book. It never was written, and, therefore, never produced by us, owing to many disturbances in the shape of immediate work, but subsequently the scenario fell into the hands of an energetic person who, probably disliking anything in the nature of waste, founded a very successful musical comedy upon our story and saved us the trouble of writing it."[33]

Behind his multiple activity, including a contract that committed Stuart to write as many as three works for Edwardes, were financial problems. Stuart's works continued to be heard around the world; but the volume of performances could not continue at the level necessary to finance a lifestyle that was getting out of control. A second news item in the July 20, 1907 edition of the *Era* gave a further indication of the problem. It concerned the sale of his future publishing rights, ending his nearly fifteen-year association with the firm of Francis, Day and Hunter: "Mr. Leslie Stuart has sold Messrs Chappell the sole right to publish all his music during the next five years. This agreement includes the songs which he has been commissioned by that firm to write for the Ballad Concerts."

Having thus won some financial breathing space, Stuart pressed on with not only *Havana* but also what was to prove his last song for Eugene Stratton. That such collaborations were now infrequent was not just that Stratton's appeal was receding in favor of newer artists and new-fangled entertainments such as the kinematograph. As Stuart himself explained, "whilst I was capable of composing many more numbers for [Stratton] than I did, he could not wean the public from those I had already written. Wherever he performed, there were incessant calls for certain numbers like 'Laguna,' etc., and only when Stratton consented to observe their demands did the audiences cease to call."[62] The *Stage* reported on the new song as it was performed at the Oxford Music Hall at Christmas 1907: "Mr. Eugene Stratton . . . is giving Leslie Stuart's melodious scena, 'I may be crazy,' with 'My 'cute Maluma girl,' a reply ditty gay in tune and treatment. Both ditties are given in Mr. Stratton's accustomed artistic style, whilst his dancing has lost none of its nimble lightness."

Havana, the one musical play that did immediately result, was somewhat more ambitious than Stuart's usual. Indeed W. H. Berry, who transferred from the cast of *The Merry Widow* to appear in it, claimed that it was intended originally for Daly's Theatre, home of more substantial musical plays. He explained that the ongoing success of *The Merry Widow* left George Edwardes seeking a solution to his contractual obligation to stage *Havana*.[5] However, Stuart's contract seems always to have been to compose for the Gaiety Theatre. George Grossmith Jr., who collaborated on the book, claims to have persuaded Edwardes to give the Gaiety public a rest from the variety-orientated musical comedies of Ivan Caryll and Lionel Monckton, usually starring Gertie Millar and Grossmith himself.[32]

At all events Edwardes arranged to send the main Gaiety company on tour in Britain and America with the Caryll/Monckton hit *The Girls of Gottenberg*, and to fill the void by mounting *Havana*. Evie Greene (the original Dolores in *Florodora*) starred as Consuelo, Lawrence Grossmith (married to Coralie Blythe, who had created the part of Wrenne in *The Silver Slipper*) played a part probably intended for his brother George. For the comedy element Edwardes engaged the lugubrious Alfred Lester as a foil to rising favorite W. H. Berry. Lester hesitated for a long while, concerned that Berry would overshadow him, but eventually agreed to a meeting. Edwardes cautioned his colleagues on no account to mention Berry's name until Lester had signed. When a page boy announced Lester's arrival, Edwardes committed one of his celebrated faux pas, saying, "I am glad to see you Berry." "Lester's face developed twice its normal length," Stuart added.[62] Lester nevertheless agreed to join the cast.

Produced by Mr. George Edwardes at the Gaiety Theatre, London,
25 April 1908

HAVANA

A Musical Play in Three Acts.
Written by George Grossmith, jnr. and Graham Hill.
Lyrics by Adrian Ross. Additional lyrics by George Arthurs.
Music by Leslie Stuart.

Jackson Villiers (of the S.Y. "Jaunty Jane")		Mr. Leonard Mackay.
Hon. Frank Charteris		Mr. Robert Hale.
Hilario	| (Bombito's Servants) |	Mr. T. C. Maxwell.
Alejandro	| |	Mr. Ernest Mahar.
Antonio		Mr. Barry Lupino.
Bombito del Campo (Mayor of Havana)		Mr. Arthur Hatherton.
The Don Adolfo (his Son)		Mr. Lawrence Grossmith.

Diego de la Concha (of Castille)		Mr. Edward O'Neill.
Customs House Officer		Mr. Lewis Grande.
Sentry		Mr. J. R. Sinclair.

AND

Nix (Bo'sun of the "Jaunty Jane")		Mr. Alfred Lester.

AND

Reginald Brown (the Yacht's Boy)		Mr. W. H. Berry.

Anita (a Cigar Seller)			Miss Jean Aylwin.
Isabelita (Bombito's Sister)			Miss Gladys Homfreys.
Maraquita (Isabelita's Duenna)			Miss Kitty Mason.
Tita	|	|	Miss Olive May.
Pepita	| (Cigarette Girls)	|	Miss Mabel Russell.
Lolita	|	|	Miss Adelina Balfe.
Mamie (Typewriter in Cigar Store)			Miss Barbara Dunbar.
Teresa (a Flower Girl)			Miss Enid Leonhardt.
Lola			Miss Florence Phillips.
Zara			Miss Jessie Broughton.
Signora Verriotti (a Fortune Teller)			Miss Kitty Hanson.
Isolda (a Spanish Dancer)			Señorita Tortola Valencia.

AND

Consuelo (Bombito's Niece)		Miss Evie Greene.

Touring Newspaper Beauties: Miss Gladys Cooper, Miss Julia James, Miss Frances Kapstowne, Miss Daisy Williams, Miss Connie Stuart, Miss Kitty Lindley, Miss Crissie Bell, Miss Phyllis Barker.

Ladies of Havana: Miss Enid Leslie, Miss Gladys Desmond, Miss Claire Rickards, Miss Eileen Caulfield, Miss Pauline Francis, Miss Sylvia Storey, Miss Pattie Wells.

Gentlemen of Havana: Mr. H. B. Burcher, Mr. Alec Fraser, Mr. W. Raymond, Mr. J. Redmond, Mr. Cecil Cameron, Mr. Sidney Lyndon.

ACT I.	Cigar Store of Bombito & Co.	Joseph Harker.
ACT II.	Patio of the Torre del Campo	Alfred Terraine.
ACT III.	The Harbour, Havana	Joseph Harker.
Orchestra under the Direction of		Mr. Carl Kiefert.
Stage Director		Mr. Edward Royce.

The story seems to have originated with Graham Hill and then been developed by George Grossmith. It tells of Consuelo, niece of the cigar-manufacturing mayor of Havana, Bombito del Campo, who is engaged to her somewhat imbecilic but influential cousin Don Adolfo, the mayor's son. The two agree that during the day before their wedding they may flirt with whomever they fancy, and Consuelo proceeds to fall for Jackson Villiers, owner of an English yacht, the *S.Y. Jaunty Jane*. When Villiers fails to respond, she determines to humiliate him. In the ensuing action the mayor mistakes Villiers for a filibuster for whom a government reward has been offered, and the *Jaunty Jane* for a gun-running American tramp ship *The Wasp* in disguise. Villiers is denounced as an "enemy of Cuba" and arrested with his friend Frank Charteris. Don Adolfo is meanwhile supposed to be involved in a revolutionary plot and is kidnapped by the crew of the *Jaunty Jane*, thereby preventing his planned marriage to Consuelo.

In a subplot, conspirator Diego de la Concha schemes to make the mayor's sister Isabelita the queen of Cuba. The lugubrious Nix, bo'sun of the *Jaunty Jane*, mistakenly believes the overbearing Isabelita to be a woman he married and deserted seven years before, before happily discovering that the woman in question was the younger and livelier Anita. Denouncing Villiers as "an enemy of Cuba," Consuelo strikes him across the face with her glove before eventually being reunited with him, leaving Don Adolfo to find consolation elsewhere.

The departure from Gaiety traditions in casting and structure was not to the liking of everyone, not least the correspondent of the *Times*, who wrote, "*Havana* is too long and too loud and too lavish and too loose-limbed. It is in three acts and four hours. . . . The old Gaiety pieces were in two acts. In the first some attention was paid to a plot; in the second, having thus done their duty and vindicated the Gaiety's right to be considered a theatre and not a music-hall, all concerned were free to get to work on their 'turns,' until, in the last five minutes, a forgetful audience had to be reminded that it really was a play they were seeing. The new plan is to have three acts and spread the plot, very thin indeed, over all three."

By contrast, the *Stage* saw the new formula as a great success. It wrote, "[*Havana*] is a great stride forward for the Gaiety. Mr. Edwardes has made something like a clean sweep of the comic shreds and patches of what must now be accounted the old style of Gaiety pieces. How ready the public was for the change, Saturday evening showed. *Havana* gave Mr. Edwardes the most successful first night that he has ever had at the Gaiety. . . . Hour after hour the piece went on, from eight o'clock until Sunday morning came, but the audience laughed and applauded and remained. Save in the stalls, the house was as crowded at the last as when the curtain first went up."

The *Era* particularly enjoyed the blaze of color when the curtain came up, noting, "The gay cigar sellers, the laughing vendors of flowers, in the springtide of their youth and beauty, seem to be having a gala day—or is it one long holiday in this land of désoeuvrement? The senoritas are arrayed in soft, deep shades of heliotrope, blue and green. The white-coated youth of Havana flirt with the dainty sylph-like creatures whose charms—every bit as much due to Anglo-Saxon as to Spanish blood are set off by confections of delightfully harmonised colour."

The *Times* reporter did at least enjoy the wealth of female beauty, venturing the thought that "there have never been so many pretty faces on the Gaiety stage." The chorus of "Touring Newspaper Beauties" was a topical touch, beauty competitions being newly the rage. Gladys Cooper was among them, while the second female chorus of "Ladies of Havana" included Sylvia Storey, who five months into the run became the Countess of Poulett. The *Times* critic also felt that there had seldom been such enjoyable music. The opening of the second act, set on the patio of a Cuban house in half-light under a purple sky, with Jessie Broughton lying under an orange tree and singing her song "Zara" to Olive May and the other beauties, was his favorite. But above all he appreciated the "turns" of Alfred Lester. "To begin with," he noted, "the very appearance of this most melancholy master of hilarity is cool and refreshing. In his dark blue jumper and reefer, with his shabby cap and his pale face, he is a place of refuge for the dazzled eye. When he speaks, he speaks to the persons he is supposed to address—not merely looks at them, which many sometimes do, but speaks to them, which he alone does. And though he has to hunt a rather feeble joke through three acts, he does it so well that he keeps it funny to the end. His skit on the 'Merry Widow' waltz is, perhaps the most ingenious and laughable of the many we have seen."

The *Merry Widow* skit was a duet between Nix and Anita. She is the cigar seller he had carelessly married on a visit to Havana seven years before and whom he is now happy to accept as his wife in the face of rival approaches from the fearsome Isabelita. In this act 3 duet, they imagine a situation where one of them has died. The musical joke is that the first six phrases of the refrain are those of the *Merry Widow* waltz, each with the sequence of notes reversed, after which the *Merry Widow* waltz breaks out unchanged at "I'm [You're] the merry widow / You're [I'm] the gay deceased."

Leslie Stuart and music from *Havana* (author's collection)

The *Times* critic also had other good things to say about the score, namely, "Mr. Leslie Stuart lifts us a little out of the cold rut; and here and there we caught a hint that he could have been even more individual if he had liked. He can write a catchy tune for Mr. Berry or Miss Aylwin; but he can also write really humorous things, like the "bomb quartette" in Act II, and really melodious airs like Miss Jessie Broughton's song; and he makes good use of his orchestra. It should be added that his orchestra on Saturday made very good use of his music."

The *Stage*, though, felt that "Mr. Stuart is no great colourist, and he does not take much inspiration from the Southern atmosphere of the piece. In this respect he is perhaps at his best in the 'Cuban Girl' solo for Consuelo and in the well-written finale to the second act." Stuart himself was struck by the way he was called upon to create a Spanish atmosphere in *Havana* and elsewhere, bearing in mind his supposed descent from Spaniards who had settled in Ireland hundreds of years before. He later mused, "It has been frequently commented upon, particularly by instrumentalists who have performed under my baton who were of Spanish nationality, that my plays, 'Florodora' and 'Havana' were the best examples of my work, had a distinct Spanish atmosphere, and suggested Latin inspiration."[62]

For *Havana*, Stuart finally had as principal lyricist Adrian Ross, who had been floated as lyricist of *Florodora* and had also done some work on *The School Girl.* The pen name hid the identity of Cambridge don Arthur Reed Ropes, who among other shows had been lyricist of the London version of *The Merry Widow*. He contributed an informative piece to the *Play Pictorial* on his collaboration with Leslie Stuart. He suggested that "*Havana* is as much light opera as *The Merry Widow*. There is a larger bulk of music, and the choral effects of the finales and opening scenes, for instance, are more elaborate and effective." He then described how the music was written:

> My method in collaboration was simple. I divided the musical numbers into classes beforehand. In one class, the musical effect was the main thing. This was especially the case in choruses and ensembles, where a stanza form was obviously unsuitable. For this class, Mr. Leslie Stuart mostly composed the music beforehand and I put words to it, trying to fit them to the dramatic situation and also to make them fairly easy to sing. . . .
>
> Another class of musical numbers was the comic songs and duets, &c. For these the words were the more important factor, and Mr. Stuart, recognising this truth, set my work with untiring energy, sometimes suggesting an alteration which was usually an improvement. For sentimental numbers we compromised, and had words or music first as we felt inspired. . . . [52]

Havana vied with *The Belle of Mayfair* as Leslie Stuart's most impressive score. In his *Composers of Operetta*, Gervase Hughes described the opening chorus as "a model of its kind."[35] In later numbers the reflective rhythms of Stuart's earlier hits give way to a more up-front, heart-on-sleeve syncopated sound. This is apparent in "Hello, People!"—one of his most obviously winning show-stoppers after "Tell Me, Pretty Maiden." Though the humor of "How Did the Bird Know That?" is hard to take now, its music is imaginatively conceived, complete with orchestral bird twittering. As for the beautifully languorous "Zara," it could hold its own among theater love songs of any period.

Arguably the most remarkable number of all is "I'm a Cuban Girl," which Evie Greene sang after entering on horseback. It's a piece of harmonically adventurous writing one would be hard pressed to find from other popular musical theater composers of the time. It begins with thirty-two bars of what would normally be the waltz refrain, modulating into a contrasted waltz section, after which comes a choral barcarolle culminating in a development of the main waltz section. That main thirty-two-bar waltz section itself is of unusually original structure. The basic melodic shape is not unlike that of Franz Lehár's "Nur die Liebe macht uns jung" from *Zigeunerliebe* of two years later, but the end effect is very different. Where Lehár's waltz has a lilt and sweep, Stuart built lovingly shaped individual phrases into an immaculately sculpted whole.

The Gaiety run of *Havana* did have one moment of near tragedy, recounted by W. H. Berry. The theater's curtain was in the form of a picture in a wooden frame, which slid up and down on wire ropes at either side. For curtain calls the company linked arms, advanced as the curtain rose, bowed, and stepped back before the curtain fell. This would happen two or three times. One night Evie Greene for some reason stepped forward again as the curtain came hurtling downwards. Leonard Mackay and W. H. Berry rushed forward and dragged her back just as the heavy curtain scraped her head, grazing her face, neck, and bosom. While Mackay carried her to her dressing room, Berry reassured the audience.[5]

When Evie Greene later left the show for health reasons, her part was taken by May de Sousa, an American from Chicago who had appeared in the previous Gaiety show *The Girls from Gottenberg*. Stuart provided a new duet for her and Courtice Pounds, who had taken over the role of Diego de la Concha.

Remarkably the first production of *Havana* outside Britain was in Berlin, less than six months after the West End opening. This was for the reopening on October 17, 1908, of the former Belle Alliance-Theater as the Berliner Operetten-Theater. The show probably never stood much chance in competition with locally grown revues and Viennese operettas

Evie Greene in *Havana*, London (author's collection)

of Franz Lehár, Oscar Straus, and Leo Fall. The *Berliner Tageblatt* admitted that "the public had a good time and laughed," but found the text tasteless and the music "essentially common." The reviewer was seemingly pleased that the overrunning of the opening night relieved him of the need to comment on the show's conclusion.

Havana closed in London in December 1908 after a relatively modest run of 221 performances that probably reflected the show's unsuitability for the Gaiety Theatre more than any shortcomings of the score. It seemed to have little appeal for the United States until comedian James T. Powers "of the expansive smile and short-cropped carroty looks" came along. In his autobiography Powers told how the Shubert brothers, Lee and Jake, sent him to London to see the show after many American managers had refused it:

> I was disappointed when I saw it at the Gaiety Theater—it ran from eight-fifteen until nearly midnight—and although it was fairly successful, the dullness at times was appalling; but the music by Leslie Stuart was beautiful. In fact, three of his songs were so catchy that I determined to cable the Shuberts that I would play it. I was called a "rube" by the managers who had refused it; but I felt that the songs "Hello People," "The Cuban Girl," and "How did the bird know that?" would make it a success in America. After the performance, I went to my rooms in the Savoy Hotel and fell asleep. I awoke at three in the morning, humming "How did the bird know that?" I . . . felt certain if I could write enough comic verses for that song, it would go far to make the play a success. . . . [46]

In rewriting the book, Powers enlarged the role of Nix for himself, dropped the boat's *Jaunty Jane* name in favor of *The Wasp*, and cut down Stuart's score from twenty-five numbers to fifteen. Lee Shubert accepted the result on the recommendation of stage director R. H. Burnside, but at the dress rehearsal at the Lyric Theater in Philadelphia the brothers were unimpressed. "It's the most amateurish performance I have ever seen," said Lee. "We're going to get in another author and have it rewritten," added Jake. Powers stuck to his guns, while harboring fears the brothers might be right. He and his wife didn't sleep a wink that night, and for hours the following day he walked the streets. He was so weak and nervous at the premiere that he had to hold onto the scenery before making his first entrance. But, from the time he and Percy Ames, as Reginald Brown, walked onto the stage in sailor costumes, the audience responded with incessant laughter and applause.[46]

Produced by Sam S. & Lee Shubert at the Casino Theatre, New York,
11 February 1909

HAVANA

A Musical Play in Three Acts. Book by George Grossmith, Jr.
and Graham Hill.

Andrew Lamb

Revised for America by James T. Powers. Lyrics by Adrian Ross and George Arthurs. Music by Leslie Stuart.

Señor Bombito del Campo, Mayor of Havana, a cigar manufacturer

	Mr. Harold Vizard.
Consuelo, his niece	Miss Edith Decker.
Isabelita, Bombito's sister, a "revolutionista"	Miss Eva Davenport.
Don Adolfo, Bombito's son, fresh from an English University	Mr. Ernest Lambart.
Anita, a cigar vendor, heroine of an obsolete matrimonial adventure	Miss Clara Palmer.
Pepita |	Miss Daisy Green.
Lolita | Cigarette girls employed by Bombito |	Miss Viola Kellogg.
Tita |	Miss Mabel Weeks.
Mamie, the stenographer at Bombino's establishment	Miss Geraldine Malone.
Gladys, a newspaper beauty from Pensacola	Miss Edith Kelly.
Señora Donna Junenez, a fortune teller	Miss Viola Kellogg.
Maraquita, Isabelita's duenna	Miss Agnes Faulkner.
Diego de la Concha, superintendent at Bombino's establishment	Mr. William Pruette.
J. de Peyster Jackson, an American yacht owner on a cruise to Cuba	Mr. Joseph Phillips.
Frank Van Dusen, his friend	Mr. William Phillips.
Reginald Brown, steward on Jackson's yacht "*The Wasp*"	Mr. Percy Ames.
Roderigo, a gallant, in love with Consuelo	Mr. Bertrand Grassby.
Hilario | employees of Bombito's |	Mr. Ernest Hare.
Alejandro | |	Mr. Ted Sullivan.
Enrico	Mr. Glen Conner.
Señor Patigo, one of the Cause	Mr. Joseph Galton.
Soldaro	Mr. Joseph Galton.
Sentry	Mr. Eugene Roder.
Officer	Milburry Ryder.
Chiquita	Little Lillie Fuehrer.
Chiquito	Master Robbie Fuehrer.
Sammy, Jr.	Master Robbie Fuehrer.
Julio, of the Havana Police	Mr. Bertrand Grassby.
Juan, servant	Mr. Harry Sulkin.

Samuel Nix, a matrimonial outlaw   Mr. James T. Powers.
and Bo'sun of "*The Wasp*"

Touring Newspaper Beauties: Miss Caroline Green, Miss Dolly Filly,
Miss Erminie Clark, Miss Elsa Croxton, Miss Cecelia Mayo,
Miss Irene Hawley, Miss Julia Mills.

Ladies of Havana: Miss Emily Monti, Miss B. Ryan, Miss Gladys Alexander,
Miss Janet North, Miss Freda Braun, Miss Helen Broderick,
Miss Marion Hartman.

Bombito's Clerks: Mr. Harold Nelson, Mr. Alfred Gerrard, Mr. Irwin Harding,
Mr. Jack Weelekin.

Gentlemen of Havana: Mr. Harold Nelson, Mr. Jack Brese,
Mr. Harold Watson, Mr. Arthur McSorley, Mr. George Allison,
Mr. Harry Sulkin.

Cuban Soldiers: Mr. Jean Roeder, Mr. Arthur Whitman, Mr. Jack Leonard,
Mr. Harry McDonough, Jr., Mr. Philip Haring, Mr. Albert Massour,
Mr. George Skillman, Mr. Milburry Ryder, Mr. Alexander Groves.

Cigarette Girls: Miss Elsie Raymond, Miss Adelaide Rossmi,
Miss Suzette Gordon, Miss Isabelle Daintry, Miss Mildred Bright,
Miss Loraine Bright, Miss Mary Murrilo, Miss Patsy O'Connor,
Miss Libbey Diamond, Miss Mona Sartoris.

Cigar Girls: Miss Hazel Williams, Miss Dorothy Sayce, Miss Ruth Elton,
Miss Irma Dixon, Miss Jeanne McPherson, Miss Holmes, Miss Isobel
Cannar, Miss Sylvia Loti, Miss Mildred Dupree, Miss Natalie Harvey.

Act I: The Cigar Establishment of Bombito, Havana. Noon.

Act II: The Patio of Bombito's Residence. The same evening.

Act III: The Harbor, Havana. The next morning.

Stage Director: Mr. Ned Wayburn.

Musical Director: Mr. Clarence Rogerson.

Scenery: Mr. Arthur Voegtlin.

"Good fun and nonsense" was how the *New York Herald* summed it up. It made it clear that Powers was the star of the show, noting, "You know him, of course—everybody does—and when he came on with the grieved, hurt expression, touched up by some carmine hair the audience gave him a royal welcome. He was funny, too, and there were laughs in the wake of his speeches, dancing, and, aye, even of his singing." As for the music, the *Herald* left no doubt what was the hit number, declaring, "'Hello, People, People, Hello!' That was the latest telephone message from *Havana*, and it was sung, danced, smiled and winked at the audience across the footlights at the Casino Theatre last night by eight young

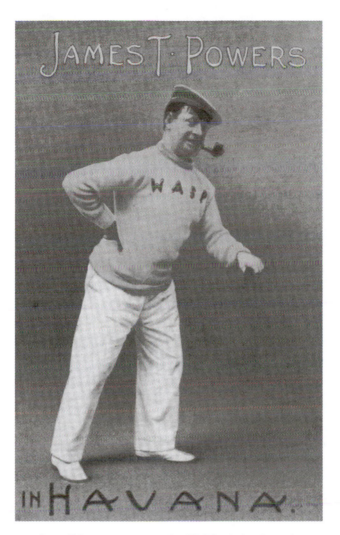

James T. Powers in *Havana*, New York (author's collection)

women possessed of waspish waists and youthful voices. . . . Later in the evening the selfsame eight sang 'Cupid's Telephone,' and there was another uproar. It subsided somewhere near the time of going to press. . . . " Of the supporting cast, it wrote, "Miss Edith Decker was a Cuban niece, with an arch expression, and Miss Clara Palmer danced with a graceful castanet and moonlight air. So did Miss Edith Kelly dance in a limber limbed manner. Mr. William Pruette sang in a deep bass voice and plotted a revolution; Mr. Ernest Lambart wore a monocle, smooth hair and a comically 'silly ass' expression, and Mr. Percy Ames helped the comedy along not a little bit. In summary, the *Herald* felt, "*Havana* is funny enough to laugh at, it's tuneful enough to make you remember it, and it's pretty and animated enough to make you wish to go again."

The *New York Dramatic Mirror* was equally enthusiastic, praising "some of the best lines, the catchiest music and the cleanest music that has resounded from the Casino walls in many years." It even ventured the view that "Hello People" "will erase the memory of "Tell Me, Pretty Maiden." The *New York Times* summarized the show as "a bright, snappy little entertainment" that was clean and wholesome enough "to get booking without difficulty—even in Trenton."

As for Jimmy Powers's "How Did the Bird Know That?" the *New York Times* considered it "quite the funniest thing of the kind heard here in a long time. . . . He has a large bundle of low-comedy tricks, and he uses them to better advantage in this piece than in anything in which he has been seen in recent years." Powers varied the song for topical effect throughout the run. He later recalled, "One grey-haired Lothario occupied a front-row seat at almost every performance, and every time I sang "How did the bird know that?" I felt ill at ease singing the same verses to him. When one of the girls told me he was a prominent New York broker, I wrote a verse especially for him, which ended with, "Buy thermometers if you're wise, for next summer they will rise—Now, how did the bird know that?" I wrote twenty-six verses for that song, and one evening, when the audience was particularly hilarious, and insisted on having another verse after I had sung fourteen, I pulled out a fire hose from the wings, pointed the nozzle, and threatened it with inundation."[46]

Acknowledging the female glamor in *Havana*, the New York press listed the performers' romantic interests. Not least they noted dark-haired, sensuous-mouthed Edith Kelly, who according to the *New York Herald* "danced with a graceful castanet and moonlight air" as leader of the line of "newspaper beauties." Edith Kelly had appeared at the Gaiety Theatre, London, in *The Girls of Gottenberg* in early 1908, and had met the young Jerome Kern, who promptly fell in love with her.[9] Alas, after *Havana*, it was not with Kern that she was romantically linked in the papers, but with Frank Jay Gould, son of American railroad speculator Jay Gould, and they were soon married. In June 1911 Frank Jay Gould sought to wrest power of London's Gaiety Theatre and replace George Edwardes with his assistant J. A. E. ("Pat") Malone, but the attempt came to nothing. Edith Kelly later married revue producer Albert de Courville, while Gould went on to develop the French Riviera resort of

Juan-les-Pins. His name lives on in the Pinède Gould, where the annual "Jazz à Juan" festival takes place to this day.

Havana ran at the Casino Theatre until July 1909, achieving a run of 177 performances. It then reopened a month later, adding a further 59 performances to make up a total of 236 performances that was an outstanding achievement for Broadway of the time. Then Jimmie Powers successfully took it on tour. Just as *Florodora* had been the first work to be recorded to any significant degree by its original London cast, so *Havana* became the first current work to be included in the series of Victor light opera selections that documented Broadway shows.

The Shubert brothers were evidently happy enough with the score. Three days after the New York premiere, they announced that they had offered Leslie Stuart an annuity for life in return for the American rights to all the music—of any kind whatsoever—that he might write in the future. Whether the offer was taken up is unclear; but it was further evidence of the financial pressures Leslie Stuart was then experiencing.

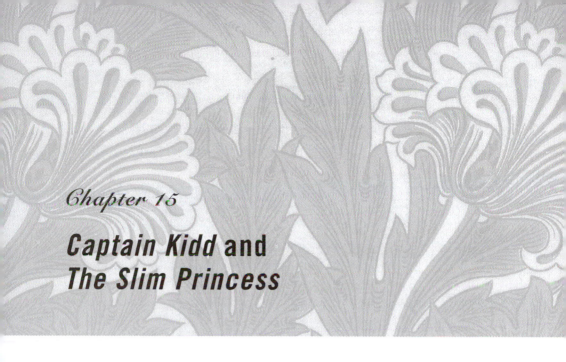

Chapter 15

Captain Kidd and
The Slim Princess

While Leslie Stuart was enjoying fame as one of the leading musical theater composers of his time, his brother Lester Barrett had been head of Francis, Day and Hunter's professional department. He also found a useful sideline in writing lyrics for songs by the company's staff composers. Particularly successful were his collaborations with the young Belorussian-born Herman Darewski.[19] These included several songs for another Lancastrian, Rochdale-born G. H. Eliot, who appeared as the "Chocolate Coloured Coon." In 1909 they produced a very considerable success in the lilting "I Used to Sigh for the Silvery Moon," a song that remained popular for many a year.

On August 31 of that same year, Leslie Stuart entered the HMV recording studios again to make recordings of some of his best-known numbers with one of his most faithful theatrical supporters. Harry B. Burcher had been in London's *Florodora* and *The Silver Slipper* and had assisted in directing the latter in New York. He had been the Earl of Mount Highgate in the New York *Belle of Mayfair*, and one of the gentlemen of *Havana* at the Gaiety. Now, in the studio, the two began a batch of recordings with the Eugene Stratton songs "The Coon Drum Major" and "I May Be Crazy." They went on through "I Want to Be a Military Man" from *Florodora*, the "Champagne Dance" from *The Silver Slipper*, "My Little Canoe" from *The School Girl*, "Come to St. George's" and "Why Do They Call Me a Gibson Girl?" from *The Belle of Mayfair*, to "Hello, People," "Way Down in Pensacola," and "Cupid's Telephone" from *Havana*. To our loss, the recordings were never released.[53]

Although Stuart still had a contract to provide further works for George Edwardes at the Gaiety, his financial circumstances evidently forced him also to seek commissions elsewhere. Thus, in May 1909, he entered into an agreement with actor-producer Seymour Hicks, who was then running a series of musical plays starring himself and his wife Ellaline Terriss. The result was *Captain Kidd*, Hicks's own adaptation of the successful 1904 American farce *The Dictator* by Richard Harding Davis. Even stripped of extraneous incident, it offered potential for a stronger story than was often the case in the musical theater. Adrian Ross was again employed to provide the lyrics, assisted as in *Havana* by Leslie Stuart's fellow Mancunian, George Arthurs.

Presented by Frank Curzon at Wyndham's Theatre, London,
12 January 1910

CAPTAIN KIDD

A Musical Play by Seymour Hicks.

Adapted from Richard Harding Davis's successful Play, "The Dictator."

Lyrics by Adrian Ross. Additional Lyrics by George Arthurs.
Music by Leslie Stuart.

Viscount Albany (*alias* Captain Kidd)	Mr Seymour Hicks
Simpson (his Valet, *alias* Jim Dodd)	Mr Hugh E. Wright
Dick Hyne (Wireless Telegraph Operator for the Red C. Line)	Mr Evelyn Beerbohm
Colonel John T. Bowie (U.S. Consul at Porto Banos)	Mr John Clulow
Duffy (a Secret Service Detective)	Mr Fred Lewis
Rev. Arthur Bostick (a Missionary)	Mr Cyril Ashford
General Santos Campos (President of San Mañana)	Mr Frank Wilson
Samuel Codman (Captain of the Bolivar)	Mr Frank Vigay
Dr. Vasques (Health Officer at Porto Banos)	Mr J. J. Hooker
Lieutenant Perry (H.M.S. Invincible)	Mr Charles Bradley

Colonel Garcia	(Aides-de-Camp to Campos)	Mr Frank Aimes
Lieutenant Manuel		Mr F. F. Holt
Teresa Glond		Miss Rosie Chesney
May Pole		Miss May Kennedy
Grace Hufnagle		Miss Doris Stocker
Rose Flipmaguilder		Miss Marie Brenda
Amy Striapolo	(Broadway Belles)	Miss Carina Cliff
Lily Friedenhamar		Miss Laurie Opperman
Anne Tique		Miss Nellie Pryor
Olga Comoff		Miss Nancie Freyne
Emmie Palorompins		Miss Asta Fleming
Sarita		Miss Florence Thurston
Mrs. John T. Bowie		Miss Sylvia Buckley
Señorita Juanita Arguilla (The Star of Panama)		Miss Hilda Guiver
Aggie Shrubb (Chief Stewardess of the Bolivar)		Miss Ivy St. Helier
Mme. Ducrot (Proprietress of the Hotel del Prado)		Miss Mollie Lowell

AND

Lucy Sheridan (a Missionary)	Miss Ellaline Terriss

The Play produced by Seymour Hicks.

The Dances arranged by Fred Farren.

ACT I.   Deck of the Steamer "Bolivar" at anchor in the Harbour of Porto Banos

ACT II.   The American Consulate at Porto Banos (Three hours later)

ACT III.   The same (Six hours later)

Time, the Present. Place—Porto Banos, Republic of San Mañana, Central America.

The Orchestra under the direction of	Frank E. Tours.
Business Manager	J. Herbert Jay.
Stage Manager	W. T. Lovell.

The plot revolves around the dashing young English nobleman Viscount Albany, otherwise known as "Captain Kidd," who believes he has killed a New York cabbie in an argument. In act 1 he is on the *S.S. Bolivar*, fleeing to Porto Banos in Central America. On board he meets

Seymour Hicks and Ellaline Terriss in *Captain Kidd* (author's collection)

pretty Lucy Sheridan, who is traveling out as a missionary to marry another missionary, Reverend Arthur Bostick. Another passenger is Colonel John T. Bowie, consul-elect in Porto Banos. Finding Porto Banos in revolt, and his ally removed by the noisy revolutionary General Santos Campos, Bowie is reluctant to disembark. By contrast, Albany is reluctant to stay on board because of the presence of a detective, Duffy. Albany and Bowie therefore agree to change places. In act 2 the disguised Albany hires a private army, settles Santos Campos and the country, and becomes for a few hours dictator. In act 3 he is rescued from ensuing revolution, and ends up claiming Lucy as his wife.

The show's on-board setting and characters are suggestive of Cole Porter's *Anything Goes*; but *Captain Kidd* enjoyed no comparable success. Playing against three big West End hits—*The Arcadians*, *Our Miss Gibbs*, and *The Dollar Princess*—it was up against stiff competition, but that alone can hardly be blamed for its dismal failure. Preproduction doubts are indicated by a note stapled into every performer's typescript libretto:

NOTE TO EVERYONE

THIS PIECE MUST BE PLAYED WITH A BANG
FROM START TO FINISH

OR IT IS NO GOOD. EVERYONE BRIGHT.
THE WHOLE NOTE THROUGHOUT BEING ONE OF
DASH AND GO OR WE SHALL DASH AND GO.

Play Pictorial summed up Hicks's adaptation by saying that he "has omitted a considerable amount of the original, and trusted to his own mother-wit to fashion a musical piece which should give free rein to his own chameleon-like style of acting." The *Times* reviewer clearly felt that was not enough:

> In pieces of this sort he is always three-parts himself to one part the character he is supposed to represent. Last night the proportion was nearer nine to one than three to one. Mr. Hicks not only rattled but ragged—there is no other word for it. He dropped unauthorised asides right and left, he addressed the audience frankly, though hurriedly, in his own person; he imitated his brother-players and his brother-artists of the variety stage. . . . Miss Ellaline Terriss . . . is more reverent in her treatment of the author, and does her sweetest for the composer; while Mr. Hicks has little or no reverence for either. . . . Mr. Hicks has taken a good farce—*The Dictator*, by Richard Harding Davis, which the American actor, Mr. William Collier, played not long ago in London—and has turned it into an average musical comedy.

The show's one undoubted bright spot was a young lady named Ivy St. Helier, a late replacement for popular soubrette Gracie Leigh as the comic stewardess Aggie Shrubb. The *Times* described St. Helier as "a very quaint little player indeed, with a fine voice and a good notion of burlesque." Overall, however, the musical adaptation stood or fell by whether audiences could stand a whole evening of Seymour Hicks in indifferent material. Understandably they couldn't, and the piece closed ignominiously after only thirty-four performances. Hicks and his wife were left to return to the variety circuit to make up their losses, though Hicks did not give in lightly with the show. In October 1910 it went on the road, with Roland Bottomley and Maie Ash playing the leading roles, but it failed again.

We cannot now judge Leslie Stuart's score in full, because it was never published, although "Nursery Rhymes" was evidently reused in his next work. Ellaline Terriss probably summed up his contribution fairly when she wrote, years later, "The music was by Leslie Stuart, but, although it was tuneful and of his best, his style was not suited to rapid farce, and the piece fell between two stools. The slow lilting melodies stopped the fun, and the elaborate plot was one to which a big musical setting should never have been wedded."[69]

The failure served to exacerbate Leslie Stuart's deteriorating financial position. When Hicks now made remarks that seemed to suggest it was the music that was at fault, Stuart did what anyone of high artistic principles and heavily in debt would do. On April 2, 1910, he sued for damages. His case was twofold: first, he alleged that Hicks was in breach of the implied terms of contract by failing to produce the show in a first rate, fit, or proper manner as regards cast, chorus, orchestra, scenery, or dresses, and that it was put on at an unsuitable theater; second, he alleged that he had been slandered by statements from Hicks that the music had been a failure.

While legal work went on, Stuart finalized the score of his second musical play to be produced within that same year. This was for the American manager Charles B. Dillingham and was Stuart's first (and, as it would turn out, only) work to receive its premiere in the United States. *The Slim Princess* was an adaptation by librettist Henry Blossom of George Ade's novel of that title, and was conceived as a vehicle for new young star Elsie Janis, celebrated not least for her impersonations. Supporting her was Julia Frary, a one-time *Florodora* girl. Besides a British composer, the show had a British director, Austen Hurgon, and a British costume designer, Percy Anderson. Its tryout opened at the Star Theatre, Buffalo, on Thursday, September 8, 1910, for three nights, and then moved to the Studebaker Theatre, Chicago, for a seven-week run beginning September 13.

The principals, who were to change significantly during the pre–New York tour, were initially as follows:

The Hon. Crawley Plumston	Mr. Ralph Nairn.
Count Louis Von Schloppenhauer	Mr. Carl Haydn.
Alex Pike	Mr. George Parsons.
"Tod" Narcross	Mr. Harry Pilcer.

Princess Jeneka	Miss Julia Frary.
Mother Saidis	Miss Florence Morrison.
The Hon. Mrs. Plumston	Miss Kate Wingfield.
Lutie Longstreet	Miss Grace King.
Princess Kalora	Miss Elsie Janis.
Prince Selim Malagaski	Mr. William Pruette.
Issit Effeadi	Mr. Sam Collins.

Act 1 is set in the oriental principality of Borovenia, where Prince Selim Malagasaka is the happy father of two daughters. The younger, Princess Jeneka, is a plump and pleasing person, while the older, Princess Talora, is perhaps more pleasing but not, alas, plump—"alas" because in Borovenia only plump girls are sought in marriage. To make matters even worse, a younger daughter may not marry before the elder. In order to surmount the former obstacle, the prince places the elder girl in the charge of one of his officials, Issit Effredi, with strict orders to have her fattened up. The princess duly appears outwardly quite plump; but she verifies accusations that her plumpness is not real by throwing off padding and appearing as slim as ever. When things seem at their worst, a young American, Alex Pike—one of the wealthy Pikes of Pittsburgh—vaults over the walls into the princess's quarters. When the guards surprise him and try to arrest him, he floors them and returns as he came—over the garden wall—but not before falling head over ears in love with the princess.

Act 2 shifts to the Chevy Chase Golf Club, in Washington, D.C. The prince has decided that his daughter must marry a German, Count Louis von Schloppenhauer. She agrees, considering herself slighted by Alex Pike, who has paid more attention to other girls in her presence. Act 3 then takes place in a ballroom in Washington, D.C., where the princess dances with various individuals, and eventually with Pike, at which a reconciliation takes place. Her father and the count object, the former because the American suitor has no titles. This is overcome when Pike advises that he is an exalted ruler of the Elks, grand master of the Freemasons, knight commander of the Knights of Pythian, and various other things. The count consoles himself with the younger princess.

After the premiere, the *Buffalo Express* dutifully informed its readers that the music was entrancing, the book clever, the heroine irresistible. At the Chicago first night the librettist and original book author were in the audience, but Percy Hammond's review in the *Chicago Daily Tribune* makes it clear that the composer was not:

> The audience approved so heartily of *The Slim Princess* at the Studebaker last evening that Miss Janis, the star, was inspired to rush around behind the scenes at the end of the second act and search for Mr Blossom, the librettist. Mr Blossom subsequently appeared with the characteristic reluctance of the man who writes the play, and graciously bestowed the credit for the evening's happiness upon others, including Mr Ade. In fact, he was of the impression that it was Mr Ade who should voice the gratitude of those concerned, since it was in Mr Ade's fantastic story that he discovered the germ of the entertainment. Whereupon a wit in the fifth row, with suspicious spontaneity, exclaimed, "Let George do it!" And so George, a modest violet beneath a mossy stone, emerged from the obscurity of a seat in the orchestra and uttered a few shrinking words of disclaimer, leaving *The Slim Princess* a waif upon our threshold to all intents and purposes. . . .
>
> *The Slim Princess* is a smart little comic opera, written with a sense of humor, its sentimental aspects mitigated by soft satire, a gay kidding of musical romance upon the stage, eliminating the purple tights, the rope ladder, and the other stigmata of the usual play with tunes.

A feature of the show was a chorus that, for dramatic reasons, was not uniformly sleek. The review noted, "The chorus of slim princesses and beef baronesses has the Dillingham 'class'—that is, it is smart and well behaved, and even the ladies of burlesque bulk are graceful and of reasonable symmetry." The review also made clear that the highlight of Miss Janis's performance was the song "O What a Chance to Take" in the last act. This "permits her to imitate Miss Barrymore, Miss Held, Mr Sam Bernard, and Mr Eddie Foy, the last in the uncanny fashion which haunts one through everything that she does!" Further claims on the audience's attention came from the comic antics of Sam Collins as the Turkish male chaperon who, "red fezzed but otherwise occidental, sings, dances, and does funny neck falls." There was further dancing from Harry Pilcer as a Pennsylvania millionaire, but the reviewer warned, "In one of his dances with Miss Janis Mr Pilcer leers, and he should be told not to do this, for when he leers he looks like a cobra."

Only then did the critic get round to the composer's contribution, writing, "Miss Frary and Carl Haydn assume the responsibilities of Mr Stuart's score, which it must be said, seems unable to emerge from the rut of his *Florodora* sextette achievement. At least three of the numbers of the *Slim Princess* take one back to that interesting number. One of his melodies, however, has had no recognizable precedent, and as sung by Mr Haydn and danced by Miss Janis and Mr Pilcer is quite Merry Widowy."

Also viewing the show in Chicago, the *New York Dramatic Mirror* was enthusiastic. It wrote, "The New Elsie Janis play is a real comic opera or opera comique. It merits all the praise which has been bestowed on it. . . . The music is both musicianly and singable." By the time the show moved to the Chestnut Street Opera House, Philadelphia, for a three-week run opening on October 31, however, the *Dramatic Mirror* had seemingly shifted its stance, writing, "The piece was well received but it was Elsie Janis who carried it to such success as it achieved. There is some tuneful music in *The Slim Princess*, a little real comedy, but it was the imitations of leading actors and actresses of today by Miss Janis which won the audience."

By now a song for four boy caddies was attracting attention and, according to the *Philadelphia Inquirer*, being "encored time and again." However, changes were now made to the cast. By the time it opened at the Nixon Theater, Pittsburgh, for the week beginning November 28, Mortimer Weldon had replaced George Parsons as Pike, and basso profundo Joseph C. Miron had taken over from William Pruette. Harry Pilcer had gone too. The show opened at the Nixon on a Monday night (football night) to a rowdy but friendly reception. Charles M. Bregg in the *Pittsburgh Gazette Times* welcomed Elsie Janis, but was less tolerant about the piece as a whole:

> Leslie Stuart, who wrote *Florodora* and that famous sextette, does not appear to be able to travel very far away from his first love. There are several pretty songs, but none that fasten themselves in the mind. Mr Stuart has set his sextette to the accompaniment of golf sticks this time, but the old air has its familiar "ear" marks. . . . *The Slim Princess*, a musical play, gets by without the aid of vocalists. This is one of the tricks of modern musical comedy. Joe Miron has a big fine bass voice, but he has practically no use for it, being given but one song. The star cannot sing at all and, like one of the leading male characters, had to

take her songs largely in a conversational tone. Julia Frary also showed symptoms of a voice in the one song allotted her. Carl Haydn, the tenor, who, by every tradition of comic opera, ought to warble the love ditties, sang but one song, in a voice that has good qualities in the making. Upon Sam Collins the fun depended, and he got away with it in great style. Mortimer Weldon is a clean-cut young actor—and there you are. A musical play with one singer.

Subsequent stops included the Grand Theatre, Cincinnati, beginning December 4, moving on to Detroit on December 12, and final pre–New York performances in Hartford, Connecticut, on December 28 and 29. During that time the show was overhauled even more radically. By the time it reached New York the romantic lead was played by Wallace McCutcheon, and the rival suitor was now a bogus Italian count, Luigi Tincagni Tomasso, played by Charles Judels. As Tod Norcross and Lutie Longstreet, the dancing partnership of Harry Pilcer and Grace King had given way to Charles King and Elizabeth Brice. Ralph Nairn remained in the supporting role of the Honorable Crawley Plumston, and Carl Haydn was also still there, but was now providing an oriental contribution as Hamdi Pasha rather than Count Louis von Schloppenhauer. That German name had been appropriated for popular "Dutch" dialect comedian Joseph Cawthorn, brought in as costar as the princesses' German tutor in place of Sam Collins. Cawthorn's wife Queenie Vassar also came in as Madame Saidis, leaving the two leading ladies as the only leading players to retain the same roles throughout.

Presented by Charles Dillingham at the Globe Theatre, New York, on 2 January 1911.

THE SLIM PRINCESS

A Musical Comedy in 3 Acts.

Book and lyrics by Henry Blossom.

Adapted from the story of the same name by George Ade.

Music by Leslie Stuart.

Hamdi Pasha, Commander of the Imperial Guards			Mr. Carl Haydn
Bokhara	|	Guards |	Mr. Neil Walton.
Baluchistan	|	|	Mr. Arthur J. Engel.
Prince Selim Malagaski, Governor-General of Borivenia			Mr. Joseph C. Miron.

Herr Louis von Schloppenhauer, tutor of the Princess Kalora	Mr Joseph Cawthorn.
The Hon. Crawley Plumston, British Consul in Borivenia	Mr. Ralph Nairn.
Count Luigi Tincagni Tomasso	Mr. Charles Judels.
Alex Pike, of Bessemer, Pennsylvania	Mr. Wallace McCutcheon.
"Tod" Norcross, of Pittsburgh, Pennsylvania	Mr. Charles King.
Harry Romaine	Mr. Eugene Revere.
Tom Golding	Mr. Sam Burbank.
Lucas, head waiter at the Golf Club	Mr. Albert Stewart.
Princess Jeneka, Kalora's younger sister	Miss Julia Frary.
Madame Saidis	Miss Queenie Vassar.
A Visitor	Miss Harriet Sterling.
The Hon. Mrs. Plumston	Miss Kate Wingfield.
Lutie Longstreet	Miss Elizabeth Brice.
Princess Kalora	Miss Elsie Janis.

Plump Ladies of the Court of Borivenia: Miss Henriette Pouts, Miss Pauline Hathaway, Miss Josephine Lachmar, Miss Jane Bliss.

Caddies: Master Albert Lamson, Master Fred Pirkuritz, Master Max Brown, Master Fred Gould.

Other Characters: Miss Mona Trieste, Miss Alus Belga, Miss Elise Steele, Miss Leila Benton, Miss Peggy Preston, Miss Estelle Perry, Miss May Fields, Miss Alice Keyes, Miss Josephine Harriman, Miss Dolly Germaine, Miss Margaret St. Clair, Miss Edna Bates, Miss Babe Beaubien, Miss Josephine Kernell, Miss Bessie Holbrook, Miss Helen Falconer, Mr. Armstrong, Mr. Burbank, Mr. Miller, Mr. Johnson, Mr. Hinds, Mr. Rose, Mr. Way, Mr. Sullivan, Mr. Schulz.

Act I.—Gardens of Prince Selim's Palace Grounds in Borivenia. Present time.

Act II.—Chevy Chase Golf Club, near Washington, D.C. Six weeks later.

Act III.—Ante-room in the Plumstons' Home, Washington, D.C. Evening of the same day.

Staged by Austen Hurgon. Costumes by Percy Anderson.

After the wholesale bloodletting, the New York reception proved favorable. The *New York Times* commented that the audience took Miss Janis to their hearts, and that most of the songs were good. The *New York*

Elsie Janis and Joseph Cawthorn in *The Slim Princess* (Harvard Theatre Collection, Houghton Library)

Herald went further, headlining a new musical play that was "crowded with good music, novelties and the pretty star's doings." It praised "songs, dances and novelties in profusion; scores of pretty girls who can dance and sing, chorus men who look like human beings, a bewildering array of costumes that made the feminine portion of the audience say 'Oh!' . . . , comedy that is worth while, whole scenes of action worth a laugh. . . . *The Slim Princess* is slim in name only. In entertainment she is stout and has a double chin." The paper reported that Miss Janis took twenty-six curtain calls.

The show settled in at the Globe as a genuine success. Six weeks into the run, journalist and future pioneer aviator Harriet Quimby added her own recommendation in *Leslie's Illustrated Weekly*: "If you happen to feel dull and out of sorts some evening, get a couple of tickets for the Globe Theater and see the three-hundred pound chorus girls dance. If you are not forced to genuine laughter by this weighty quartet, consider your case hopeless."[47]

The published score of *The Slim Princess* does not assign songs to characters, which in view of the wholesale plot changes is perhaps not surprising. The music is attributed entirely to Stuart, apart from a single vaudeville number, "My Yankee Doodle Girl," composed by John Golden and sung by the princess and her Pennsylvania suitor just before the act 1 finale. However, Edward N. Waters revealed a curious thing about the score in his biography of Victor Herbert. He states that the collection of Herbert's autographs in the U.S. Library of Congress includes an elaborate second act finale for *The Slim Princess* in Herbert's own hand. Waters describes this finale as "full of dramatic effects in the orchestra, snatches of recitative and sung dialogue, short dance episodes, a choral ending, and a heavy flourish by the orchestra alone." He adds, "At the . . . entrance into the choral ending . . . the music swings into an arrangement of the refrain of Golden's 'My Yankee Doodle Girl,' quite spirited enough to bring down the curtain with bursts of applause."[75] Golden himself explained that Herbert incorporated the song into the finale at Dillingham's request.[75]

In Stuart's absence, it is perhaps not surprising that such assistance should be needed. Though individual numbers could be moved around between characters and performers, changes on the scale of those in *The Slim Princess* would almost certainly have needed amendment of an elaborate act 2 finale. Stuart would surely have been happier to have Victor Herbert do the work than anyone else. Herbert may have done it for a fee or, perhaps, out of friendship for Stuart. It may not be without significance that the young Victor Herbert had been among the composers featured in Leslie Stuart's Manchester concerts, his "Andante" and "Serenade" being performed on November 26, 1892, by the young Belgian cellist Jean Gérardy.

Although the score was still very largely Stuart's when the show opened in New York, it seems to have been treated to the inevitable insertions thereafter. The only two numbers from the show recorded during the New York run were "Let Me Stay and Live in Dixieland" and

"That's Ever-Loving Love," written and sung by Charles King and Elizabeth Brice. Later, when Janis and Cawthorn toured the show with some changes of cast, Janis recorded a further two pieces supposedly from it and credited to herself: "When Angelo Plays the 'Cello" and "Fo' de Lawd's Sake, Play a Waltz."[48] One can only imagine what Leslie Stuart might have thought about that. Yet, even though *The Slim Princess* never made it to European stages, it managed a creditable three-month Broadway run and continued to run successfully in the United States for many months afterward.

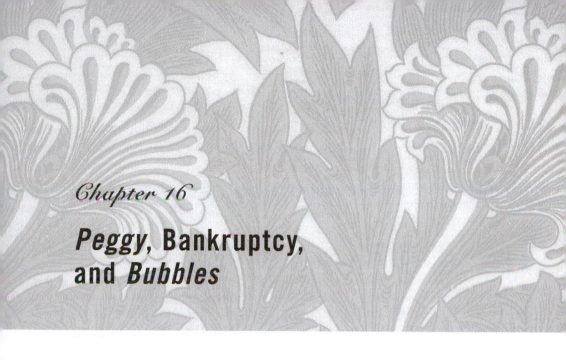

Chapter 16

Peggy, Bankruptcy, and *Bubbles*

By 1910, Leslie Stuart's lavish living had left him heavily in debt, and his recourse to moneylenders meant that his debts were increasing fast. He seems initially to have sublet part of his home in West Hampstead and to have sold it by 1910 in favor of a town house at 21 Russell Square, London. However, he still retained an impressive country residence, The Elms, at Crawley, between London and Brighton, where he continued to demonstrate outward signs of prosperity. At one dinner party at the Elms, in October 1910, his guests included two London members of the world-famous art dealing Duveen Brothers company, together with the novelist Horace Annesley Vachell. That very week two representatives from Duveen Brothers' New York operation were arrested for supposedly defrauding the U.S. Customs by falsely undervaluing a painting. According to Stuart, Vachell used the explanation given by the two guests after dinner that night as the basis of his 1915 play and novel *Quinneys'*.[62]

The artistic result of Stuart's precarious financial position was that, instead of producing one work every two years or so, he achieved three premieres within just fourteen months. The third took him back to George Edwardes and the Gaiety Theatre. After *Havana*, Edwardes had reverted to his tried-and-tested formula, producing *Our Miss Gibbs* with a score by Ivan Caryll and Lionel Monckton and a company headed by Gertie Millar, George Grossmith Jr., and Edmund Payne. It proved to be the best remembered of the Caryll and Monckton series, but also the last. Caryll went off to America, and Monckton to other things: *The Arcadians,* for Robert Courtneidge at the Shaftesbury Theatre, and (with Gertie Millar—Mrs. Lionel Monckton) *The Quaker Girl* for Edwardes at the Adelphi Theatre.

With *Havana,* Stuart had license to produce something radically different from the Gaiety's norm. Now he sought to produce a more traditional Gaiety mix. In September 1910, the *Era* announced a musical adaptation of a French play by Léon Xanrof and Gaston Guérin called *L'Amorçage* (The Bait). Xanrof, a highly successful literary figure of Bohemian Paris, was really named Léon Fourneau, his nom de plume being the reverse of Fornax, the Latin form of his surname. The announcement in the *Era* promised a show in the Gaiety's traditional two acts: one in the vestibule of a well-known London hotel, the other on the seafront at Dieppe. Eventually, act 1 of *Peggy* was set in a lounge at the "New Hotel, London" and act 2 on "the plage at Friville," but that earlier announcement shows what the show's creators had in mind. Alongside Gaiety veterans George Grossmith and principal comedian Edmund Payne, Edwardes brought in glamorous young Phyllis Dare to replace Gertie Millar as leading lady.

Produced by Mr. George Edwardes at the Gaiety Theatre, London, 4 March 1911.

PEGGY

A New Musical Play in Two Acts.

Book by George Grossmith, Junr., founded on Xanrof and Guérin's *L'Amorçage.*

Lyrics by C. H. Bovill.   Music by Leslie Stuart.

Auberon Blow (A Street Hawker)	Mr. Geo. Grossmith, Jnr.
Hon. James Bendoyle, M.P., M. F. H.	Mr. Robert Hale.
Montagu Bartle (of Buenos Ayres)	Mr. Herbert Jarman.
Aristide Picot (Maire of Friville)	Mr. Arthur Hatherton.

Phonso (Mr. Umble's Assistant)	Mr. Ernest Mahar.
Marquis of Didsbury	Mr. Guy Struthers.
Emil (Manager of New Hotel)	Mr. Harry B. Burcher.

AND

Mr. Albert Umbles (Hairdresser at the New Hotel)	Mr. Edmund Payne.

Polly Polino (of the Vaudeville Stage)	Miss Gabrielle Ray.
Doris Bartle	Miss Olive May.
Diamond (Barmaid at the New Hotel)	Miss Enid Leslie.
Lady Florence Alister	Miss Nancy More.
Mrs. Ware-Wills	Miss Ruby Kennedy.
Miss Vooch (of Cincinatti)	Miss Madge Melbourne.
Jinnie	Miss Dorothy Selbourne.
Ethel		Miss Blanche Stocker.
Cecilie	(Manicure Girls)	Miss Marie Mitchell.
Rosie		Miss Gertrude Thornton.
Maud		Miss Connie Stuart.
Nini (Bathing Woman)	Miss Gladys Ffolliot.
Jeannette (Fleuriste)	Mdlle. S. Bourcard.

AND

Peggy Barrison (Manicurist at the New Hotel)	Miss Phyllis Dare.
ACT I.—Lounge at the New Hotel, London	(Joseph Harker.)
ACT II.—The Plage at Friville	(Joseph Harker.)

Stage Director: Mr. Edward Royce.

Musical Director: M. Leopold Wenzel.

The story concerns Peggy Barrison, a pretty manicurist at London's New Hotel, who is engaged to marry Albert Umbles, the hotel's hairdresser. She doesn't quite know why she's marrying him, except that her mother has told her it is the right thing to do. She could certainly find herself someone wealthier, because almost every young man whose nails she trims tends to fall for her charms. One such is the Honorable James Bendoyle, a sporting member of Parliament and man about town, who has tried in vain to win her. Bendoyle chances to meet his old friend Auberon Blow, who is down on his luck and is forced to scrape a living as a street vendor. Bendoyle offers Auberon money to help him win Peggy. Their plan revolves around the fact that Umbles has a millionaire uncle, Montague Bartle, who is expected to arrive at any moment from Buenos Aires. Bendoyle offers to provide Blow with funds to enable the latter to impersonate the uncle and shower Peggy with gifts. He will then cut off the supply of favors, so that Peggy will turn to Bendoyle and his money instead.

By the time the company migrates to the *plage* at Friville, Blow is enjoying himself too much with Peggy to care about the reason for his affluence. Moreover, Umbles has lost his heart to a pretty young vaudeville artiste, Polly Polino. Things go even more awry with the arrival of the real uncle and his charming daughter Doris Bartle. Fortunately, Bendoyle promptly falls for her, leaving everyone to pair off happily.

Edwardes chose to delay the first night until after the 1911 general election, an event that traditionally put a damper on theater attendance. The wait doubtless added to the sense of anticipation that, according to the *Times*, was readily apparent in the opening night audience. "Before the play began the house throbbed with the excitement proper to a Gaiety first night," the review read. "Continual bursts of clapping broke out as some popular Gaiety favourite made her way to her place in boxes or stalls or Mr. Leslie Stuart appeared at the conductor's desk."

The *Stage* confirmed its pleasure that the traditional Gaiety formula was intact, noting, "*Peggy* ... contains all the ingredients that go to the making of a genuine up-to-date Gaiety success.... Mr Edwardes has once again provided an Aladdin's feast of dainty songs and dances, together with wit and general sparkle, set amid beautiful surroundings...."

The *Stage* also considered the story "a distinctly good one," though the *Times* man reckoned the high level of enthusiasm in the first act was not sustained. He wrote, "In the second [act] it cooled slightly, but perceptibly, and when the curtain finally fell, after being raised several times, not all the hearty applause of boxes and stalls and dress circle could drown the discordant sounds that came from the upper regions. And the performers as they bowed their way along the footlights were obviously affected by the signs of disapproval. Even Mr. Edmund Payne looked almost dejected, and neither Mr. Edwardes nor Mr. Grossmith responded to the calls for a speech."

Fête at Friville in act 2 of *Peggy*, London (author's collection)

The *Times* reviewer felt that Grossmith's production was sadly lacking in humor. Moreover, the plums he had given Edmund Payne were not very good ones: "It is not very witty to sing that when you were at Eton you coxed the eleven and kept wicket for the eight, nor to say, as an answer to a riddle, that the fruit on a penny is a date." He also wondered why the setting had moved to France for the second act, although he did appreciate "as brilliant a show of beautiful dresses and pretty faces as even Mr Edwardes has ever put upon the stage." Even he conceded that, "with the exception of the rude people up above, the audience really seemed to be hugely entertained."

As for the music, the *Times* found it "not very catchy, but always bright." On the other hand, *The Stage* considered that "Leslie Stuart has provided some of his most melodious and characteristic music." The *Era* agreed that *Peggy* "contains some of the most dainty melodies that Mr Leslie Stuart has ever written," associating this with praise for the lyrics of C. H. Bovill, which "have all the desirable 'lilt' and neatness of phrase." The *Sunday Times* was even more enthusiastic: "It is a long time since I have heard Mr Stuart in a more spontaneous vein."

Reviews singled out two songs for particular mention. The first was Peggy's enthusiastically encored act 2 waltz, "Ladies, Beware! (When the Lights Are Low)." Considered by the *Observer* to be "a musical gem," this was sung to a group of girls reclining on their chaises longues on the Friville sands. It had a violin obbligato played by Walter de Groot, who later became a celebrated orchestra leader at London's Piccadilly Hotel. On the little finger of his right hand he wore a big diamond ring that sparkled as he played. The second outstanding song was Doris Bartle's act 1 song "The Lass with the Lasso," during which she lassooed various gentlemen of the company.

Among other songs that attracted attention was a waltz serenade, "Juliet and Romeo," for Peggy and Albert Umbles in a mock balcony scene in act 1 that ended up with each catching cold from the night air. Also in act 1 was a lively trio, "Uncle Monty," for Peggy, Auberon Blow, and Albert Umbles. Arousing particular mention from act 2 was "Go Away, Little Girl" for Polly Polino, which the *Weekly Dispatch* considered "a real gem." A duet, "Pierrot and Pierrette," featured Umbles as a sailor dummy, burlesquing a current music-hall turn. The beach setting also provided the opportunity for a Bathing Trio ("Three Little Pebbles on the Beach"), showing off the talents of not only "three girls ... attired in most becoming bathing costumes" but also choreographer Edward Royce.

The opening chorus was in typically more ambitious Stuart vein than was usual for the Gaiety. Thereafter Leslie Stuart's fingerprints were less readily apparent than usual, perhaps due to the need to turn out material speedily. The *Sunday Times* reference to the score's spontaneity is apt, and it is also rather easier for the average pianist to play than was usual for Stuart's music. Although "The Lass with the Lasso" stands out as the act 1 showstopper, it is the reflective slow waltz "Ladies Beware!" in act 2 that is the real gem. It is far from surprising to find Stuart as joint lyricist, with Bovill, for this number, providing further evidence of how much more perfect a musical statement emerged when both words and music were conceived together.

Peggy produced a more extensive selection of original cast recordings than for any of Stuart's shows after *Florodora*. In March 1911, with the show little more than two weeks old, Phyllis Dare recorded "Ladies, Beware!" and, with George Grossmith, the duet "You're the One Man I'm Looking For." Grossmith recorded, as a solo, the sextet "Be a Lady All the Time" and, with Edmund Payne, their duet "I Beg Your Pardon." Olive May set down "The Lass with the Lasso" and, in August, Robert Hale added "Whistle and the Girls Come Round." In May, following the

Andrew Lamb

example of Victor in the United States, HMV's Light Opera Company recorded two sides of "Vocal Gems."[53]

Peggy ran happily through the summer, with the customary alterations to keep it fresh. However, interest began to sag rather earlier than usual for Gaiety shows, and Edwardes came up with the drastic remedy of writing in a new part for the old Gaiety Theatre favorite, Connie Ediss. The significant thing about her two solos is that they were composed by Philip Braham (future composer of "Limehouse Blues") and not by Stuart, who in normal circumstances would have gone to considerable lengths to avoid interpolations by others. Moreover, although Stuart still had one work to write for the Gaiety under his three-show contract, Edwardes announced that Paul Rubens would compose the next show. It was seemingly in relation to Stuart's critical financial position that, according to his later testimony, pressure was brought upon him by another person to induce him to cancel the contract. Who this other person was is unclear.

While awaiting a New York production of *Peggy*, Stuart apparently also had a song performed on Broadway in one of the Shubert shows. *The Kiss Waltz* was an adaptation of a Viennese operetta composed by C. M. Ziehrer, with supplementary numbers nominally by Jerome Kern. However, Stuart was credited with a number called "Belle of Vienne," sung by Adele Rowland as the first number after the opening chorus. Produced at the Casino Theatre on September 18, 1911, *The Kiss Waltz* was rapturously received by the first night audience and ran for eleven weeks. Then followed *Peggy* in a production by the faithful Thomas W. Ryley. Though based on the original Gaiety production, the New York production varied in numerous ways, most obviously in that Albert Umbles now became Cecil Custard Caruthers.

Produced by Mr. Thomas W. Ryley at the Casino Theatre, New York, 7 December 1911.

PEGGY

A Musical Play in Two Acts.

Book by George Grossmith, Jr., founded on *L'Amorçage* by Léon Xanrof and Gaston Guérin

Lyrics by C. H. Bovill.   Music by Leslie Stuart.

Captain James Bendoyle   Mr. Farren Soutar.

Auberon Blow, a street hawker   Mr. Charles Brown.

Cecil Custard Caruthers	Mr. Harry Fisher.
'Phonso, barber at the New Hotel	Mr. Jules Charmettes.
Emil, manager of the New Hotel	Mr. A. Hylton Allen.
Montague Bartle of Buenos Aires	Mr. John W. Ransome.
Man about town	
Official at the Casino	Mr. Lew Quinn.
Marquis of Didsbury	Mr. Tom Dingle.
Aristide Picot, collector	Mr. Jules Charmettes.
Rastus	Mr. Tom Dingle.
Lady Snoop	Miss Alva York.
Peggy Barrison, manicurist at the New Hotel	Miss Renee Kelly.
Polly Polino, the American dancer	Miss Louise Alexander.
Doris Bartle	Miss Vida Whitmore.
Diamond, barmaid of the New Hotel	Miss Esther Bissett.
Lady Frederick	Miss Rose Winter.
Miss Vooch, of Cincinatti	Miss Margaret Rutledge.
Dolly	Miss Elise Hamilton.
Ruby — manicure girls	Miss Maud Brown.
Nini, bathing woman	
Jeannette, fleuriste	Miss Blanche West.

Society Ladies: Miss Isabel Congleton, Miss Betty Adams, Miss Jeannette Clark, Miss Adelaide Croker, Miss Grace Williams, Miss Ruth Cardon, Miss Josephine Angela, Miss Janet Marran, Miss Kelcey Staunton, Miss Madeleine Ottie.

Manicure girls: Miss Flora Ottie, Miss Anna Watson, Miss Billie Hunter, Miss Olive Carr, Miss Minerva Walton, Miss Marguerite Dana.

English Pony Ballet: Miss Ada Robertson, Miss Dorothy Marlow, Miss Louise Hawman, Miss Seppie McNeil, Miss Nellie Wilkie, Miss Eva Marlow.

Guests: Miss Gertrude Thurston, Miss Jane Arrol, Miss Clara Lloyd, Miss Marie Garland, Miss Katharine Grant, Miss Faith Powell, Miss Eleanore Gray, Miss May Thompson, Miss Elsie Weller, Miss Aimee Montague, Miss Joan Sherman, Mr. Arthur Wells, Mr. Oliver Van Der Burgh, Mr. Frank Caruso, Mr. Byron Bell, Mr. Arthur J. Richter, Mr. William J. de Forest.

Officers: Mr. W. M. Benedict, Mr. Waldo Heinemann, Mr. Paul Riblet, Mr. Billy Faye, Mr. Angelo Caruso, Mr. Charles Gurney.

Waiters: Mr. Genarro Marino, Mr. Joseph Luna, Mr. Paul Profatta.

ACT I.—Lounge at the New Hotel, London.

ACT II.—The Plage at Trouville.

Stage Director: Mr. Ned Wayburn.   Musical Director: Silvio Hein.

Scenery: Ernest Albert, Lee Lash Studio.

This time the New York press did not mince words. "Queer mixture" was the headline in the *New York Times*. "Pretty, but that is about all" said the *New York Herald*. After praising "Leslie Stuart's very agreeable music," the *New York Times* laid its cards on the table:

> Here the familiar attempt of transforming what Americans do not want to what the producers insist that they do want has resulted in about as curious a jumble as has been seen in many a long day. . . .
>
> One of the most remarkable features of the performance resided in the fact that here we had a musical comedy in which the prima donna does not sing—mind, it is not said that she cannot sing. Prima donnas of that sort are not rare. But Miss Renee Kelly, late of the Drama Players and recruited at the eleventh hour, didn't even try. And so Peggy's best song was sung by Vida Whitmore, with Peggy herself held in the arms of her lover up-stage, where the light from the calcium shone. Miss Kelly was pretty to look at and agreeable to hear when she was speaking, and, after all, she will at least enjoy an unusual advantage as regards prima donnas as she will not have to read any bad notices of her singing.

The paper further exemplified its theme of a queer mixture by citing "the presence of M. Maurice, a really remarkable turkey-trotter and tango-er, who, with his dancing partner, Mlle. D'Arville, has been summoned from a restaurant cabaret where he has been the bright particular idol for some time." Even Maurice's turkey-trotting could not rescue a show from such an unenthusiastic reception; it limped into the new year, before closing on January 6, 1912 after only thirty-seven performances. By then the London show, too, had ended after a run of 280 performances that was good for most shows but disappointing for the Gaiety.

It was the last straw for Stuart's finances. In September 1911 his daughter May had become the the first of his children to marry. May had made her debut on the London musical stage in 1909 as Beauty in Frederic Norton's children's musical *Pinkie and the Fairies*, and her husband was also from the theater. He was Cecil de Bensaude, who as Cecil Cameron had appeared in *The Belle of Mayfair* and *Havana,* and was the son of Violet Cameron, who had played in *The School Girl.* At her wedding, May gave The Elms in Crawley as her home address, but that impressive residence also soon went as her father's financial position reached crisis point.

On February 3, 1912, Stuart signed a contract with the Shuberts in New York for a comic opera of at least ten numbers to a scenario already submitted.[54] However, on June 13, 1912, a receiving order was made on the petition of a firm of moneylenders. At the first meeting of creditors on June 28, 1912, the official receiver told a sorry story of financial mismanagement, reported thus in the following day's *Times*:

> His royalties were from 3 to 5 per cent on the gross receipts, and until 1908, although he was sometimes pressed for money, all his royalties were free. About that time he gave a charge for £3,300 to moneylenders over 60 per cent of his income from all sources, and a charge over a further 20 per cent of his income to secure a bank overdraft of £2,000. Other bankers afterwards paid off these sums and took a transfer of the charges.
>
> The remaining 20 per cent of his income was insufficient to meet his household and personal expenditure, and in 1909 or 1910 he obtained £2,000 further on his agreeing to pay £3,000 representing a one-half share of the revenue of *Captain Kidd.* As additional security he had to charge 50 per cent of his uncharged interests and 50 per cent of the revenue from future compositions and productions. After allowing for agents' charges, this left him with only 7½ per cent of his revenues. A receiver of his income was subsequently appointed, and since then he had received neither income nor account. . . .
>
> [He] estimated his liabilities at £5,000, arising primarily from his having lived above his income in certain years, but more particularly from heavy interest and bonuses paid for the accommodation of money, and from the agreements for the repayment of money borrowed. . . .
>
> [His] assets comprised the lease of premises in Russell-square, valued at £700; the equity of redemption of his interests in a large number of musical works, which he estimated to produce a surplus of £1,000; and an operetta called *The Final Waltz*, not yet published. . . .

[He] had the definite offer of contracts to write operas for Mr George Edwardes and Mr. Charles Frohman, and a sketch for Mr Stoll, which should bring him in from £8,000 to £10,000. His earnings had never been less than £4,000 or £5,000 a year, but, of course, it was difficult for him to settle down and write music while he was being pressed by creditors.

Of the works and contracts mentioned, *The Final Waltz* was perhaps the work for the Shuberts, the Frohman work probably *Nina*. The sketch for Stoll would presumably have been for the Coliseum.

The meeting was adjourned for the submission of a scheme of arrangement; but early projections proved wildly optimistic. On July 23, 1912, a statement of affairs showed liabilities of £12,075 5s 7d—equivalent to over £500,000 in year-2000 terms. Assets other than from interests in musical plays (whose value Stuart was unable to estimate) amounted to little more than an eighth of that.

Subsequent meetings revealed details of Stuart's income over the years, figures that need to be multiplied over forty times to arrive at year-2000 equivalents. Between 1885 and 1896 he earned about £10 a week by teaching and composing church music and songs. *Florodora* had brought in from first to last about £20,000, while his other stage works apart from *Captain Kidd* had produced on average £3,400. "The Soldiers of the Queen" had brought in £2,600, though he reckoned his loss of royalties as a result of music piracy to be about £20,000, in addition to many hundreds of pounds paid out in efforts to suppress music piracy. His average income during the thirteen years before the receiving order was £3,300 per annum. His retainer from Chappell and Company to write exclusively for them had been worth £800 per annum until January 1911, when it was reduced to £400 with a bonus of £500 and royalties for every opera he wrote. Since 1910, he had practically lived on borrowed money, to secure the payment of which he had charged 90 percent of the revenue from his royalties. During that period, he had been pursued by creditors and had nine bankruptcy petitions presented against him.

The formal bankruptcy proceedings were not altogether solemn. At a meeting of creditors on September 26, 1912, Stuart complained that he had been unfairly treated by the press, and that the unnecessary publication of his arrangements with certain managers had caused contracts he was making to be canceled. The official receiver replied that he had his remedy. To laughter, Stuart asked whether the court would finance him in an action for libel.

In October 1912, a scheme of arrangement was put forward involving the payment of 7s 6d for the pound (37.5 percent). The official receiver advised that it seemed to offer greater benefits to the creditors than if the estate were administered in bankruptcy, and it was therefore agreed. However, in January 1913, counsel advised that he would not be in a position to carry out his proposal and withdrew the application for its approval. Leslie Stuart was thereupon declared bankrupt.

The action against Seymour Hicks over *Captain Kidd* was still outstanding, and Hicks now took action to get it removed. On February 3, 1913, he took out a summons for an order that the trustee in bankruptcy should within one month obtain and serve an order to carry on and prosecute the proceedings in the action, and that in default thereof the action should stand dismissed. The result was a farce perhaps better than *Captain Kidd* had ever been. The trustee in bankruptcy obtained agreement to proceed with the case but failed to take the appropriate steps in time. The master of the rolls exercised his discretion to refuse an application for an extension of the time, and the case was therefore laid to rest.

By now it was not only Leslie Stuart's financial position that was in disarray but also his personal life. During the years of prosperity his wife Kitty had enjoyed the high life; but when things began to turn sour she was driven wild by her husband's contempt for bank accounts and savings.[67] Alcohol, too, was a problem, and Stuart was reputed to have been consuming a bottle of whisky before breakfast. It was thanks to Father Bernard Vaughan that he was persuaded to sign the pledge and abstain from alcohol.[67] A letter to her mother from the youngest daughter Lola, away at school, had exemplified the family's hopes. After commenting on prospects of letting The Elms, she went on, "Isn't it ripping about the temperance business? I am delighted. I am sure you have been worried about this bankruptcy business. Don't you think Father will ever drink any more? I do hope not."[67] For a time, Leslie Stuart drank only ginger beer. Then, alas, someone spiked his drink, and the problems began anew.

Stuart also had a reputation as a ladies' man. According to one family anecdote, Kitty attended a first night and saw one of the girls on stage wearing a brooch the same as her husband had bought her for her last birthday. During the interval she went backstage and snatched it off.[67]

Stuart's bankruptcy made it necessary for him to earn money when not only was his personal life in tatters but musical fashions were changing with the advent of ragtime from America. Moreover, his personal pride and refusal to bow to his reduced circumstances meant he burned his boats with many impresarios. Hilda Brighten, née Cohen, noted, "He was difficult to handle, and towards the end of his career, when asked to add some numbers to a musical play (Father had suggested to George Edwardes that Leslie Stuart was being lost to the public, that he could do with the money, and would add prestige to the production) Leslie's answer was, 'I write the whole opera or nothing. Leslie Stuart does not interpolate.'"[10]

Stuart's efforts to put his name back before the public resulted in periodic sightings on both sides of the Atlantic thereafter, without him ever achieving any further major success. On January 12, 1914, for instance, he had a song, "Whistle," in a show at New York's Globe Theatre called *The Queen of the Movies*, an English-language version of a German musical with music by Jean Gilbert. However, the show's producer was Thomas W. Ryley, who may simply have been trying to extract extra value from "Whistle and the Girls Come Round" from *Peggy*.

Later that year, too, Stuart also reappeared as composer of a complete theatrical work. However, its scale, its performers, and its place of production were a far cry from what he was used to. One-act theatrical revues, forming just a part of an evening's entertainment and incorporating snappy songs and topical references, were very much in vogue, and his circumstances forced him to conform. Curiously, Lauri Wylie, the author and driving force behind this and similar touring revues, was—like Stuart himself—from Southport. Born Morris Lawrence Samuelson Metzenberg, the son of a Jewish refugee from Prussia who had become a tobacconist in the Lancashire resort, Wylie entered the theater in the footsteps of his elder brother Julian.[28]

Presented by Messrs. S. G. Chamberlain and J. L. Davies

at the New Theatre, Northampton, on 27 April 1914

BUBBLES

A New and Original Burlesque in Six Puffs.

Written by Lauri Wylie and Alfred Parker. Lyrics by George Arthurs.

Music Composed and Arranged by Leslie Stuart.

	Bubbles blown by	
	HORACE LANE	
Oliver Round	Mowbray Macks	Ruth Trafford
Harold Loscombe	Ethel Darsley	The Kentucky Trio
Will Bishop, jun.	Felice Forvar	Ella Kay and
	VIOLET LLOYD	
1st Puff	The Eugenic City	Scenery by Bruce Smith
2nd Puff	A Roadside	" " E. H. Ryan
3rd Puff	A Fortress	" " Bruce Smith
4th Puff	John Bull's Bedroom	" " E. H. Ryan
5th Puff	Bubbles	" " Bruce Smith
6th Puff	The Garland Club	" " E. H. Ryan
Conductor: Phil Saxe.		Stage Direction: A. E. Dodson.

The *Stage* declared the show "mightily entertaining." There was "no pretence at coherent plot," but the show lived up to its title in that "as light illuminates the soapy product of the bubble-maker's pipe, so are the scenic settings and dresses kaleidoscopically beautiful and effective." The first scene depicted young inhabitants of a eugenic garden city, with all the handsome young inhabitants wearing the picturesque costume of Parisian art students. Much fun was derived from a baby show. The second scene's roadside setting offered a gigantic property motor car and a comic routine tracing devious routes for a lost motorist.

In the third scene the whole company appeared as toy soldiers in a typical Leslie Stuart concerted number. Considered by the *Stage* the best scene was the political skit in John Bull's bedroom. Bull is discovered in bed, with his various medical advisers—the Parliamentary leaders—recommending courses of treatment. Eventually General Public makes his appearance and convinces John Bull that the best course of action is to throw over his "doctor" and get up. The final two scenes provided settings for song items, the first with an accompanying effect provided by the blowing of bubbles.

Though advertisements declared the music to be "composed and arranged" by Stuart, there is no obvious indication where composition ended and arranging began. The *Stage* commended "the lilting melody of the ballad-like 'Bubble girl,' the martial ring and taking tune of 'Where

Are the Soldier Boys?' [and] the haunting chorus of 'You've Got Me Good.'" In somewhat lighter vein, it welcomed "I'd Like to Be a Boy," "Tinker with Your Automobile," and "Colonel Swank." Alas, its prediction of "a long and successful run, and . . . London appearance" proved overconfident. Despite being renamed *Colonel Cobb*, *Bubbles* soon evaporated. Only "Where Are the Soldier Boys?" was published, the result of an increased interest in soldier songs created by Britain's declaration of war on Germany in August 1914.

Chapter 17

World War I, America, and *Nina*

The outbreak of war between Britain and Germany gave a new life to "The Soldiers of the Queen," but now as "The Soldiers of the King." Under that title it was republished by Francis, Day and Hunter, and it was among the numbers Leslie Stuart conducted at the Coliseum in August 1914 in an entertainment devised by Italian impresario Arturo Spizzi. Featuring a "grand patriotic chorus of 100 voices" and soloist Jamieson Dodds, it included the national anthems of Belgium, Russia, France, and Britain, as well as other patriotic airs. It ran for weeks at the Coliseum and then toured.

The novelist Horace Annesley Vachell was one who saw the Coliseum show at the end of August 1914. He later recalled, "The huge theatre was packed from stalls to gallery. Tears rolled down the cheeks of the women, and I saw many men furtively wiping their eyes. I wiped mine more than once. Then I supped alone with Stuart, and he asked me to put words to a recruiting song. Next day, we spent hours together. He sat at his piano, playing each bar over and over again till I found words for it."[74] This was "Who Said You Never Would Go?" and it was sung by Ouida Macdermott, daughter of "The Great Macdermott," who had made famous the song "We Don't Want to Fight, But By Jingo If We Do." "It warmed my heart to get a telegram saying that our recruiting song had been a great success in Manchester," recalled Vachell, adding that Stuart wrote to say that the song was to be sung at all recruiting stations.[74]

Vachell was also involved with another song, revived by May Leslie Stuart and published by Francis, Day and Hunter in 1915 with two sets of words. Those of "Is That Mr. Riley?" were by Lester Barrett, those of "Is That You, O'Riley?" by Stuart himself. According to May, this was one of her father's earliest songs, dedicated in his youth to the landlord of the Slip Inn, who was evidently a fellow Irishman:

> It became very popular amongst the customers and in the market. Of course, it was not published then. After Father left the Slip Inn, I imagine it was forgotten.
>
> During the 1914–18 War, Father, Horace Annesley Vachell and I were sitting on the terrace of our house in Regent's Park when a contingent of Canadian troops passed by, whistling. Father jumped out of his chair. "That tune, Horace, what is it?" he asked.
>
> "American, old as the hills," and he sang the words.
>
> "American?!" shouted father. "My brother and I wrote that years ago when we were kids."
>
> Vachell said he had heard it in California, cowboys sang it on the ranches. How a song can go round the world, no radio, no gramophone, not even published. Father did publish it, with new verses and the same old chorus he wrote all those years ago as a joke.[65]

The idea than an unpublished song from many years before could thus appear on the lips of Canadian troops seems preposterous. Yet the basic facts of the story are verifiable. The fact is that the song "Is That Mr. Riley?" was popularized in America during the 1880s by an Irish-born song-and-dance man named Pat Rooney. Rooney died in 1891, but his name lived on through his son and grandson, the former of whom played Arvide Abernathy in the first production of Frank Loesser's *Guys and Dolls* in 1950.[8] Twenty-four years after the first Pat Rooney's death, "Is That Mr. Riley?" was revived with revised words as a morale-boosting song for the troops in World War I. In its issue of May 28, 1915, *Variety* reported that it "has replaced 'Tipperary' in the affections of the combined armies fighting Germany."

Of this 1915 revival, Douglas Gilbert wrote in his history of American vaudeville that "during the World War a controversy raged over the origin of the song 'Is that Mr. Riley?'" A number of people in America, and even in Europe, claimed authorship."[29] Pat Rooney himself seems never to have do so, and we cannot now prove that Leslie Stuart actually composed it in his Manchester days. However, he very clearly believed he had. With his strong views on piracy, he would never have sought to appropriate someone else's song. Equally, he would have done all he could to assert ownership he believed was his. Hence the two versions published in his name in 1915, one laying claim to the original song "Is That Mr. Riley?" and the other to its reincarnation as "Is That You, O'Riley?" Incidentally, "Is That Mr. Riley?" tells of an innkeeper with ambitious ideas beyond his means. Authorities cite it as the source of the phrase "living a life of Riley."[44]

War also created renewed interest in shows of earlier days. Thus, on February 20, 1915, theater manager J. Bannister Howard enchanted London theatergoers by reviving *Florodora* at its original Lyric Theatre home. Evie Greene played her original role of Dolores, and Leslie Stuart conducted the first night. It had been intended that Ada Reeve should repeat her original role of Lady Holyrood, but, when ill health prompted her to decline, May Leslie Stuart took her place. Indisposition also caused Edward Lewis, who had made the part of Tweedlepunch very much his own on tour, to drop out during the run. He was replaced by Ben Nathan, who had often played the role during the original run. May had a new song, "Jack and Jill," which she recorded with orchestral accompaniment conducted by her father. There was also another new song, "My Garden Girl," with words by Lester Barrett, for Jamieson Dodds as Abercoed. After running a creditable couple of months and a total of sixty-two performances, the show transferred to the Aldwych Theatre for a further twenty-eight performances.

May Leslie Stuart had toured the variety theaters in 1914 with her husband Cecil Cameron; but their marriage then foundered. She had always been close to her father, and the idea now arose for Leslie Stuart to try to recoup some of his losses by going onto the variety circuit, accompanying May in a program of his songs. They opened at Golders Green Hippodrome on April 26, 1915. First they performed old favorites with Stuart conducting the orchestra, and then he accompanied his daughter at the piano in new songs such as "Don't Blame Eve" ("a particularly attractive example of the effect of ragtime on the Stuart method," according to the *Stage*), "My Beautiful Witch," and "Heligoland." This last was a topical number, with May dressed as a naval officer serving in the battle of Heligoland in August 1914.

Manchester welcomed the couple at the newly rebuilt Palace Theatre in the week of May 10, 1915, in a program headed by the Jersey-born, naturalized American actress Lillie Langtry. It was overshadowed by widespread shock at the German sinking of the *S.S. Lusitania,* with the loss of 1,467 people. Among them was producer Charles Frohman, whom Stuart remembered fondly, later writing, "All Frohman's engagements with his stars were made verbally. . . . In my case I did not have anything signed at all, yet it is computed that out of the 'Belle of Mayfair' and the 'School Girl,' I must have received thousands of pounds from Frohman. . . . Charles Frohman's word was his bond."[62] Stuart also had a more immediate reason for lamenting Frohman's death: "He had the manuscript of a book by Cosmo Hamilton, on which I was immediately to commence work on his arrival in London."[62] Presumably that book was of *Nina.*

With the outlook in London increasingly unpromising, Stuart now decided to try his luck again in America. Traveling alone, he took up residence in New York, where he was joined for a time by the elder of the two sons surviving after the death of the handicapped Vaughan. Both sons had received a good Jesuit education: the elder, Leslie, at Stonyhurst College in Clitheroe, Lancashire, and the younger, Stephen ("Chap"), at Beaumont College, Windsor, where in 1914 he was stroke of the college boat. Stephen was to see service in both World Wars, being recalled to the colors in 1938 and becoming a lieutenant colonel in the Royal Artillery. However, Leslie was shell-shocked and never saw active service. After joining his father in New York, he moved on to Hollywood and was engaged in film production for some twenty years, working with Charlie Chaplin, among others.[67]

Stuart's prime objective in New York was to achieve production of his beloved *Nina,* which had already simmered in his mind for a dozen years. For a book around his scenario, he enlisted Cosmo Hamilton, with whom he had worked on *The Belle of Mayfair* and the aborted *The Little Governess,* and who had traveled to New York with his wife and family in October 1915. Hamilton evidently thought highly of Stuart, and in his memoirs he summed up his character as well as anyone:

> [T]here was one man in New York, whom I was delighted to meet
> there shortly after my arrival, who seemed to me to be as unconscious

Andrew Lamb

Leslie Stuart rehearsing with his daughter May in 1915 (author's collection)

of the war as though he were living on a South Sea Island with a piano in his bungalow. . . . I found Leslie Stuart comfortably ensconced in a studio in the middle West Forties, knee deep in new and mellifluous numbers and the fag ends of a thousand cigarettes. And there, in the pleasant intervals of business, I drew together the unknotted ends of a formerly discussed story which, in due time, became a play called *Nina*, in composing the music of which Stuart outdid himself. In addition to the fact that he had never grown up and was an Irish-Liverpudlian, Stuart was a man of strange impulses and odd complexities, difficult therefore to deal with, though a lovable, loyal, and most attractive creature, fair of hair and blue of eye, who came up smiling even after he had been knocked completely through the ropes. His resilience and capacity for work were quite remarkable, and when any other man who had never stirred from a seat at a piano for twenty-four hours would have fallen face down on a bed, Stuart had an astonishing way of turning a lineless and cherubic face to his interrupter, lighting one more cigarette, and playing over all the neat pages of the score that he had written with the fresh enthusiasm of a well-slept man.[33]

On March 31, 1916, Hamilton and Stuart signed a contract with the Shubert Theatrical Company for production "in a first-class New York theatre, preferably the Casino, and with the usual adequate chorus and orchestra, usually provided for Stuart productions." A rider provided for the music to be published by G. Schirmer. The contract was signed on the basis of Stuart's own scenario, about a romantic attachment between a Monte Carlo gambler and the Italian girl he meets who is disguised as a boy in a group of traveling musicians. The score Stuart developed for *Nina* seemingly included numbers already heard either in *Bubbles* in 1914 or in May Leslie Stuart's appearances with her father in 1915.

Stuart's work on *Nina* did not prevent him entering fully into American musical life. He was evidently happy to join up with fellow composers whose campaign for authors' rights had recently led to the formation of the American Society of Composers, Authors, and Publishers. With some of them, he was recruited in March 1916 for a novelty Sunday evening performance at Charles Dillingham's New York Hippodrome for the benefit of the Actors' Fund. At the top of the bill was Mary Pickford, so-called queen of the movies. Besides Sousa's Band, which had been appearing at the Hippodrome since September 1915, there was a supporting ensemble that included New York's original *Merry Widow* Danilo, Donald Brian, and boxing, stage, and vaudeville celebrity James J. Corbett. Billed as a further attraction were "the Greatest AMERICAN COMPOSERS in person, each playing his most famous melody."

The *New York Herald* reported thus:

> With Miss Mary Pickford herself in overalls, a quorum of the world's best known composers seated at fourteen pianos arranged in battery across the stage, and Oscar Hammerstein in a little sentimental scene, . . . "Composers' Night" at the Hippodrome last evening passed into stage history as a pleasing and unique event. . . .
>
> When the curtain disclosed the fourteen composers, seated at their pianos, every one wondered if they would all play together, and they did. There must have been about a million dollars' worth of conflicting royalties in those finger tips, but they all worked together on one another's music. Each played in turn some popular air of his own composition, then led his fellow-composers in a piano chorus. The composers were Gustav Kerker, Irving Berlin, John L. Golden, Raymond Hubbell, Silvio Hein, Louis Hirsch, Jerome D. Kern, Alfred Robyn, A. Baldwin Sloane, Leslie Stuart, Rudolph Friml, Hugo Felix and John Philip Sousa and Mr Hammerstein. . . .
>
> Mr Berlin forgot how to play his own piece "Alexander's Ragtime Band," but the gallery whistled it to a finish. Mr Stuart, from England, was distinguished by an elaborate accompaniment which the others played to his tune from *Florodora*.

Leslie Stuart later recalled:

> For the occasion of this matinee there was one piano "downstage," apart from the others, and at this each composer sat in turn and played his favourite composition. In the ensemble he was supported by the rest, and each received his ovation. When it came to the turn of Irving Berlin to go to the piano "downstage," it was immediately after Friml, who is one of the most accomplished pianists in America. As an introduction to his then famous number "I Want Sympathy," Friml gave a remarkable display of technique. Then Berlin sat at the piano and immediately had the house in a roar with an imitation of Friml, a joke that Friml equally enjoyed. Berlin's contribution was his first success, "Alexander's Ragtime Band." We all had to transpose into his own key of six flats when the time came to join him in the ensemble.[62]

Oscar Hammerstein I at the piano with (from left to right) Jerome Kern, Louis A. Hirsch, A. Baldwin Sloane, Rudolf Friml, Alfred Robyn, Gustave Kerker, Hugo Felix, John Philip Sousa, Leslie Stuart, Raymond Hubbell, John Golden, Silvio Hein and Irving Berlin, New York Hippodrome, March 26, 1916 (courtesy Gerald Bordman)

The father figure at the gathering was impresario Oscar Hammerstein, grandfather of the celebrated lyricist. He was then in the midst of a bankruptcy petition and, after playing his waltz *Louise*, he was jokingly presented with a summons. This turned out to be an expression of esteem from the other fourteen composers. The whole occasion was commemorated in a photograph of the composers gathered around Hammerstein at the piano. Stuart stands proudly with arms folded, a diminutive figure with John Philip Sousa on one side and Raymond Hubbell and John Golden on the other.

Evidently the occasion was a sufficient success for a similar gathering to be arranged for the eleventh anniversary celebration of the Hippodrome on Easter Sunday, April 16, 1916. This time there was no Hugo Felix or Oscar Hammerstein, but Victor Jacobi was added to the party. The *New York Herald* reported,

> Each of these composers, who have written the music for hundreds of musical comedies and thousands of songs for the dance halls and cabarets, had a chance to conduct the band through one of his own works, while Mr Sousa sat down next to the harp player and watched.
>
> When they were all through he began to direct his own band in one of his own marches, *The Bride Elect*. He had only played a few bars when out came the twelve, baton in hand, forming a row between him and the footlights. With their backs to the audience they followed Mr Sousa's motions bar for bar. The band had thirteen conductors, probably the largest number that has ever conducted one organization at the same time.

Not content with success at the Hippodrome, the twelve composers then moved on to the Century Theatre. There they joined in a benefit performance for the Actors' Fund, featuring such stars as Marie Dressler, Elsie Janis, Alla Nazimova, Blanche Bates, Herbert Beerbohm Tree, and representatives from the Metropolitan Opera Ballet and various Broadway shows. "Then came that battalion of composer pianists," reported the *New York Herald*. "It went big. No doubt it was the hit of the night."

For Leslie Stuart it must have been marvelous to be in the limelight in New York after all his troubles. He was particularly gratified by the account of the Easter Sunday Hippodrome event in the *New York Sun*, which noted, "Thirteen composers directed their famous popular compositions as performed by Sousa's band at the Hippodrome the other night, and when they got through everybody in the house would have bought tickets for a *Florodora* revival if some manager had announced one. The joint efforts of the composers simply proved that there have been a lot of popular tunes but none ever, before or since, to equal the "Tell me, pretty maiden" song. . . . Leslie Stuart, stocky and blond, anything but emotional and composer-like, bringing out with perfect effect the delicious, inconsequential, vagrant, matched-up melodies of the "Pretty maiden" sextet, and the big house fairly rose to its feet to demand encores." It was no small tribute that Stuart could eclipse some of the best names of American popular song. Together with the photograph from the earlier gathering, signed by all the participants, this report remained a treasured possession of Leslie Stuart and, after his death, his daughter May, to the extent that it received pride of place in May's will.[67]

During the summer of 1916, publisher J. W. Stern issued a Leslie Stuart waltz song, "Sweet Rose O'Mally," a collaboration with Russian-born lyricist L. Wolfe Gilbert, who was already famous for "Waiting for the Robert E. Lee" and would later collaborate on "Ramona" and "The Peanut Vendor." Shortly afterward, Stuart decided to follow his British variety theater appearances with a similar venture into American vaudeville, appearing at the Majestic Theatre, Chicago, with May de Sousa, the local singer who had appeared in *Havana* in London. After the first night on July 31, 1916, Percy Hammond of the *Chicago Daily Tribune*, who had six years earlier reported on *The Slim Princess* under the heading "*The Slim Princess* Cheers if It Does Not Inebriate," confirmed himself the master of the succinct headline with "Giving Leslie Stuart Three Clammy Cheers":

> I envied nobody on Monday afternoon at the Majestic theater so little as I did Mr Leslie Stuart, the affluent [*sic!*] and eminent English composer of *Florodora*. A scared alien on a bleak frontier, he was making his debut in the varieties, confronting the cold, critical Chicago first day audience which foregathers at that imposing sanctuary of vaudeville.
>
> When he was introduced in the orchestra pit, directing the band as it played selections from his works, he was received with all the warmth that Joe Howard, for instance, would get if he did a similar thing at the Palace music hall in London. Only one handclap, and that from an embarrassed usher, greeted him; and he looked very frightened and miserable and lonely. . . .

Miss De Sousa, however, soon rescued him. She is a home girl, a product of the north side, and her father, a good policeman, once ornamented the local gendarmerie. Miss De Sousa has charm and a voice, and she addressed both of these attributes to Mr Stuart's polite songs. . . . At the Majestic in Chicago . . . she is somewhat of a prophet without honor on her own stamping ground. What she and the estimable Mr Stuart need to make their act more popular is a bit of ginger and vulgarity. They are a trifle too nice and too slow for American vaudeville.

A less public engagement that Stuart recalled from that same year was an invitation from the Mutual Welfare League to help with a concert in the notorious Sing Sing prison, thirty miles north of New York City:

It was a Christmas Eve entertainment in the year 1916. . . . During the rehearsal prior to the concert we were waited on by two or three dapperly-dressed men, one of whom turned over the music as I played the piano. I naturally presumed they were officials, but imagine my surprise when during my conversation with one of them . . . regarding prison life, I was asked by the Governor not to make inquiries of the prisoners as it was not in accordance with prison discipline, and it tended to embarrass the inmates.

Then I discovered that the superior-dressed individuals . . . were under sentence. They were known as "trustees," being men who could be trusted to go out of the prison into the village for cigarettes or even into the city of New York, on parole, without fear of them breaking it. . . .

[One] of the well-tailored, sweetly-mannered "trustees" acted as master of ceremonies to us in the ante-room, and he suggested the various songs we were to include in the programme. For this polyglot collection of humanity he selected the most doleful, miserable, dirgeful, and melancholic numbers it was possible for mind to remember as having been set to music.

When he noticed the amazement of the company of ten at the selections he had made, he charmingly explained that songs of home and mother and son stuff about being away from children were practically the only songs the convicts would stand for. He said they would just gulp these down like drinking good wine, whereas anything of a lively, cheerful nature they would give the bird to. I was more than ever impressed with this psychology when I learned that out of all the seven or eight hundred men in the gaol, most of whom attended the concert, at least twenty of the audience were men who were awaiting the electric chair.[62]

Progress toward production of *Nina* came with extension of the Shubert contract for four months from January 8, 1917. Soon afterward it went into rehearsal, with a company led by Wilda Bennett, John Rutherford, Joseph Latora, and Bennett Parker. The musical director was Max Steiner,[54] famous later for the film scores of *Gone with the Wind* and *Casablanca*. Cosmo Hamilton recalled the ups and downs of rehearsal:

I directed the book in the many strange places that are invariably allotted to rehearsing companies—basements, smoking-rooms and the like—and Leslie Stuart and his conductor coached the chorus in his music. Great enthusiasm prevailed and optimism grew stronger daily as the story emerged and the melodies took a greater hold. I shall never forget attending a music rehearsal one night in the vast cellars of the Forty-fourth Street Theatre which were called the Little Club, and being swept off my feet by the lilt of those numbers, the thrill of Stuart's masterly finales, orchestrated for fifty voices and all the instruments of a full band.

Just at the moment when all that we needed to proceed to a production were the scenery and clothes, in walked a stage director of the old barn-storming bully type attended by a play-doctor who, from force of habit and of custom, is sent to inject a million microbes collected from the old, old book of jokes into the veins of supposedly frail pieces. Not being able to understand that this appearance was simply part of theatrical routine, the outcome of the usual pessimistic report on the book and the company, we gazed at them with great amazement and a rising temperature, but proceeded with the rehearsal in the endeavour to forget. In the afternoon, however, the blood went to our heads when the barn-stormer stalked over to the piano, gazed over the shoulder of the conductor at the orchestrated score in front of him and called out: "Cut everything out except the top-line. Rehearsal dismissed until this evening. Eight sharp." This meant that with one devastating sweep of an ignorant blue pencil all Leslie Stuart's harmonies were to be swept away as valueless, leaving the unorchestrated melody to the voices and the band. A bomb dropped into the middle of an art gallery, destroying all the precious exhibits and leaving merely the bare walls of the building, was precisely the effect of this absurd and emasculating order upon the many months of labour that had resulted in this score.

Well, waiting until this hectoring housebreaker had removed himself from the staggered stage, I then proceeded to collect every scrap of the music, every page of the book, and all the actors' parts, and with this huge bundle Stuart and I, feeling rather like Don Quixote and Sancho Panza, walked out never to return. When the hectoring gentleman "who knew his business" put in an appearance at eight sharp he found a blank piano, an even blanker company, no book to cut to ribbons, and no score to emasculate.[33]

Documents in the Shubert Archive fill out the story. On February 15, 1917, J. J. Shubert wrote to Cosmo Hamilton about changes he required to the script. He objected to characters becoming strolling musicians, feeling that "it is stretching a point too far to expect a modern audience to accept a condition of that kind." He also felt that some of the speeches were too long, and added, "This play needs a great deal of time and attention, and we have been wasting so much valuable time up to the present that we had better get down to business as quickly as possible." He was also worried about the music, writing, "I think Mr. Stuart has given very little attention to this play. He seemed to be very anxious to have it produced but now keeps away entirely. From what I have heard of the chorus singing I think some of the musical numbers could be improved upon. . . . Mr. Temple will meet Mr. Stuart at any time to go over the matter with him, but Mr. Stuart must make up his mind that he has got to devote some time to the proposition, otherwise it will lag along indefinitely."[54]

Hamilton replied the next day that he had already made the changes J. J. had requested, and with some irritation he referred to delays in engaging the remainder of the cast. Then, it seems, the stage director and the play doctor—evidently Edward P. Temple and Edgar Smith, respectively—walked in, prompting a heated, handwritten, hand-delivered note from Hamilton to Shubert on the afternoon of Friday, February 16, 1917 that read, "I give you notice that if Mr. Smith or any other of your fixers who are responsible for all your failures, puts one line into my book of 'Nina' I shall hold you in a court of law immediately as having broken your contract and injunct you against producing. If any alterations, cuts &c are to be made they must be made by me & I am willing, unless the suggestions are obviously ignorant & foolish to make them."[54]

Replying immediately, Shubert acknowledged "your most extraordinary communication . . . , in which you object to Mr. Smith's lining the play with laughs, etc." He declared that "under the terms of our contract I can do anything I like with the manuscript," and, since Hamilton felt so keenly about the matter, he would return his manuscript if the latter would send back his advance. He added that, "I take exception to your remark that our many failures were caused by Mr. Smith. Mr. Smith has never yet given me a book that I have made a failure of, and furthermore, all our musical plays have been successes."[54]

In a further handwritten note that afternoon, Hamilton pointed out that the contract stated that Stuart and he were the owners of the book and music. He added that Shubert was not at liberty to do anything to his book, and that "the small sum paid on account is not returnable in any event." The following day Hamilton and Stuart withdrew the work, leaving Max Steiner to inform Shubert that "I was unable to continue rehearsals of the musical production 'Nina' this afternoon because Mr. Leslie Stuart took the music away with him and failed to return it at 2 o'clock. As the music was incomplete and he often took the music away with him to finish it up, I did not hesitate to give it to him."[54]

For all the acrimony, Hamilton tried to revive the contract for production of *Nina* in June 1920, but in vain. As it was, he recorded, "*Nina* was dead, as dead as a doornail, but the poor little soul was buried with full honours in the studio with all her limbs intact. Every member of the company attended the funeral, deeply sympathetic for all that they had wasted several good weeks of their time and energies."[33]

Those 1917 cast members included various young people for whom Stuart had written parts. Hamilton recalled, "A homogeneous person who was happiest when surrounded by young people who loved music and could sing, his studio very quickly became the collecting place of innumerable aspirants for parts in the gradually erected musical play on which he was at work. Among these, many of whom have since had the satisfaction of seeing their names in electric lights, was a quiet, eager, fur-coated young man who wanted to sing but had no voice, wanted to act but was without experience, and finally wanted to dance, which he did extremely well. Day after day he hung about the studio, more and more wistful, more and more eager, more and more inarticulate, but never any less glossy of hair or furry of overcoat."[33]

For this young man, Leslie Stuart incorporated a tango into the act

1 finale of *Nina*. He was Rudolph Valentino, whom Stuart remembered as follows:

Leslie Stuart

> While I was in New York, there came to me for a job a young man
> of very smart appearance who had been washing dishes in a restau-
> rant in the city. His ambition to get higher than the wash-sink
> caused him to approach me for a job in my chorus. He was a natural
> dancer, and even though he were hungry he was always well
> dressed.... He lived with me in 31, West 47th-street, New York,
> for nearly two years, as did now one of the most famous screen
> lovers—Norman Kerry.... Both he and Kerry were introduced,
> by me, to the greatest theatre-owners in the world, the Shubert
> brothers, to be engaged by them for small parts in a play I was then
> writing them....
>
> "Ruddy" ... many times came into my studio immaculately dressed
> *en route* for some cabaret up town, where he had arranged to dance
> with, always, a new partner. It was difficult for me to persuade him to
> take a taxi in the rain, and he never once betrayed that he may not
> have the wherewithal. He would return in the early hours, enter my
> bedroom and unburden himself of some complication or of some
> story of a new infatuation. For hours I remained awake giving him
> lectures and much unheeded advice.
>
> Finally I put a severe and final admonition on him—I said he must
> quit New York at once—make for Chicago to join a company then
> playing there—and then on to ... California, where my son, Leslie
> junior, was the guest of Charlie Chaplin and "Doug" Fairbanks. He
> was immediately introduced to the producer of "The Four Horsemen
> [of the Apocalypse]," who said, "You are the type I have been waiting
> for." The rest is history recorded throughout the world.[62]

Cosmo Hamilton recorded that, after *Nina*, "Leslie Stuart sat down in order to recover his breath. I regret to say that he never succeeded in doing so. He hung around New York for a considerable time waiting for someone to tread on the tail of his coat, while he wrote enough delightful music to fill half a dozen new light operas."[33] Edward B. Marks casts further light on how Stuart had pushed his luck just once too often, writing, "Leslie Stuart ... was [an] idol of the hour; a keen, dapper Englishman who insisted upon a full orchestra of forty men that he might score his work properly. The Shuberts raved protest at this unheard-of extrava-gance, but Stuart had his way. It was a costly way for him. In after years, when he had dissipated the profits of *Florodora* and *Havana*, he found the cards stacked against a comeback. He had bucked the theatrical autocrats. In the end, he ate at Offer's, a low-priced table d'hôte on Forty-Sixth Street, every noon—at friends' expense. He never complained as long as he had a pint of California claret with his simple meal.[41]

There were, of course, some bright spots. One commission clearly owed much to Billie Burke, whom Stuart had given a first break in *The School Girl* and then the lead role in *The Belle of Mayfair*. She had since progressed to being Mrs. Florenz Ziegfeld, as well as entering into lucrative film contracts:

> On my arrival in New York in 1916 Billie Burke and Ziegfeld, I learned, had been telephoning all over New York to invite me to their marvellous mansion at Richmond, on the Hudson, about thirty miles from New York City. Ziegfeld called for me in his car and drove me to his home. The approach to the house was a replica of an Arabian Nights picture. The house itself was lighted up and it became a veritable fairy palace.
>
> Billie Burke showed me through the home, which was replete with priceless pictures and works of art purchased on Fifth-avenue at enormous cost. I have been through palaces, real palaces, and more than one compared with the grandeur of Billie Burke's Hudson River home. . . . I congratulated her on their magnificent surroundings and her wonderful achievement in acquiring such luxury. Her reply was: "This grandeur you are speaking of would never have been brought into being were it not for that fateful knock you gave on my door at the Pavilion music-hall."[62]

The result was that, in December 1917, Stuart's name appeared with those of writer Gene Buck and composer Dave Stamper among the credits for the *Ziegfeld Midnight Frolic*. This was a midnight cabaret that Ziegfeld had established in January 1915 at the roof theater of the New Amsterdam Theatre, accommodating 480 people on the floor of the cabaret and 280 in the balcony. There was no traditional stage, but a four-foot-high platform with steps. A new edition of the show was generally introduced twice each year, and it was to the sixth edition, produced on December 29, 1917, that Stuart contributed a song called "Cutey," and possibly more. The production had its problems. Two days before its opening, a fire destroyed most of the costumes. Then the cold weather delayed the arrival of the scenery from Boston, so that it arrived only two hours before the opening. As a final blow, the weather meant the demand for cabs was such that people couldn't get to the theater on time.[78]

As for the rest of his time in the United States, Stuart was at least able to make some interesting acquaintances. He recalled being invited to lunch by the "five and dime" stores entrepreneur Frank W. Woolworth in the fifty-nine-story Woolworth Building, which at that time was New York's highest:

> At this time Woolworth had developed a vanity that caused him to be regarded as a man whose intellect was weakening. His magnificent room, amongst his offices, was an exact replica of Napoleon's room in the palace at Versailles. A more than life-sized portrait of Napoleon decorated one of the walls. The chairs, after the fashion of those in the historic French palace, bore the letter "N" embossed on them. The carpet was a copy to a degree of minute exactitude of that which is so admired at Versailles. Even the inkstand and the pens bore the embossed "N. . . . "
>
> The conduct of his business was on the characteristic American scale. Lunch over, he suggested to me that I should write a song on his enterprise for his sole manipulation, guaranteeing me a three millions circulation, with a royalty of one cent per copy. To say he was surprised when I rejected the offer is to put it mildly. I believe he really felt I had taken leave of my senses, as I was turning down 30,000 dollars for what I could have done in an hour or two's work. I knew, what he could not understand, that once I did such a thing as he had suggested I would have been ostracised by all the reputable music publishers of Europe and America.[62]

Perhaps he should have taken the deal and run.

There was also another famous personality he encountered: "My experience with Theodore Roosevelt, when I lived out at his house at Oyster Bay, which some of my friends rented from him, was when he used to run over and spend some time with us. He used to attend service at the church close by and then come along to see us. He was a man of broad views and had the courage of his convictions. I have played before him, and his favourite numbers of my composing were 'Shade of the Palm' and the sextette from 'Florodora.'"[62]

Fortunately, too, the Shuberts had not completely washed their hands of Leslie Stuart. On February 19, 1919, Lee Shubert acquired from Tom B. Davis the production rights for *Florodora* in the United

States and Canada.[54] The result was a major revival of *Florodora*, with which they were able to recoup some, or all, of their losses on *Nina*. After tryouts in Atlantic City; Philadelphia; Washington, D.C.; and Baltimore, the production reached the Century Theatre, New York, on April 15, 1920. Eleanor Painter played Dolores, Walter Woolf was Abercoed, and George Hassell was Tweedlepunch. In the *New York Times,* Alexander Woollcott made it clear that the show had not lost its appeal, writing, "The expertly heralded revival of *Florodora* packed the Century Theatre last evening with an audience as large and as alive as the Alumnus Association of the original sextette. There was great rejoicing, for this favorite of twenty years ago, now sung and mounted and played far better than ever it was in its youth, proved to be an abundantly entertaining piece with no disappointment." At the same time, he recognized the show's weaknesses: "*Florodora* was never a mine of laughter and, though its timeworn script has been industriously refurbished with new jokes, it is not convulsing even now."

Stuart's original score was supplemented with interpolations such as "Come to St. George's" and "Hello, People," but it was the sextet that everyone had come to see, and the Shuberts triumphantly managed to trump expectations. As the *New York Times* review noted, "It was the 'Tell me, pretty maiden' melody for which last night's audience was waiting and there was a great hullabaloo when it began, with the heads nodding and the hats lifting as of yore. But the greater excitement was manifested in the more elderly bosoms when, for an encore, there emerged from the wings six pompadoured girls, clad in flapping hats and long black gloves and flowing trains of the first sextette. When *Florodora* was new these costumes seemed very saucy indeed, but now they suggest nothing so forcibly as an A. B. Frost illustration for a story by Alice Brown. Not that all the elements of the original enchantment were present. For where are the waistlines of yesteryear?" Nor was that all. Children's acts were all the rage at that time, being cheap as well as crowd-pulling. There was therefore a third double-sextet performed by children, among them future television comedian Milton Berle.[42] The whole lavish production enjoyed a remarkable run of 150 performances.

In 1921, Leslie Stuart did a coast-to-coast American tour, registering surprise and pleasure at the number of former pupils, or sons of former pupils, he met in out-of-the-way places. Then he returned to Britain for good.

Chapter 18

Death and Legacy

While Leslie Stuart was in America, his daughter May remarried. Following her appearances with her father in 1915, she had taken the title role in Horace Annesley Vachell's *The Case of Lady Camber*. At one of her stage appearances a young man named James Mayhew Balls was in the audience and took a fancy to her. Her mother frowned on the romance. Not only was May still married to Cecil Cameron, but Jim Balls was five years younger than she was. Worst of all, he was a Protestant. When May sought to include him in a family gathering in 1916, her mother refused, whereupon May revealed that she was pregnant.[67] She had to wait for divorce from Cecil Cameron before marrying Jim Balls on January 17, 1917. By dint of the groom generously overstating his age by a year and the bride reducing hers by two, they managed to reduce their age difference on the marriage certificate to two years. Their first child, Mary (always known as "Treasure"), was born less than four weeks later.

An auctioneer and surveyor like his father, Jim Balls had money. To facilitate his return to Britain, therefore, Leslie Stuart asked May and Jim to help him obtain release from his 1913 bankruptcy. The Bankruptcy Court heard the application on June 15, 1920, when the Official Receiver advised that a dividend of four or five pence on the pound (2 percent) was expected. The registrar reiterated that the bankrupt's trouble appeared to have been reckless extravagance. As he had been undischarged for nearly eight years, the discharge would be granted on his consenting to judgment for £500. Jim Balls came up with the money. [67] That Stuart's daughter May remained his closest ally was a symptom of the fact that he was now estranged from Kitty, though, as Roman Catholics, they would never divorce. Their separation was deeply regretted by Kitty's sister Connie, who had never married and had been very close to her sister and her family. She was fond of her brother-in-law, and on one occasion she sought to arrange a reunion between the estranged couple. Alas, Leslie Stuart turned up with his current lady friend, and Kitty walked out.[67]

Stuart returned in 1921 to a Britain where many of his old colleagues had died, most notably Eugene Stratton. In 1915 Stratton had retired, due to ill health, to Christchurch in Hampshire, where he died on September 15, 1918 at the age of fifty-seven.[4] However, as May Leslie Stuart later related, her father had fallen out with Stratton some time earlier, when "one day he and Gene quarrelled about a horse running in the 2:30 race at Hurst Park. It seemed a trivial, unimportant thing—but they never spoke again and never saw each other. Gene would have made it up. He came to me, said how sorry he was for his part in the quarrel, and how much they needed each other. Father set his jaw and said I was never to mention Gene again."[65]

It's unclear just when this breach occurred; but any suggestion that it curtailed the creative relationship should be resisted. Their major successes had come during the 1890s, their last, "I May Be Crazy," in 1901. Stuart's absence in America for the last two-and-a-half years of Stratton's life could have been a factor in there being no reconciliation. In any event, Stuart wrote generously and affectionately of his old friend in his memoirs, just a few months before his own death.[62]

During Stuart's absence in America, a few of his songs were apparently heard in the British provincial tour of *Toto* in 1919. This was a show that had enjoyed only limited success at London's Duke of York's and Apollo Theatres in the spring of 1916 but proved a successful touring show for some time afterward. Seemingly the appearance of W. Louis Bradfield, seasoned performer of Stuart's songs, led to his music finding a place there. But Bradfield, too, died in August 1919, at the age of only fifty-three. There were also Stuart songs in the short-lived *Jenny*, which opened at the Empire Theatre on February 10, 1922, among them the song "Cutey," which had already been heard in New York's *Midnight Frolic*.

Later that same month, Stuart made what was to prove his final bow as composer for a West End musical play. The show was *The Lady of the Rose*, adapted from a German musical comedy *Die Frau im Hermelin*, composed by Jean Gilbert and produced in Berlin in 1919. An English version by Harry Graham opened in Manchester on December 26, 1921, and reached Daly's Theatre on February 21, 1922. It was a big success, playing for 514 performances in London, with many more on tour before and after. It was produced in Australia and was brought back to Daly's in 1929. Its hit numbers included Stuart's "Catch a Butterfly If You Can," an *alla marcia* number with typical dotted rhythms. Evidently he had softened his "Leslie Stuart does not interpolate" stance, and the result must have rekindled memories of past glories. Ivy Tresmand sang it and also recorded it for Columbia. Stuart's final contribution to the musical theater was one of his most typical, and one of his best.

On February 13, 1923, his daughter May's family, now including four children, changed their name by deed poll from "Balls" to "Mayhew," this being Jim Balls's middle name. With Stuart's financial problems continuing, May's husband also came to the rescue once more. On April 6, 1923, he set up a company called Mayball Limited to administer Stuart's finances and copyrights.[67] Stuart returned once more to the variety theater, this time at the Alhambra with baritone Harry Barratt on July 9. His subsequent tours took him back twice to Manchester after a break of eight years, the second time—in September 1923—accompanying Powell Edwards. Later that year, he similarly acted as accompanist to Hayden Coffin, his old colleague from the days of *An Artist's Model*.

All this time he was still composing, and in July 1923 a new Stuart musical with the title *The Girl from Nyusa* was announced, apparently for production by James White—yet another fellow Lancastrian—who had recently taken over Daly's Theatre. The show was seemingly no more than a revision of *Nina*, with some new numbers. The new title derived from the notion of the heroine having been left at a convent with a box of clothes labeled "Miss Nina, N.Y.U.S.A." Instead of the actual "New York, U.S.A.," the initials were misinterpreted as a place called "Nyusa." The new title may have been a deliberate attempt at distancing from the work developed with Cosmo Hamilton and contracted to the Shuberts. However, talk of production in the autumn of 1923 again came to nothing.

On September 13, 1924, Stuart's brother Steve—"Lester" Barrett—died at his home at 40 Thorney Hedge Road, off Chiswick High Road, London, of Bright's Disease, from which he had suffered for fourteen years. He had run the professional department at Francis, Day and Hunter for twenty years until his retirement in 1919, and he left his widow, Hetty, and five children (four sons and a daughter), all married. The funeral at Acton Cemetery on September 17 followed a service at Chiswick Catholic Church. Immediately below the notice in the *Era* of Lester Barrett's death appeared the announcement of a further Leslie Stuart engagement at the New Oxford Theatre from Monday, September 29, 1924. Poignantly, this theater was the remodeled Oxford Music Hall, where his melodies had been sung so often and so successfully by Eugene Stratton.

Stuart's very last major London appearance came in a revue, *Palladium Pleasures*, written by Lauri Wylie, Greatrex Newman, Gilbert Lofthouse, and Ronald Jeans, with music by Vivian Ellis. It opened at the London Palladium on February 24, 1926, and W. Macqueen-Pope has left a vivid memoir of the occasion:

> Tremendous spectacle filled the mighty stage at the command of the producer Harry Day and the chief of the Palladium, Charles Gulliver. Big, colourful scenes of lavishly dressed and beautiful girls followed closely one upon the other. Anton Dolin danced. . . . And then, the curtain rose once more and an audience, almost sated with sensation, found itself gazing in astonishment, not on crowds of gay and dancing beauties, not on speedy and complex ballet, not on jovial comedians, but on an elderly, silver-haired, sad looking man, sitting all alone at a grand piano. His strong mouth was closed in a firm line, his eyes gazed far away as if oblivious of his surroundings. The audience looked and wondered. Then, quite softly, he began to play. The audience stilled, and listened. From his skilful fingers, ranging over the keys, came the strains of the songs he had given to the world, songs that audience had known and remembered from childhood. Many of them had never seen him before, but they knew his songs. He wove a spell around them and that great audience began to nod and move in time to the music. And then—it began to sing.

The man at the piano played on and on, seemingly unconscious of the evergrowing excitement and enthusiasm around him as one well beloved melody followed on another. Leslie Stuart, as he sat there playing, must have seen his whole life pass in review before him as that vast crowd began to cheer and acclaim him. He crashed out some chords on the piano, the orchestra joined in, curtains behind him swished up and the stage was filled with The Soldiers of the Queen (or rather of the King). Amidst that mimic pageantry he must have visualised another great day in June, 1897, when the bands of the whole Empire played that music hall song of his and the remembered cheers of those Victorian crowds of London must have blended with the actual cheers which rose from a frenzied house giving him once more an accolade for himself and for those great Music Hall Melodies of his which had indeed lingered on—unforgettably.[38]

Stuart's success at the Palladium in February 1926 was such that the Columbia recording company invited him into its studio on March 17 to record a selection of his songs on two 78-rpm sides. Side 1 comprised "Little Dolly Daydream," "I May Be Crazy," "Shade of the Palm," and "Lily of Laguna." Side 2 covered "Tell Me, Pretty Maiden," "My Little Octoroon," and "The Soldiers of the Queen."[53]

Much of his time in London now seems to have been spent around London's version of Tin Pan Alley, off Charing Cross Road. One who recalled meeting Stuart in Denmark Street during the great strike of May 1926 was Tolchard Evans, who went on to compose such songs as "Lady of Spain," "If," and "My September Love." "I'd just written my first world hit, a thing called 'Barcelona,'" recalled Evans, "and there was a pub opposite called Peck's Wine Bar, and in this bar you met everybody. Classical writers, popular writers, everybody congregated there. And I went in, and he was introduced to me. And he had a tremendous overbearing personality, and he suddenly picked on me, and gave me a lecture. He said, 'Do you know, young man, with this song you could make a lot of money. But don't you go mad! Don't you go and buy a lot of sports cars and live with women and commit other dreadful sins!' To my amazement, the following year he went broke for doing the same thing that he lectured to me about."[25]

Quite what Evans meant by saying that Stuart "went broke" the following year is unclear. Proud and combative to the end, Stuart continued his appearances on the variety circuit, his visits to such theaters as the Argyle in Birkenhead, the Empire in Liverpool, and the Metropole in Bootle enabling him to renew acquaintance with Liverpudlian friends. His tour with *Palladium Pleasures* also took him, on June 6, 1927, to Manchester, which hailed him as "The Greatest Living Melodist." However exaggerated that may have been, the *Manchester Guardian* report supports Macqueen-Pope's account of his reception, describing how Stuart "sat at the keyboard, his eyes fixed on vacancy." This visit to Manchester also took Leslie Stuart back to his boyhood. It was Whit Week, and on the morning of Whit Friday he walked in the Roman Catholic procession with the young people of St Patrick's in Ancoats as he had done as a boy fifty years before.

Stuart maintained his Irish nationalist support, too, and in August 1927 he walked to Euston Station with T. P. O'Connor, journalist and father of the House of Commons, as the remains of Charles Stewart Parnell's successor John Dillon began their journey to Dublin for burial.[62] Between August and November 1927, moreover, he provided fourteen weekly episodes of reminiscences for the Sunday newspaper *Empire News*, providing a wealth of background information on his life. But then his health broke down. In December 1927, his daughter May took him into her home at Downe Lodge, 122 Richmond Hill, Richmond.

On January 21, 1928, Stuart drew up a new will, appointing as executors and trustees his solicitor, William Greenwood Curtis, together with Walter Westmoreland, quantity surveyor. After payment of funeral expenses and debts, he left one-third of his estate to his wife, and one-fifth to Mrs. Elizabeth Kennedy of 3 Greek Street, Soho "in recognition of the valuable services she has rendered me for some years past." We are left to imagine what those services were. The remainder was to be divided between just three of his children—May, Stephen, and Lola. The other two—Leslie and Dolly—were excluded, and the result was to be bitter wrangling in the years after his death, based on the contention that May had unduly influenced the will's terms.[67]

On Monday, March 26, 1928, Queen Surayya of Afghanistan was in the royal box for a program at the Coliseum Theatre, London. Herman Darewski and his band included "The Lily of Laguna" in their selection of pieces, to great enthusiasm. Performers and audience were unaware of the seriousness of Leslie Stuart's condition; but the following evening's press carried the announcement that, at 3:00 A.M. on Tuesday, March 27, he had died at May's home in Richmond. Members of his family were with him when he died.

It was reported that Stuart had been ill for some two or three weeks with liver trouble, but that toward the end of the previous week he had felt so much better that he left his bed. He was reportedly seen on Friday, March 23, by his Liverpudlian friend Francis J. Cox, and sent a number of messages to Liverpool and Birkenhead theater managers. He then contracted a chill, which developed into pneumonia and pleurisy, causing him to lose consciousness. They were classic symptoms of the alcoholism that had killed his father. His doctor certified the causes of death as broncho-pneumonia, jaundice, and cirrhosis of the liver.

The following Friday a requiem mass took place in the Church of St. Elizabeth, Richmond. The organist played "O for the Wings of a Dove," "Pie Jesu," and "Requiem Eternum." To the strains of "O Rest in the Lord" the coffin was borne out of the church, and it was followed by Stuart's widow, two sons, and two daughters, Lola being absent through illness. In the church or at the graveside were colleagues representing various aspects of his career. Among them were composer Guy d'Hardelot, Hayden Coffin, songwriter Emmett Adams, journalist Hannen Swaffer, Sydney Ellison, John Lawley (a former choirboy in Salford), Francis J. Cox (representing the founders of the Old Xaverian Athletic Association), Charles Lucas (representing Francis, Day and Hunter), and Jacques Greebe (his musical arranger). Floral tributes came from Sir Oswald and Lady Stoll, the Gatti brothers, Herman Darewski and his wife Madge Temple, Zélie de Lussan, David and Frederick Day, and the staff of Francis, Day and Hunter, as well as other relatives and friends.

The *Era* reported that the sun shone brightly and a lark sang an anthem overhead as Stuart was laid to rest in Richmond Cemetery. A prelate of the Catholic Church, whose purple robes stood out in vivid relief against the fresh green of the turf, pronounced the last rites. Thomas Augustine Barrett, alias Leslie Stuart, was left to rest in a plot that remains today without a headstone but is readily locatable and tidily looked after.

Obituaries remembered the time long gone that his music represented. The *Manchester Evening News* perhaps got the right balance of the pros and cons in his makeup: "Quick-tempered, argumentative, yet easy to appease, and generous to a ludicrous extent, Leslie Stuart was as genuine as his music. . . . He was a delightful raconteur, and a charming companion, and gathered round him a large number of friends." James Tevnan, who had collaborated on those autobiographical articles in the

Empire News, sought to distinguish Tommy Barrett, the perpetually cheerful, generous, and effervescent raconteur, from Leslie Stuart. The latter was one moment confident that he would again be the idol of the West End and Broadway, the next full of doubt and jeopardizing his prospects through his pride and obduracy.[70]

Perhaps the most heartfelt tributes were in the *Manchester Evening Chronicle*, which read, "Bohemian in character he retained all the old-fashioned dignity and courtliness of manner. He had all the waywardness and loveableness associated with great artists, and his kindliness endeared him to all who had his acquaintance."

There followed a memoir from "a friend":

> If there was one quality that endeared Leslie Stuart to all who knew him it was his joy in life. He was always ready for a "lark," and would entertain the company for hours at the piano just for the sheer fun of playing. Stuart was the essence of the erratic genius, and although when the notion seized him he could produce such tantalising tunes as those of *Florodora*, he would not—could not—write to order, and the offers he refused from managers would make the mouth of Croesus water. The magic flow could not have been so vivid if it had not flowed of its own accord.
>
> He was the lovable Peter Pan who never properly grew up, and if he sometimes drove producers nearly mad because he could never be found when he was wanted, they loved him just the same. No one could help liking Leslie Stuart.

The "friend" who penned those comments was probably his old performing colleague Phil Herman. Certainly Herman provided the paper with detailed reminiscences, giving a personal example of how, even when in desperate financial straits himself, Stuart's natural generosity to any of his friends who fell on hard times was undiminished.[40]

As for Liverpool, the London correspondent of the *Liverpool Post and Mercury* observed, "The late Mr. Leslie Stuart had the heart of an Irishman and the mode of speech of a Lancastrian, and between the two with all his great melodic ability he found difficulty in getting on with the theatrical world which he had once conquered. . . . The whole character of light music changed during his lifetime, and Leslie Stuart declined to change with it. The consequence was that in recent years managers would not give him a chance. . . . His personal extravagances were almost childish, such as his habit of wearing a newly-bought collar every day. He was a most lavish host, and his house was Liberty Hall to all sorts of people."

Friends and colleagues remembered him with equal affection. Even Seymour Hicks, who never mentioned *Captain Kidd* in his several volumes of memoirs, had kind words, noting that Stuart, "a small, dapper fair-haired little fellow, always slightly more of his native Manchester than of London . . . took a delight in entertaining all and sundry, and it was owing to his over-generous nature that he died with little or no money."[34] George Grossmith, who after appearing in Stuart's shows had helped introduce the works of Jerome Kern, George Gershwin, and Vincent Youmans to Britain, wrote, "no composer (not even Sullivan) had such a distinct individuality in his work. Play sixteen bars of anything he wrote . . . and though you never heard it before you would say immediately: 'Leslie Stuart, of course.' Though English or Irish, whichever you prefer, he composed much in America, and there is little doubt he inspired to a great extent Gershwin, Kern, Youmans, and other modern American composers."[32]

In its coverage, the *Manchester Evening News* expressed surprise at the information that, on the Friday before his death, Stuart had signed an agreement for the production of his opera *Nina*. The title was unknown to the managers of the city's Palace and Prince's Theatres, who expressed the view that they would not hesitate to produce a new Stuart work. The manager of the former added that about three years before it had almost been agreed to produce *The Girl from Nyusa* at the Palace Theatre, but that negotiations had been dropped at the last moment. "Almost" and "negotiations dropped" were the story of Stuart's last fifteen years.

Whether or not a contract was actually signed at that time, one certainly was on June 29, 1928, between Stuart's Executors and the Shubert Theatrical Company. May Leslie Stuart obtained Rowland Leigh for an updated libretto, and wrote on August 17 to J. J. Shubert, "I really think you will be pleased with the "book", which is practically finished. While the original story remains, there is such an entirely different construction that you need have no fear that Hamilton could make *any* claim. . . . Rowland Leigh, as you may know, is half American. His Grandfather was General Gordon who did great things in the Civil War and his people own practically the whole of Savannah, consequently he writes more as an American than an Englishman. . . . The music is ready, the lyrics are completed, the orchestration is entirely ready for either 37, 24 or 15 pieces. . . . You never can have any idea what chaos all the music was in. It was all over London and Manchester, held sometimes in pawn, sometimes he just forgot it."[54]

On September 5, the Shuberts signed a contract with Leigh, and on September 6, May wrote again to say that the material was being sent to New York. She declared that the act 1 finale was orchestrator Jacques Greebe's masterpiece, and that "there is no doubt it is the greatest tour de force that Father ever wrote and will be a sensation." However, the Shuberts cabled that they were not satisfied with the book. May referred the matter to her solicitors, who wrote on her behalf on November 24: "Mrs. Mayhew expresses surprise at this, as she is more than pleased with same." The Shuberts responded on December 3, 1928, "We did cable that the book was inadequate. It is absolutely without any merit so far as an American audience is concerned. There is hardly any premise for a story for American consumption. . . . Also note you say that Mrs. Mayhew is very well pleased. Unfortunately Mrs. Mayhew is not putting up the money to produce this play. . . . I regret exceedingly that Mrs. Mayhew did not take the gentleman she had in mind at first to do this play. Mr. Leigh was merely to do the lyrics." Once again matters developed into acrimonious argument (and eventually a writ), but not to production.[54]

The Girl from Nyusa, too, was announced for production in 1930, but again without coming to anything. Precisely how this differed from *Nina* it is now scarcely possible to know, but surviving synopses make the link unmistakable. Seemingly the latter title was used in America, the former in Britain, although May referred more than once to there being more than one unproduced work. Alas, the mass of disorganized material and May's readiness to present it in new forms in the hope of getting it produced scarcely make it possible to disentangle everything now. The BBC did apparently broadcast songs from *The Girl from Nyusa* in performances by Olive Groves and John Rorke. *Follow My Lady* and *Lovelight* are other titles found on surviving *Nina* synopses.

Noël Coward's use of "The Soldiers of the Queen" in *Cavalcade* in 1931 was to be only one of such uses on stage, screen, and radio over the years to recapture the atmosphere of the Boer War. Also, in July 1931, there was a London revival of *Florodora*—again under the management of J. Bannister Howard—at Daly's Theatre, with George Graves as Tweedlepunch and "topical lyrics by Arthur Klein." Though officially there was no film version of *Florodora*, a 1925 Australian film called *Painted Daughters* claimed in its advertising to be based on the show. As for Hollywood's 1930 offering *The Florodora Girl*, it included a performance of "Tell Me, Pretty Maiden" alongside some very non-Stuart numbers. The double sextet had become so very much a part of American vaudeville performances that the show was widely assumed to be of American origin, and it had a further summer revival by the Shuberts in the 1930s.

It was also in America, in August 1941, that the composer's widow, Kitty, died. She had been taken there on the outbreak of World War II by her youngest daughter, Lola, who in 1934 had married Francis Worthington Hine, son of a treasurer of Bankers Trust. Kitty Stuart's remains were buried in the Cemetery of the Gate of Heaven in Westchester County, New York, in 1946.[67]

Meanwhile, in May 1938 Alderman Joseph Toole, deputy lord mayor of Manchester, announced a subscription for funds for a plaque to commemorate Leslie Stuart. On April 12, 1939, Toole presented the resultant bronzed plaster plaque for exhibition in the Henry Watson Music Library. Designed by John Cassidy, it was duly hung in the corridor of the second floor of Manchester Central Library, but was eventually vandalized and damaged beyond repair.

Nostalgia induced by World War II helped keep the memory of Leslie Stuart and his times alive in Britain. In 1940 a film biography was released by British Lion, under the title *You Will Remember*, with Robert Morley as Leslie Stuart and Tom E. Finglass as Eugene Stratton. Finglass had built up a career impersonating Stratton and was able to boast a letter from Stuart, dated September 23, 1927, certifying that he had his permission to use his songs at any time. The film was typically loose with the facts, one scene finding Stuart in jail for debt. In 1945 Aubrey Danvers-Walker wrote the script for a radio show, *Hullo, Yesterday*, featuring Leslie Stuart's best-known songs, and this led in the spring of 1946 to May's radio adaptation of *The Girl from Nyusa*, renamed *Treasure of Pearl* after the big waltz song. In November 1950, May introduced a series of three hour-long biographical radio programs on her father written by Leslie Baily.

After the war, Stuart's songs retained familiarity in Britain, not least for "olde tyme" dances. During the 1960s, "Lily of Laguna" was still being sung by Britain's blackface troupe "The Black and White Minstrels," before political correctness eventually brought that to an end. In the spring of 1978, the BBC produced an eight-part television series called *The Songwriters*, written by Tony Staveacre, who also wrote an accompanying book.[69] The first songwriter featured was Leslie Stuart, the other programs being devoted to Lionel Monckton, Noël Coward, Ray Noble, Ivor Novello, Lionel Bart, John Lennon and Paul McCartney, and Tim Rice and Andrew Lloyd Webber. The Stuart program, on June 15, 1978, included several numbers that were by then long forgotten. Besides a snatch of "Soldiers of the Queen" (evoking Queen Victoria's Diamond Jubilee procession), it featured "Is That You, O'Riley?" (evoking the Slip Inn), "The Little Mademoiselle," "The Girl on the Ran-Dan-Dan," "Sweetheart May," "Is Yer Mammie Always with Ye?" "Little Dolly Daydream," "The Cake Walk," "I May Be Crazy," "Tell Me, Pretty Maiden," "Shade of the Palm," "Lily of Laguna," "In Montezuma," "The Gibson Girl," and even a snatch of the tango for Rudolph Valentino in *Nina*.

Florodora had meanwhile achieved a British touring production in the 1950s, albeit in much revised form, but thereafter disappeared almost completely along with others of its ilk as Britain succumbed to the craze for American musical theater. The only subsequent appearance of music from *Florodora* on the London stage seems to have been when "The Fellow Who Might" was included in Harold Fielding's spectacular extravaganza *Ziegfeld* at the London Palladium in 1988. In America, by contrast, the rediscovery of theater scores of the past did not ignore *Florodora*. An Off-Off-Broadway production by Bandwagon on February 20, 1981, was followed in 1996 by a revival by the Catholic University of America as part of its Musical Theater Research Project.[2]

Leslie Stuart's children—at odds as a result of their father's excesses and his divisive will—were reconciled by the 1940s, though the family's nature meant its members would always blow hot and cold toward each other. Of the five who reached adulthood, the first to die was Marie Roze ("Dolly") in 1949, followed by Stephen in the early 1950s, and May in 1956. Following the death of May's husband in 1960, her children sought once more to arouse interest in the *Nina* music, imagining that the "Treasure of Pearl" theme running through *Nina* might become a ballad for Perry Como or Frank Sinatra. They submitted manuscript copies of the music, together with privately made recordings of *Nina*, to both Chappells and EMI, only to elicit the inevitable response that the music was "hopelessly out of date."[67]

The death of Leslie Stuart Jr. in 1970 left Lola as the only surviving child, and on August 23, 1988, a curious item appeared in the "Peterborough" column of the *Daily Telegraph* referring to a ninety-two-year-old lady in Sevenoaks, Kent, who was about to send a cable to American presidential candidate George H. W. Bush. In it she declared herself "Aunt Lola" Stuart-Hine, who had taught Bush tennis at Kennebunkport, Maine.[17] This was indeed Lola, who had got to know the Bushes through her husband's banking connections. A photograph exists of her relaxing with George Bush's mother, Dorothy, and aunt, Nancy Walker. After the death of her husband, Lola had lived in an apartment on Park Avenue until her sister Dolly's son Ross de Havilland and his wife Barbara installed her in the Sevenoaks nursing home when her health began to fail in 1985. George Bush duly replied to Lola on September 8, 1988.[67] By the time he was elected the forty-first president of the United States, however, she was no longer around to bask in the reflected glory, having died at her Sevenoaks nursing home on October 3, 1988.

Compact disc has now made some early recordings of Stuart's music conveniently available again. Pavilion Records reissued the original cast recordings of *Florodora,* along with Stuart's early piano solo recordings, and Pearl Records has released the complete original Victor Light Opera selections from the pre-electric era, including both *Florodora* and *Havana*. Some of Eugene Stratton's recordings, as well as Peter Dawson's 1929 recording of "The Bandolero," have also reappeared.

Moreover, for all that Leslie Stuart's music has fallen out of fashion, there still are those who do treasure it—and in elevated circles, too. Eric Sams, German Lieder specialist and Shakespeare scholar, considers him "one of the supreme melodists of the age, who ought to be sung and lilted more often than he is." Most remarkably, perhaps, in December 1998, the *Times* began a short series called "Unsung Heroes," celebrating long-forgotten figures of twentieth-century arts. The first contribution was by the paper's esteemed opera critic, Rodney Milnes, who devoted his contribution not to some forgotten opera singer, but to Leslie Stuart. It brought him a bigger reader response than anything else he had written for the *Times*. He explained his choice as follows:

> Back in the late 1940s, when television programmes—on one channel!—were broadcast for a few hours each evening, the rest of the day was filled with what I think were called test transmissions, half a dozen or so items of wide variety to demonstrate the wonders of the new medium. Then as now in thrall to the box, I sat transfixed, watching them over and over again (anything rather than work). . . .

But the test transmission that riveted me then and rivets me still was a little number called *Tell Me Pretty Maiden* ("are there any more at home like you?"), performed in stately Players Theatre fashion, all eyes, teeth and winsomeness. I can see it now. The tune was catchy— it has never left me and never will—and part of its fascination, which perhaps I instinctively realised at the time but certainly did not rationalise until much later, was that the phrases were uneven: they did not fall into the normal eight-bar patterns, but followed the text, the decorously flirtatious conversation between clean-limbed boys and gels ("there are a few," the latter replied coyly).[43]

Milnes went on to tell readers something of Leslie Stuart's career and Eugene Stratton's songs. He confessed that he had read the synopsis of *Florodora* four times, stone-cold sober, and still couldn't make head or tail of it, and he then analyzed its music, noting, "*Tell Me Pretty Maiden* is the stand-out. It's interesting to learn that it was one of the few numbers for which Stuart also wrote the words—so *that's* why the music is shaped by the text. A Sondheim *avant la lettre*, a Wagner after the event. Stuart knew exactly when to give a number a lift with a modulation or a frisky harmonic sidestep: there are other numbers in *Florodora* with oddly uneven phrase structures, some scrunchy, decidedly adventurous chromatic progressions, and nice major-minor alternations. Stylistically, he is streets ahead of his contemporaries and marks a significant advance even on Sullivan, who was essentially a conservative composer, looking back to Gounod and Donizetti both for inspiration and material to parody."[43]

Milnes advocated a fresh look at Stuart's shows, putting in a particular plea for *Havana,* with its "elaborately worked-out finales ... , one smashing waltz song ('I'm a Cuban Girl'), and one rather good joke." Altogether he made an eloquent case for rediscovery, claiming that "in Stuart, certainly in his rhythms, you can hear seeds of early Jerome Kern, who travelled regularly to London to learn what was going on this side of the pond. Kern, admittedly a far better composer, went on to *Show Boat*, and the modern musical was born. By all of which I suppose I am suggesting that it would be nice if, instead of endlessly recycling the obvious standards, producers took another look at Stuart, a palpable missing link in the development of the popular musical. Apart from anything else, designers could have fun with the frocks—all those tall, hourglass showgirls, padded top and bottom, front and back, huge picture hats and every now and then a glimpse of well-turned ankle."[43]

One can scarcely say fairer than that. Yet it is also easy to argue that Leslie Stuart's stage scores were not his greatest contribution to posterity. After all, he was only *one* of the finest musical theater composers of his time, whereas in the field of music-hall scenas he was unique. If Eugene Stratton could have committed to film his performances of "Little Dolly Daydream," "Lily of Laguna," and "I May Be Crazy," is it too fanciful to suggest that they would have become artistic treasures admired every bit as much as Charlie Chaplin's clowning or Busby Berkeley's Hollywood choreography?

Sources

1. John Abbott. *The Story of Francis, Day and Hunter*. London: Francis, Day and Hunter, 1952.
2. Ellwood Annaheim. "*Florodora*: Musical Theater Research Project." Online at www.geocities.com/musictheater/floro/floro.html (1996).
3. Rudolph Aronson. *Theatrical and Musical Memoirs*. New York: McBride, Nast, 1913.
4. Tony Barker. "Eugene Stratton," *Music Hall* (London) 12 (April 1980).
5. W. H. Berry. *Forty Years in the Limelight*. London: Hutchinson, 1939.
6. W. H. Boardman: *Vaudeville Days*. London: Jarrolds, 1935.
7. William Boosey. *Fifty Years of Music*. London: Ernest Benn, 1931.
8. Gerald Bordman. *American Musical Theatre*, 3d ed. New York: Oxford University Press, 2001.
9. Gerald Bordman. *Jerome Kern: His Life and Music*. New York: Oxford University Press, 1980.
10. Hilda Brighten. *No Bridge to Yesterday*. London: Victor Gollancz, 1949 .
11. Billie Burke, with Cameron Shipp. *With a Feather on My Nose*. London: Peter Davies, 1950.
12. Neville Cardus. *Autobiography*. London: Collins, 1947.
13. Neville Cardus. *Second Innings*. London: Collins, 1950.
14. James Coover. *Music Publishing, Copyright and Piracy in Victorian England*. London: Mansell Publishing, 1985.

15. Robert Courtneidge. *I Was an Actor Once*. London: Hutchinson, n.d. [1930?].
16. *Daily Mail* (London), May 15, 1906. "Leslie Stuartism: Is It Real Music?"
17. *Daily Telegraph* (London), August 23, 1988: "Peterborough: Late Call."
18. Robin Daniels. *Conversations with Cardus*. London: Victor Gollancz, 1976.
19. Herman Darewski. *Musical Memories*. London: Jarrolds, 1937.
20. Clara Novello Davies. *The Life I Have Loved*. London: William Heinemann, 1940.
21. *The Era*, June 3, 1899. "Popular Composers: Mr Leslie Stuart."
22. *The Era*, November 23, 1901. "A Chat with Lester Barrett."
23. *The Era*, October 18, 1902. "A Chat with Leslie Stuart."
24. *The Era*, January 27, 1906. "The Music Piracy Trial: Mr Leslie Stuart's Views."
25. Tolchard Evans. Comments in *Desert Island Discs*, BBC Radio 4, April 1976.
26. Herman Finck. *My Melodious Memories*. London: Hutchinson, 1937.
27. Kurt Gänzl. *The British Musical Theatre*. London: Macmillan, 1986.
28. Kurt Gänzl. *Encyclopedia of the Musical Theatre*, 2d ed. New York, Schirmer, 2001.
29. Douglas Gilbert. *American Vaudeville: Its Life and Times*. New York: Whittlesey House, 1940.
30. James M. Glover. *Jimmy Glover: His Book*. London: Methuen, 1911.
31. George Graves. *Gaieties and Gravities*. London: Hutchinson, 1931.
32. George Grossmith. *"G. G."*. London: Hutchinson, 1933.
33. Cosmo Hamilton. *Unwritten History*. London: Hutchinson, 1924.
34. Seymour Hicks. *Vintage Years*. London: Cassell, 1943.
35. Gervase Hughes. *Composers of Operetta*. London: Macmillan, 1962.
36. *Illustrated Mail*, January 19, 1901. "A Chat with Mr Leslie Stuart."
37. "Limelight." Online at www.abc.net.au/limelight (2001).
38. W. Macqueen-Pope. *The Melodies Linger On*. London: W. H. Allen, n.d. [1950/51].
39. *M.A.P.*, October 28, 1899, and November 25, 1899. "Leslie Stuart."
40. *Manchester Evening Chronicle*, March 31, 1928. "Song That Set Nation Singing."
41. Edward B. Marks, with Abbott J. Liebling. *They All Sang: From Tony Pastor to Rudy Vallée*. New York: Viking Press, 1934.
42. Brooks McNamara. *The Shuberts of Broadway*. New York: Oxford University Press, 1990.
43. Rodney Milnes. "A Toast to the Florodora man," *Times*, December 30, 1998.
44. William and Mary Morris. *Morris Dictionary of Word and Phrase Origins*. New York: HarperCollins, 1988.
45. *Music Trades Review*, April 15, 1898. "The Song Copyright Question."
46. James T. Powers. *Twinkle Little Star*. New York: G. P. Putnam's Sons, 1939.
47. "Harriet Quimby—In Her Own Words." Online at www.harrietquimby.org (2001).
48. Jack Raymond. *Show Music on Record: The First One Hundred Years*. Washington, D.C., 1998.
49. Ada Reeve. *Take It for a Fact*. London: William Heinemann, 1954.
50. Arthur Roberts. *Fifty Years of Spoof*. London: The Bodley Head, 1927.
51. T. Roberts. "Stories of Some Successful Songs." *Royal Magazine*, 1900.
52. Adrian Ross. "Havana," *Play Pictorial* 71 (1908).
53. Brian Rust, with Rex Bunnett. *London Musical Shows on Record, 1897–1976*. Harrow: Gramophone, 1977.

54. Shubert Archive, New York. Contracts and correspondence.

55. *Southport Guardian*, March 2, 1901. "'Florodora': Its Producer and Composer."

56. *Southport Guardian*, March 6, 1901. "Local Jottings."

57. *Southport Visiter*, March 2, 1901: "'Florodora'—Interview with Mr Leslie Stuart."

58. *Spy* (Manchester), November 21, 1891. "Mr T. A. Barrett."

59. Tony Staveacre. *The Songwriters*, BBC Television, June 15, 1978, and accompanying book. London: British Broadcasting Corporation, 1980.

60. Leslie Stuart. "Beggared by Piracy," *Daily Mail*, January 9, 1906.

61. Leslie Stuart. "In the Days of My Youth: Chapters of Autobiography," *M.A.P.*, October 5, 1901.

62. Leslie Stuart. "My Bohemian Life-Story," *Empire News* (Manchester), August 14–November 13, 1927; fourteen weekly installments.

63. Leslie Stuart. "Personal Reminiscences," *Liverpool Review* 35, no. 1816 (April 26, 1902).

64. Leslie Stuart. Scrapbook of telegrams and press cuttings (author's collection).

65. May Leslie Stuart. "The Irishman Who Made the World Sing: The Story of Leslie Stuart," radio script, n.d. [1940s?].

66. May Leslie Stuart. Contributions to Leslie Baily: "The Life of Leslie Stuart," radio script, BBC Home Service, November 12–26, 1950 (three weekly installments).

67. Stuart family documents and anecdotes.

68. Mark Sullivan. *Our Times*, vol. 3, *Pre-War America*. New York: Charles Scribner's, 1930.

69. Ellaline Terriss, with others. *Ellaline Terriss*. London: Cassell, 1928.

70. James Tevnan. "Leslie Stuart and Tommy Barrett," *Empire News* (Manchester), April 1, 1928.

71. Vesta Tilley [Lady de Frece]. *Recollections of Vesta Tilley*. London: Hutchinson, 1934.

72. W. R. Titterton. *From Theatre to Music Hall*. London: Stephen Swift, 1912.

73. Harry S. Truman. Letter in "Truman File." Online at www.whistlestop.org (2001).

74. Horace Annesley Vachell. *Distant Fields*. London: Cassell, 1973.

75. Edward N. Waters. *Victor Herbert: A Life in Music*. New York: Macmillan, 1955.

76. *Woman's Life*, February 8, 1902. "How I Wrote 'Tell Me, Pretty Maiden.'"

77. *The World*, June 19, 1901. "Mr Leslie Stuart 'At Home.'"

78. Richard and Paulette Ziegfeld. *The Ziegfeld Touch: The Life and Times of Florenz Ziegfeld, Jr*. New York: Harry N. Abrams, 1993.

Compositions

Pre-1885 (as T. A. Barrett)

Hearts Ever True [cited in *Spy* article, 1891]

John Malone [cited by Phil Herman as written for the opening of Manchester Town Hall, 1877]

Meet Me To-night [cited by Phil Herman]

Mr. O'Shay's Little Shop [cited by Phil Herman]

Rocking the Baby to Sleep [cited by Phil Herman as from 1876]

Walking on the Promenade [cited by Phil Herman]

Wake, Lady, Wake (serenade) [dedicated: from T. A. Barrett to K. Fox, September 15, 1884]

1885 (as T. A. Barrett)

Bounding o'er the Deep (words: Leon Desmond)   J. B. Cramer

1888–89 (as Leslie Stuart)

Cherished Vows [dedicated to Lady Stafford] (words: Leslie Stuart) J. B. Cramer

Queen of the Night (trio) [concert, Manchester, November 30, 1889]

1892 (as T. A. Barrett)

The Holy Name (grand motets and benedictions)   R. Cocks

> No. 1. Tantum Ergo (four voice chorale with solos) [dedicated to Father Bernard Vaughan]
>
> No. 2. Ave Maria (soprano and tenor duet and chorus)
>
> No. 3. O Salutaris (tenor and bass duet)
>
> No. 4. Peuri Hebraeorum (anthem for Palm Sunday)
>
> No. 5. O Salutaris (tenor solo and chorus) [dedicated to Father Zulueta]
>
> No. 6. O Cor Amoris (men's voices)
>
> No. 7. Salve Regina (solos and chorus)
>
> No. 8. Ave Verum (bass solo and chorus)
>
> No. 9. Jesu Dulcis Memoria (chorale)
>
> No. 10. Tantum Ergo (solo and chorus)
>
> No. 11. Ave Regina (quartet)
>
> No. 12. O Salutaris (soprano solo and chorus)

1892 (as Leslie Stuart)

Molly (words: Leslie Stuart)	R. Cocks
The Vales of Arklow (words: Leslie Stuart)	R. Cocks
Were I a King (words: Leon Desmond)	J. B. Cramer

1893–96 (as Lester Thomas)

The Lads of the Village [listed in Pazdírek's *Universal-Handbuch der Musikliteratur*]	E. Ascherberg
Katie, I Love You True (words: Felix McGlennon)	Francis, Day and Hunter
Sheelagh Magee (words: Lester Thomas)	Francis, Day and Hunter
Eily Riley (words: Lester Thomas)	Francis, Day and Hunter
McGinnis's "At Home" (words: Lester Thomas)	Francis, Day and Hunter
Baby Eyes (words: Lester Thomas)	Francis, Day and Hunter
By the Sad Sea Waves (words: Lester Barrett)	Francis, Day and Hunter
I Didn't Know Till Afterwards, or, I Laughed (words: P. Sweeney)	Francis, Day and Hunter
Some Danced the Lancers (words: Lester Barrett)	Francis, Day and Hunter
Louisiana Lou (words: Lester Thomas)	Francis, Day and Hunter
The Little Mad'moiselle (words: Lester Thomas)	Francis, Day and Hunter
In a Cottage By the Sea (words: Lester Barrett)	Francis, Day and Hunter
All for Me (words: Lester Barrett)	Francis, Day and Hunter
They're All Fine Girls (words: P. Sweeney and Lester Barrett)	Francis, Day and Hunter
De Missis ob de House (words: Malcolm Arnold)	Francis, Day and Hunter

1894 (HEREAFTER AS LESLIE STUART)

The Bandolero (words: Leslie Stuart)   Chappell

Why So Late? (words: Leslie Stuart)   R. Cocks

1895

> **Baron Golosh** *(Swansea, New Theatre, 15 April 1895)*
>
> Unidentified songs

I Went to Paris with Papa (words: Leslie Stuart)   Francis, Day and Hunter

Oh! Venus, Let Me Call You Sal   Francis, Day and Hunter
  [The Limelight Man's Lament]
  (words: Leslie Stuart)

> **An Artist's Model** *(second edition; Daly's Theatre, September 28, 1895)*
>
> The Military Model (words: Leslie Stuart)   Francis, Day and Hunter
>
> The Soldiers of the Queen (words: Leslie Stuart) Francis, Day and Hunter
>
> Trilby Will be True (words: Leslie Stuart)   Hopwood and Crew

Sweetheart May (words: Leslie Stuart)   Francis, Day and Hunter

The Donna Señora of Gay Seville   Francis, Day and Hunter
  (words: Leslie Stuart)

I Never Saw a Girl Like That (words: Leslie Stuart)   Francis, Day and Hunter

If You Were Me (words: R. Martin)   Boosey

1896

Rip Van Winkle (words: Leslie Stuart)   Chappell

Is Yer Mammie Always with Ye? (words: Leslie Stuart) Francis, Day and Hunter

The Willow Pattern Plate (words: Leslie Stuart)   Francis, Day and Hunter

> **The Ballet Girl** *(Wolverhampton, Grand Theatre, March 15, 1897)*
>
> She's an English Girl (words: Leslie Stuart)   Francis, Day and Hunter
>
> De Baby Am a Cryin', Mommer Come
> (words: Leslie Stuart)   Francis, Day and Hunter

The Girl on the Ran-dan-dan (words: Leslie Stuart)   Francis, Day and Hunter

Dear Boy, Ta-ta!   Francis, Day and Hunter

> **Babes in the Wood** *(Manchester, Prince's Theatre, December 1896)*
>
> Opening chorus, scene 7

1897

In the Summer (words: Leslie Stuart)   Francis, Day and Hunter

> **The Circus Girl** *(London, Gaiety Theatre, December 5, 1896)*
> She May Not Be That Sort of Girl   Francis, Day and Hunter

> **The Yashmak** *(London, Shaftesbury Theatre, March 31, 1897)*
> The Silly Old Man in the Moon   Francis, Day and Hunter
> (words: Leslie Stuart)

Little Dolly Daydream (words: Leslie Stuart)   Francis, Day and Hunter

> **Lost, Stolen or Strayed (A Day in Paris)** *(London, Duke of York's Theatre, April 27, 1897)*
> The Goblin and the Fay (words: Leslie Stuart)   Francis, Day and Hunter

The Valleys of Eden (words: Leslie Stuart)   Boosey
The Dandy Fifth (words: Leslie Stuart)   Francis, Day and Hunter

> **Puss in Boots** *(Manchester, Prince's Theatre, December 23, 1897)*
> Opening chorus, act 1
> Finale, act 1, scene 2
> Haymakers' chorus, act 2

1898

From Skies to Earth Again (words: Leslie Stuart)   Francis, Day and Hunter
The Lily of Laguna (words: Leslie Stuart)   Francis, Day and Hunter
The Down on the Butterfly's Wings
   [announced as sung by Elaine Ravensberg]
The Girl with the Roses Red [A Story of Far Alsace] Francis, Day and Hunter
   (words: Leslie Stuart)
Just the Tale by Night and Day [A Lady in the Case] Francis, Day and Hunter
   (duet) (words: Leslie Stuart)
The Little Anglo-Saxon Every Time   Francis, Day and Hunter
   (words: Leslie Stuart)
The Cake Walk (words: Leslie Stuart)   Francis, Day and Hunter
Drummer Dick [Oxford Music Hall, November 7, 1898]
   (words: Beatrix M. DeBurgh)
I Must Love Some One; It Might As Well Be You
   [announced as sung by Vesta Tilley]

1899

The Coon Drum Major (words: Leslie Stuart)   Francis, Day and Hunter

My Little Octoroon (words: Leslie Stuart)   Francis, Day and Hunter

A Soldier's Sin [reportedly sung by Richard Hoodless,
    Kennington Theatre, August 1899]

Florodora *(London, Lyric Theatre, November 11, 1899)*   *Francis, Day and Hunter*

ACT 1

Flowers A-Blooming So Gay (chorus) (words: Ernest Boyd-Jones)

The Credit's Due to Me (sextet) (Clerks) (words: Ernest Boyd-Jones)

The Silver Star of Love (Dolores) (words: Leslie Stuart)

Somebody (Dolores, Abercoed) (words: Leslie Stuart)

Chorus of Welcome (words: Ernest Boyd-Jones)

Come and See Our Island (English Girls, Clerks) (words: Leslie Stuart)

When I Leave Town (Lady Holyrood) (words: Paul Rubens)

Galloping (Angela, Donegal) (words: Ernest Boyd-Jones)

I Want to Marry a Man, I Do (Lady Holyrood, Tweedlepunch, Gilfain)
(words: Paul Rubens)

The Fellow Who Might (Angela, chorus) (words: J. Hickory Wood)

Phrenology (Gilfain) (words: Ernest Boyd-Jones)

When an Interfering Person (Lady Holyrood, Donegal, Angela)
(words: Paul Rubens)

The Shade of the Palm (Abercoed) (words: Leslie Stuart)

Finale: Hey! Hey! A-lack a-day! (words: Ernest Boyd-Jones)

ACT 2

Come Lads and Lasses (chorus) (words: Ernest Boyd-Jones)

Tact (Lady Holyrood, chorus) (words: Paul Rubens)

The Millionaire (Gilfain) (words: Ernest Boyd-Jones)

Tell Me, Pretty Maiden [I Must Love Some One] (English Girls, Clerks)
(words: Leslie Stuart)

Mysterious Musicians (Dolores, Tweedlepunch) (words: Ernest Boyd-Jones)

Land of My Home (Abercoed) (words: Leslie Stuart)

Finale: The Millionaire (words: Ernest Boyd-Jones)

1900

Florodora   *Francis, Day and Hunter*

SUPPLEMENTARY NUMBERS

We Get Up at 8 A.M. (Valleda, Leandro) (words: Leslie Stuart)

He Didn't Like the Look of It at All (Donegal) (words: Frank A. Clement)

I Want to Be a Military Man (Donegal) (words: Frank A. Clement)

He Loves Me, He Loves Me Not (Dolores) (words: Ernest Boyd-Jones)

Willie Was a Gay Boy (Whistling Song) (Angela) (words: Alfred Murray)

When We Are on the Stage (Dolores, Tweedlepunch) (words: Paul Rubens)

I Don't Know Nobody (words: Richard Morton)   Francis, Day and Hunter

The Banshee (words: Leslie Stuart)   Francis, Day and Hunter

1901

The Silver Slipper *(London, Lyric Theatre, June 1, 1901)*   *Francis, Day and Hunter*

ACT 1

Our College Gowns (chorus) (words: W. H. Risque)

To-Night's the Night (Sir Victor, chorus) (words: W. H. Risque)

[We'll Just] Let It Go At That (quintet) (words: W. H. Risque)

When No One Knows (Louis, Brenda) (words: W. H. Risque)

That's the Way That's Sure to Pay (Miss Jimper, Berkeley, Twanks) (words: W. H. Risque)

If I Were a Girl Instead (Wrenne) (words: Leslie Stuart)

A Glimpse–impse–impse (Stella) (words: W. H. Risque)

Hunt the Slipper (concerted number) (words: Leslie Stuart)

Good Behaviour (Miss Jimper) (words: George Rollit)

Finale: We Don't Intend to Stay (words: Leslie Stuart)

ACT 2

Hi! Hi! Hi! Hi! (chorus) (words: W. H. Risque)

The Tup'ny Show (Wrenne) (words: W. H. Risque)

Come, Little Girl, and Tell Me Truly (double sextet) (words: Leslie Stuart)

Two Eyes of Blue (Louis) (words: Charles H. Taylor)

Marche Militaire—Danse Parisienne

Four-and-Twenty Little Men (Stella, men's chorus) (words: W. H. Risque)

She Didn't Know Enough about the Game (Berkeley, chorus) (words: George Rollit)

Class (Miss Jimper) (words: Charles H. Taylor)

SUPPLEMENTARY NUMBERS

We Work at Play [Toys?] (quartet) (Berkeley, Tiraupigeon, Roland, Harry)

My Studio (Berkeley) (words: Charles H. Taylor)

The Detrimental Man (Berkeley) (words: Charles H. Taylor)

The Baby with the Dimple and the Smile (words: Charles H. Taylor)

Compositions

I May Be Crazy, But I Love You (A Mexican Romance) Francis, Day and Hunter
(words: Leslie Stuart)

1902

Waiting for Jack (A Skipper of the Blue)   Francis, Day and Hunter
(words: Leslie Stuart)

The Silver Slipper *(New Haven, Connecticut, Hyperion Theatre, October 21, 1902)*

Mad'moiselle Éternelle (words: Charles H. Taylor)   Francis, Day and Hunter

---

Robinson Crusoe *(Manchester, Prince's Theatre, December 1902)*

Fear Not the Twilight (duet) (act 1, scene 4)

1903

The School Girl *(London, Prince of Wales's Theatre, May 9, 1903)   Francis, Day and Hunter*

ACT 1

Gaily Rings the Bell (chorus) (words: Charles H. Taylor)

The Honeymoon Girl (Cicely) (words: Charles H. Taylor)

When I Was a Girl Like You (Mother Superior) (words: Charles H. Taylor)

The Daughters of the Guard (Lillian) (words: Leslie Stuart)

Chorus (Stockbrokers' Clerks and Visitors) (words: Charles H. Taylor)

Chickoo (We're Only Just Sixteen) (American girls) (words: Charles H. Taylor)

Belinda on the Line (Sir Ormesby) (words: Paul A. Rubens)

From Skies to Earth Again (Verney) (words: Leslie Stuart) [see 1898]

Looking for a Needle in a Haystack (Tubby) (words: Charles H. Taylor)

Call Round Again (Lillian) (words: Leslie Stuart)

Finale: We're Going to Be at Least (words: Leslie Stuart and
Charles H. Taylor)

ACT 2

Étudiant des Beaux Arts (chorus) (words: Charles H. Taylor)

My Little Canoe (Mamie Reckfeller) (words: Leslie Stuart)

Clytie (Lillian) (words: Charles H. Taylor)

Just the Tale by Night and Day (Lillian, Verney) (words: Leslie Stuart and
Charles H. Taylor) [see 1898]

There's Nothing Like a Wife (quartet and dance) (words: Charles H. Taylor)

Tarantella, Valse and Cake Walk

One Girl Too Many (Tubby) (words: Charles H. Taylor)

La Rosière (Lillian) (words: Adrian Ross)

If Ma Says "No" (words: Percy Greenbank)   Francis, Day and Hunter

1904

My Little Black Pearl (words: Leslie Stuart)   Francis, Day and Hunter

1906

There's Nothing Like Your First Love after All   Francis, Day and Hunter
  (words: Richard Morton)

The Belle of Mayfair *(London, Vaudeville Theatre, April 11, 1906)   Francis, Day and Hunter*

ACT 1

Opening Chorus (words: Basil Hood)

Bells in the Morning (Pincott) (words: William Caine)

I Am a Military Man (Lord Mount Highgate) (words: William Caine)

Eight Little Débutantes Are We (concerted number)
(words: William Caine)

In Gay Mayfair (Julia) (words: William Caine)

What Makes the Woman? (Raymond) (words: George Arthurs)

The Matron and the Maid (Lady Chaldicott, Comte de Perrier)
(words: Charles Wilmott)

Welcome to Princess (chorus) (words: Basil Hood)

Said I to Myself (Princess) (words: Basil Hood)

Where You Go, Will I Go (Julia) (words: Basil Hood)

What Will the World Say? (Meredith) (words: Basil Hood)

Come to St George's (Julia, Princess, Raymond, Meredith)
(words: Leslie Stuart)

Finale (words: Basil Hood)

ACT 2

Opening Chorus (words: Basil Hood)

My Little Girl Is a Shy Little Girl (Pincott, Simpson)
(words: Basil Hood)

I'm a Duchess (Duchess) (words: Basil Hood)

Hello! Come Along, Girls (Meredith) (words: Leslie Stuart)

We've Come from Court (Julia, Princess, Lady Chaldicott, Comte de Perrier, Theobald) (words: Basil Hood)

Play the Game (Julia) (words: Basil Hood)

And the Weeping-Willow Wept (Princess) (words: George Arthurs)

In Montezuma (Julia) (words: Leslie Stuart)

I Know a Girl (Raymond, Meredith, Comte de Perrier, Lord Mount Highgate) (words: Leslie Stuart)

Finale: Come to St George's (words: Leslie Stuart)

SUPPLEMENTARY NUMBERS:

Why Do They Call Me a Gibson Girl? (Duchess) (words: Leslie Stiles)

I'll Wait For You, Little Girlie (words: George Arthurs)

She Always Does the Right Thing (words: George Arthurs)

1907

The Belle of Mayfair   *Francis, Day and Hunter*

SUPPLEMENTARY NUMBERS

The English and French Maid (words: George Arthurs)

Do You Waltz? (words: George Arthurs)

Come Back to Pierette, Pierrot! (words: George Arthurs)

The Girlie in the Goggles and the Veil (words: George Arthurs)

Military Mad (words: George Arthurs)

The Pine Girl (words: George Arthurs)

Six Little Pantomime Boys (words: Leslie Stuart)

If You Must Sigh (words: Leslie Stuart)

On the Road to Tipperary (words: George Arthurs)   Chappell

The Old Shield (words: Leslie Stuart)   Chappell

1908

My Cute Maluma Girl (words: Leslie Stuart)   Chappell

Havana *(London, Gaiety Theatre, April 25, 1908)*   *Chappell*

ACT 1

'Tis Noon, the Noon of Tropic Day (chorus) (words: Adrian Ross)

If I Was a Ruler Despotical (Bombito, girls' chorus) (words: Adrian Ross)

My Husband (Anita, chorus) (words: Adrian Ross)

The Yacht, sextet (Tita, Lolita, Pepita, Bombito, Hilario, Alejandro) (words: Adrian Ross)

I'm a Cuban Girl (Consuelo, chorus) (words: Adrian Ross)
Hello, People! (Adolfo, girls) (words: George Arthurs)
And Then That Cigar Went Out (Jackson, chorus) (words: Adrian Ross)
According How You Take 'em (Reginald, Nix) (words: Adrian Ross)
Finale, act 1: The Girl with the Yellow Roses (words: Adrian Ross)

ACT 2

The Sun Is Down and over the Town (chorus) (words: Adrian Ross)
Zara, Creole song (Zara) (words: Adrian Ross)
Little Miquette (Consuelo) (words: Adrian Ross)
Filibuster Brown (Reginald, chorus) (words: Adrian Ross)
The Slopes of Denmark Hill (Anita, Reginald) (words: Adrian Ross)
Beware of the Bomb (Anita, Pepita, Frank, Reginald) (words: Adrian Ross)
Cupid's Telephone (Adolfo, girls' chorus) (words: George Arthurs)
A Little Supper-Table for Two (Frank) (words: George Arthurs)
Finale: Welcome to the Lovely Bride (words: Adrian Ross)

ACT 3

The Morning Breaks upon the Shore (chorus) (words: Adrian Ross)
The Merry Widow (Anita, Nix) (words: Adrian Ross)
How Did the Bird Know That? (Reginald) (words: Adrian Ross)
Way Down in Pensacola (Pepita, chorus) (words: Leslie Stuart)
Waiting for Me (Consuelo) (words: Adrian Ross)
Would You Like to Motor with Mater? (chorus)
(words: George Arthurs)
Finale: I'm a Cuban Girl/If You Want to Motor with Me
(words: Adrian Ross and George Arthurs)

1909

Mighty Mother England (words: Fred E. Weatherly)   Chappell

1910

Captain Kidd *(words: Adrian Ross; London, Wyndham's Theatre, January 12, 1910)*

ACT 1

Opening Chorus: Haul in the Line
Entrance of Show Girls: The Broadway Belles
Octet: What Are You Going to Do?
Oh! What a Chance to Take! (show girls)
A Honeymoon in Peru (Lucy, show girls)

Um-te-ay (Lucy, children)

Johnny on the Spot (Kidd, chorus)

You Could Do Wonders with Me (Lucy, Kidd)

Quintet: Nursery Rhymes (Lucy, Kidd, Jim, Hyne, Aggie)

Finale: All Ashore for Porto Banos!

ACT 2

Opening Chorus: Work Together Quick and Steady

My Mascote (Hyne)

The Star of Panama (Juanita, chorus)

When Love Is King (Aggie)

The Constant Lover (Kidd)

In Yucatan (Lucy)

Wireless Telegraphy (Kidd, Lucy)

March Chorus: We're the Dashing Military

I'm the King of the Corderillas (Kidd)

Finale

ACT 3

My Affinity (Aggie), plus other unidentified numbers

The Slim Princess *(Buffalo, September 8, 1910)*   *Chappell*

ACT 1

The Plumes of the Palm Trees (Jeneka and chorus)
(words: Henry Blossom)

Patrol and Soldiers' Song: When the Guards Go Passing By (male chorus)
(words: Henry Blossom)

I Like 'em Plump (words: Henry Blossom)

Love's Lesson (quartet and chorus) (words: Henry Blossom)

A Little Pot of Tea (Consul) (words: Henry Blossom)

Kalora's Entrance (ensemble) (words: Henry Blossom)

Finale (words: Henry Blossom)

ACT 2

Opening Chorus (words: Henry Blossom)

We Will Not Live in a Bungalow (duet) (words: Henry Blossom)

Nursery Rhymes (quartet) (words: Henry Blossom)

I'm Glad My Home Is in the States (words: Henry Blossom)

The Land of the Free (words: Henry Blossom)

Do You Belong to Anyone Particular? (octet) (words: Henry Blossom)

A Certain Sort of Father (words: Henry Blossom)

O What a Chance to Take (words: Henry Blossom)

Queen of My Dreams (solo and chorus) (words: Henry Blossom)

1911

Peggy (London, Gaiety Theatre, March 4, 1911)   *Chappell*

ACT 1

The New Hotel, the New Hotel (chorus) (words: C. H. Bovill)

Whistle and the Girls Come Round (Bendoyle, chorus)
(words: C. H. Bovill)

Off We Go, the Festive Four of Us! (Polly, Didsbury, Diamond, Bendoyle)
(words: C. H. Bovill)

Daily We Are Found, Neatly Gowned (manicure girls)
(words: C. H. Bovill)

Come to Friville (Peggy) (words: C. H. Bovill)

Juliet and Romeo (operatic duet) (Peggy, Albert) (words: C. H. Bovill)

Tomorrow's My Big Day (Auberon) (words: C. H. Bovill)

The Lass with the Lasso (Doris, chorus) (words: C. H. Bovill)

Uncle Monty (Peggy, Auberon, Albert) (words: C. H. Bovill)

Finale: Who Is That Person Over There? (words: C. H. Bovill)

ACT 2

Oh, Friville, Friville (chorus) and For, I Am the Maire (Maire)
(words: C. H. Bovill)

Three Little Pebbles (bathing trio) (Doris, Peggy, Polly)
(words: C. H. Bovill)

You're the One Man I'm Looking For (Peggy, Auberon)
(words: C. H. Bovill)

I Beg Your Pardon (Auberon, Albert) (words: C. H. Bovill)

Danse Fascination

Go Away, Little Girl—Go Back to School (Polly, chorus)
(words: C. H. Bovill)

Ladies, Beware! [When the Lights Are Low] (Peggy)
(words: Leslie Stuart and C. H. Bovill)

Be a Lady All the Time (sextet) (words: C. H. Bovill)

The Fête (concerted number) (words: C. H. Bovill)

Pierrot and Pierrette (Doris, Albert) (words: C. H. Bovill)

Finale: Oh, Uncle Monty! (words: C. H. Bovill)

The Kiss Waltz (New York, Casino Theatre, September 18, 1911)
  Belle of Vienne

1914

Bubbles *(Northampton, New Theatre, April 27, 1914)*
  Opening Chorus: Eugenics! Eugenics!
  Colonel Swank
  What Will the Robins Do Then?
  Tinker with Your Automobile!
  Where Are the Soldier Boys? (words: George Arthurs)   B. Feldman
  There was a Little Girl!
  A Man is Just as Old as He Feels! (words: George Arthurs)
  I'd Like to Be a Little Boy!
  Bubble Girl
  Chorus: You've Got Me Good

1915

Florodora *(London, Lyric Theatre, February 20, 1915)*
  Jack and Jill (words: Leslie Stuart)   Francis, Day and Hunter
  My Garden Girl (words: Lester Barrett)   Francis, Day and Hunter

Is That You, O'Riley? (words: Leslie Stuart) /   Francis, Day and Hunter
  Is That Mr Riley? (words: Lester Barrett)
Who Said You Never Would Go?   Ascherberg, Hopwood and Crew
  (words: Horace Annesley Vachell)
Don't Blame Eve (words: Leslie Stuart)   Francis, Day and Hunter
Heligoland [sung by May Leslie Stuart]
My Beautiful Witch (words: Leslie Stuart)   Ascherberg, Hopwood and Crew
The Nautical Girl
  [sung by May Leslie Stuart]
Of All the Girls I Know I Love You Best [sung by May Leslie Stuart]
Memoire Triste, valse intermezzo   Ascherberg, Hopwood and Crew

1916
The Good Old Days of To-Morrow   Francis, Day and Hunter
  (words: Leslie Stuart)
Sweet Rose O'Mally (words: L. Wolfe Gilbert)   Jos. W. Stern

Nina *(later* The Girl from Nyusa*)*

ACT 1

Ensemble Entrance: Play the Tables

How Did You Leave Them on Broadway?

Napolitana

Wanderlust

Open Road to Bohemia

The Magazine Girl

Treasure of Pearl

Finale, Act 1

ACT 2

Put a Ticket on Yourself Marked 'Sold'

Lovelight in Your Eyes   Ascherberg, Hopwood and Crew
(words: Leslie Stuart)

plus other unidentified numbers

Midnight Frolic (New York, New Amsterdam Theatre Roof, December 29, 1917)

Cutey

1922

Jenny *(London, Empire, February 10, 1922)*

Cutey [see 1917] and other unspecified songs

The Lady of the Rose *(London, Daly's Theatre, February 21, 1922)*

Catch a Butterfly While You Can!   Ascherberg, Hopwood and Crew
(words: Leslie Stuart)

1924

Love's Debutante (words: Leslie Stuart)   Herman Darewski

UNDATED

My Cherokee Rose (words: Leslie Stuart)

Vera Cruz (instrumental) [ms]

What's Goin' to Happen When Ragtime's Gone? (words: Leslie Stuart)

Index

Concert and theater programs are indexed only for names that appear also in the main text or illustrations. Illustrations are indicated by page numbers set in *italic*.